COMING HOME

FREDDIE FLINTOFF

COMING HOME

THE MOMENTS THAT MADE ME

First published in the UK in 2025 by Blink Publishing
An imprint of Bonnier Books UK
5th Floor, HYLO, 105 Bunhill Row,
London, EC1Y 8LZ

A CIP catalogue record for this book is available from the British Library.

Hardback ISBN: 9781785127458
Trade Paperback ISBN: 9781785127465

Also available as an ebook and an audiobook

1 3 5 7 9 10 8 6 4 2

Design and Typeset by Envy Design Ltd
Printed and bound in Great Britain by Clays Ltd, Elcograf S.p.A.

Every reasonable effort has been made to trace copyright holders of
material reproduced in this book, but if any have been inadvertently
overlooked the publishers would be glad to hear from them.

The authorised representative in the EEA is
Bonnier Books UK (Ireland) Limited.
Registered office address: Floor 3, Block 3, Miesian Plaza,
Dublin 2, D02 Y754, Ireland
compliance@bonnierbooks.ie

www.bonnierbooks.co.uk

CONTENTS

CHAPTER 1

A SPLIT-SECOND DECISION

A split-second decision is all it takes. A decision that can change the course of a cricket match. Maybe even change the course of your life. Or save you from death.

Jamaica, Sabina Park, 2004. England against the West Indies in the first Test of the series. There I am, bat in hand, sunlight bouncing off the pitch and a passionate crowd restless in the stand. That low-level hum of anticipation crackling in the air.

I stand at the crease, heart thumping, sweat prickling at the back of my neck, and the world outside the boundary feels impossibly far away. From the sidelines it's been looking brutal – Nasser and Butcher battered by pace, the ball flying through chest-high, the kind of session that makes you doubt your sanity for choosing this sport. Fidel Edwards, the West Indies quick, steams in from the far end, all coiled energy and menace.

COMING HOME

I watch him unleash another short one – Butcher is hopping again, fending balls that rear up at throat height. Nasser looks twitchy at the other end, gloves adjusting, eyes narrowing – the kind of body language that tells you this is a proper scrap. I can feel that knot of anxiety tightening somewhere deep.

Butcher doesn't last much longer – gloves one to the cordon. Nasser follows not long after, done in by the lift and nibble. And just like that, I'm out there – pads on, adrenaline up, heart hammering – joining Chris Read at the other end. England are wobbling at around 209 for five – not in full freefall, but dangerously close, and it's me at the crease, trying to slow the skid, absorb the heat, maybe even fight back. The wicket's spicy, the ball's taking off, and part of me wonders if I'd rather be anywhere but here.

But then again, no.

Because once you walk out, once you mark your guard and face that first delivery, it's never as bad as you've built it up to be. The opposite, in fact. One ball – just one – and something inside you shifts. This is all right, you think.

Better than all right.

This is where you belong.

There's a little ritual to taking guard, a sequence you fall back on. Bat tucked under your arm, you ask the umpire for middle stump, maybe leg, sometimes two, just to find your bearings. You move about, a shuffling dance, searching for the sweet spot that makes you feel settled. You look around – sometimes you give the bat a little tap, scan the outfield, see what the fielders are plotting, sneak a glance at the crowd. Maybe you share a word with your partner – mine was

Chris Read. It's my own little routine, though every batter has theirs. There's a strange, unspoken comfort in these moments, as if each tiny act grounds you in the present.

And then you step into your stance. For me, it's bat pressed into the earth, head bowed for a beat, shutting out everything that isn't absolutely necessary. When I look up, Edwards is miles away – so far back I can barely see him. But you can see he's ready. There's always a group in the crowd having a pop – throwing out a bit of stick, reminding you they're not your fans, not today. But I grew up in Preston, fought my way on to cricket pitches from council estates, so some loudmouths don't rattle me. I've heard worse. I've fought for my right to play this game, so the jeering fades into the background.

Inside, I'm repeating it: I'm not giving up, I'm not giving up. A private mantra. Then Edwards sets off, and something shifts. The atmosphere compresses. You zone in, everything tightening into a point of focus so sharp you could cut yourself on it. It's strange – I couldn't even tell you what I'm looking at. People always say you should watch the bowler's hand, try to read the grip, pick the variation, but I just stare forward, eyes locked on the space where ball and hand will separate. Sometimes it feels like instinct rather than conscious choice.

As Edwards charges in, something in me sharpens. The rest of the ground blurs away, a watercolour wash. There's a split second of silence inside my head – a kind of auditory tunnel vision. I don't hear the crowd now. I don't even hear anything apart from my own heartbeat thundering in my chest.

And then the ball leaves his hand.

This is where everything happens, and nothing happens. Are my eyes locked on the ball? I think so, though truthfully sometimes it feels like my focus is everywhere and nowhere, like the act of seeing has become muscle memory. Some batters swear they read the seam, watch the rotation, clock the way it comes out – vertical seam, tilted, cross-seam. Sometimes I see it, sometimes I don't. There are days you can pick a bouncer before it's even released, spot a cutter from the wrist, sense a slower ball from the pause in the action. There are little tells – a change in stride, a fractionally higher arm, the angle of the seam – that your eyes register long before your mind can translate them. If it's a spinner, I'm watching the seam, trying to judge which way it will turn, reading the revolutions – or trying to.

The seam itself is rarely perfectly upright. Swing bowlers tilt it, work their magic – one angle to take it away, another to bring it back in. Sometimes they go cross-seam, just to get the ball to grip unpredictably. I'm reading these signals, consciously or not, adjusting my stance, recalibrating my options. If it's swinging out, I want to let it go or guide it in that direction. If it's cutting back in towards me, I meet it head-on, bat angled to deaden the threat. If it's spinning, I'll adjust – sometimes with my feet, sometimes just my hands, always fighting the urge to overthink.

And yet, from the moment the ball leaves Edwards' hand to when it thuds into the bat – if it does – it's less than half a second. 0.4, maybe 0.5 of a second. In that sliver of time, the mind is doing a hundred calculations. Where's the bounce? What's the speed? What's the angle? Where are my feet?

Where's my head? Where are my hands? Can I get my bat down in time? Will it rise? Will it nip away? Should I leave it? Play late? Defend? Attack? All those decisions – and then, with luck or judgement, the bat comes down, the ball cracks off the middle, races away for four, and suddenly the crowd's roar is back and you're in it, fully alive.

We'd go on to win that series 3-0. As far as that first Test was concerned, I ended up scoring 46 runs off 50 balls before being dismissed – caught by Ryan Hinds off the bowling of Ramnaresh Sarwan – and every ball was like that. Maybe every ball I ever faced. It all came down to split-second decisions.

Same with my accident.

Okay. Word of warning before we go much further: this isn't my accident book. I'm referring to the car accident I went through while filming an episode of *Top Gear*. The one that turned me over in more ways than one. This book definitely *involves* the accident, in the sense that what I went through informed and continues to inform my life, but although I reserve the right to talk about the crash when it's relevant, there will be no blow-by-blow account here.

What I will say, though, is that the same split-second decision-making at the crease came into play during the crash, where suddenly the car was going, rolling, and the world was all slow-motion chaos. When everything in me slowed right down, and I knew, somehow, exactly what was coming. I knew the options:

If I stuck my arm out, I'd lose it.

If I didn't brace, I'd snap my neck.

So I made the call. I shut my eyes and flung up my left

arm, with the thinking being that as a right hander, I was prepared to lose my left.

The car dragged me underneath for 50 metres, face skidding, body flipping. Minus two degrees, busted face, but alive – because in that instant, my mind, honed on cricket's demands, made the right call. A split-second decision. One that saved my life, and changed it.

It's bonkers what the human brain can do in a moment. They say we only use 10 per cent of it. Maybe that's true. All I know is that for all the talk about instinct and calculation, sometimes life is a string of split-second decisions – on the field, on the road, in the middle of chaos. I've always trusted mine, whether it was picking a strike or bracing for impact. These days, maybe I'm a bit more reflective, maybe I think a little longer before making a move. Age does that. But deep down, I know it's still in there – that flicker of instinct, the willingness to trust in a decision you make without thinking. The same reflex that helps you read the ball, see the seam, move your feet, keep your head still and put everything on the line for the game you love.

CHAPTER 2

THE FIRST BALL

Back, back in time. And here I am again, only this time I'm six, not 26, and I'm standing on a cricket pitch in summertime. Damson trees rustle in the evening breeze, branches heavy with fruit, and some of the kids are still picking them – eating some, pocketing the rest. And there are midges, plenty of midges. And this being a cricket pitch in England in summer – the ever-present smell of cut grass.

There would have been conversations about the weather, of course. Scratch a cricketer, you'll find a weatherman beneath, experts at shielding their eyes, squinting at clouds and predicting a shower at four. Maybe ten past, like.

But I'm not thinking about that. Not rain or damsons or midges. I'm thinking *What the bloody hell is happening?* Because I am literally playing cricket.

I hadn't come to play. Just to watch. My brother, Chris, was playing. I'm sitting on the grass with Mum and Nana and all the chairs they'd brought – fold-out ones with faded patterns and cup holders and all the bits they thought made summer better. But someone's not turned up. One short. And now I'm standing on the edge of the boundary in a black and red Manchester United tracksuit that doesn't even fit properly. Hand-me-down from the Smiths across the road. I'm not even a United fan. Liverpool and Preston are my teams. But here I am.

My heart's going like mad. Everyone's acting normal. Like it's no big deal. But I can feel the grown-ups watching. Not in a bad way. Just curious. What's he doing out there, then?

I hear my brother shout something. His voice carries from the other end of the field, a mix of bossy and proud. He's in the slips, sleeves rolled up. He belongs out here. I'm still figuring out where to stand. Someone tells me to stay deep. Fine by me. Safer.

The batter's a big lad. Bigger than me, anyway. Thwack – the ball's hit hard, over my head. I run, but I know I'm not getting there. It flies past and thuds against the fence. No one says anything. Not really. Just a bit of laughter. I breathe again.

Overs tick by, and I change ends. The scoreboard's made up of 'tins' – black rectangles with numbers painted on the front – and every over, someone goes out to change them, hooking the right tin onto the board. Sometimes the wrong number goes up and there's a bit of an uproar, umpires waving their arms, everyone shouting from the field, and a ripple of laughter across the ground.

I catch Mum's eye. She's in her chair with a cup of tea. She smiles, gives me a little wave. I wave back.

Now we're batting. I'm told I'll go in last, if we get that far. We do. Pads too big. Bat too heavy. The lad bowling has sideburns. I swing. I miss. The bails fly.

Out.

One ball.

Doesn't matter.

I trudge back to the pavilion, heat in my face, not sure whether to be embarrassed or proud. My brother says something about the ball being quick. He's kind. Dad gives my hair a ruffle. I sit down next to the urn, still fizzing with energy.

Next time, I think.

Next time I'll hit it.

* * *

The year was 1986, the place was Harris Park in Fulwood, just outside Preston (you'll have seen it if you watched *Field of Dreams*), and by then cricket was already written into my DNA like words in a stick of seaside rock. It was family, mostly – Dad doing the ground and maintenance, Mum and Nan sorting out the teas, my brother playing, the whole lot of us turning up with our chairs and our habits. I can still picture it: there are photos of me and my brother being pushed round the ground in prams while Mum, Nan and my Auntie Ennis scoped out the best spot for the afternoon. The ritual was always the same – before the season started, they'd choose which chair to claim for the summer, and every year the chairs got a bit more elaborate. One year it would be a simple garden seat, next a pull-down recliner, then something with arms and a footrest. They'd sit for hours, their own sort of committee, calling out encouragement and keeping an eye on everything.

We still do it now, to be honest – picking the chair for the summer has become a tradition in its own right. As kids, we'd spend whole evenings on the sidelines, watching or half-watching, then graduating to the nets, me and my brother usually ending up in a row over whose turn it was. It was a kind of progression: from prams, to chairs, to the nets, and then finally out onto the pitch for a match.

The club drew in all sorts, including Patel family – there were five or six brothers – and the Dyers, a West Indian family. I remember it as a happy a place where people got on with things in their own way. That was grassroots cricket – proper, no frills, a club pieced together by people who turned up, rolled up their sleeves and did what needed doing. I'd grown up on the sidelines, listening more than talking, always around cricket whether I was playing or not.

I tried scoring before I ever played, mostly because my brother had done it, earning himself a fiver and a free tea on Saturdays. He could keep up with it, sitting with the scorebook, marking every ball and run, making sure the tins on the scoreboard were right. I never stuck at it – I couldn't sit still, couldn't see the point, and usually got the numbers wrong anyway. If I was roped in when they were desperate, I'd do it, but I'd be itching to get away, not cut out for all that detail. When you got it wrong, you'd know about it – the umpire striding over, people shouting from the field, the old tins clanging as you swapped the numbers for the next over. The scoreboard was a bit of a show in itself, black tin numbers the size of your lap, hanging from hooks, swaying in the wind.

It was that day at Harris Park that I properly started, but really, it had all been building for years – Mum with the teas, Dad with the mower, my brother in the team, and me drifting from sidelines to nets to the outfield. Those early games didn't matter for the score. What mattered was being there: learning to watch, listen and, in time, take part. Those long evenings with the smell of cut grass, the clatter of tins and the low hum of family chatter – these are the memories that stay with me.

CHAPTER 3

DAD

To misquote *Goodfellas*: as far back as I can remember, I always wanted to be a cricketer. And though there have been times when we grew apart, when maybe I should have called more than I did, me and cricket have always come back to one another. After family, it's the one constant in my life, the one thing that's always been there. After all I've been through, it's my happy place, my comfort blanket, my safety zone, my bliss.

And the thing is. I really can't remember a time when it wasn't. It was always there, in my life. Always the family talk and the focus of almost every day. Thinking about it, talking about it, playing it, watching it. I remember seeing Ashes matches in the early 1980s, standing in front of a shop window in the St George's Shopping Centre in town while my mum went shopping. I didn't want to be dragged round Marks & Spencer, BHS or Debenhams; I just wanted to watch Terry Alderman of Australia play the series of his life – getting Graham Gooch out lbw over and over again.

It had all begun with Dad, of course. My mum, my grandparents, my brother and the people around the club – they're all in there, in the mentor mix. But it starts with him, because although he didn't exactly teach me cricket – not in the formal sense – what he did was imprint the game into me, purely and simply because his love for it was so infectious. And that sort of passion – when it's genuine, when it lives in someone's DNA – can't help but rub off. Dad knew the basics of the game, of course, and he passed those on, but he wasn't in a position to coach me properly. What he did was to keep the game alive in word and thought and deed, which was more than enough.

There was a thing I told him once – and I think he laughed, but it was true – that if I played a bad shot, I'd sometimes hear a little clap from his chair. Not a cheer, not encouragement, more like, 'We're not doing that, are we?' He didn't need to say anything. Just that one clap.

He took me everywhere. To every practice, every game, wherever I needed to be. I later found out that when I was staying in team hotels, Mum and Dad would sometimes sleep in the car. They didn't say anything about it at the time, but we weren't flush with money, and they just got on with it. That's how much they wanted me to have the opportunities. They never made a show of it, never looked for credit.

And they never put pressure on me. Which might be the best thing they ever did for me, looking back. They wanted me to do well, obviously. You could feel that. But it wasn't pressure. Not in the way you sometimes see it now, where parents are living through their kids. They just gave me support, quiet encouragement and space. I try to remember that with my own kids.

Dad could be tough too. Three years in a row I went to the Dartford Festival, which was a long-running junior cricket tournament that brought together county-level players from all over the country.

It was a proper test for young cricketers, and at the end of the week they'd pick a representative side, a sort of best-of-the-best match, and I got picked all three years, which was rare, especially at that age.

I remember one year – I was nine – and Dad was hitting me catches in the warm-up when I caught one between my fingers and split the webbing of that hand. It was pretty horrible, and unsurprisingly, I was in a bit of a state about it, but Dad had the solution: he taped them fingers together and cut my batting glove so I could hold the bat, 'You're good to go,' he said, and that was Dad. He wasn't going to let split webbing stop me. At the time, I didn't question it. Looking back now, with kids of my own, I think, *Would I do that?* Probably not, if I'm being honest (sorry, Dad), but it stayed with me all the same. You get on with it. 'Good to go.' That's what I learned. Advice that helped me play injured nearly all my career.

Another lesson I got from him was the fact that sometimes the mistakes aren't necessarily down to a lack of effort. It's not that you're not trying – it's that you're trying too hard. You want it so much, you get in your own way. That was me at times. Chasing it instead of letting it come. I'd be pushing for the big score, and I'd forget to play the game that was in front of me.

Dad got that. He was passionate but sensible. Measured. When I retired from playing, I think he was sadder about it than I was. All those years of coming to matches, watching me play for England suddenly over, and there I am, jumping about on the telly. That was never going to be his thing. Again, sorry, Dad. But you know what? Cricket never left me. And I did, eventually, find my way back.

CHAPTER 4

BEGINNINGS AT LANCASHIRE

If my dad was the first, he was far from the only. Mentors came in different forms as I got older – coaches, captains, teammates – anyone who took the time to help without making a fuss about it. Some of them probably didn't even realise they were doing it, but they all made a difference. Massive, in many cases.

I was about 13 or 14 when I started to get actual coaching – not just tips from the sidelines or advice in the car on the way home, but proper, structured sessions. Some were through school, some paid for, and a few came through Lancashire. They all played their part, but there was one coach in particular, Jim Kenyon, who was proper cricket through and through. I think he'd been a decent player in his day – places like Blackburn, then Leeds – though not at county level. He also worked for Radio Lancashire. Saturdays, they'd cover the local league matches and Jim was one of the voices on the mic.

But where he really made his mark was in the winter sessions. Every Sunday, he'd put on training at an indoor school. It wasn't flashy – nothing in cricket is flashy at that level – but the standard was good. You'd have top local league players turning up, sometimes a couple of county pros, and a handful of the best young lads from the area. It cost three quid. I still remember my dad handing over three pound coins every week.

I started in the kids' net, but I didn't stay there long. Jim moved me up into the adults pretty quickly. That was his way. He didn't believe in mollycoddling. If you were going to make it, you needed to face it. Literally. No helmet, no coddling, just full-pace bowling from blokes trying to hit you in the head. That was the test. Welcome to the world of adult cricket.

You know what I realised? The main difference was in the bounce. In kids' cricket, the ball didn't come up much. You played on decent pitches and getting hit wasn't a big worry. But then you're in against grown men and suddenly you're thinking about your ribs, your chest, your face. It changes things. Jim didn't ease me in. He just said get on with it. Sink or swim. I got through it – bruised but still there – and kept coming back.

Looking back, that period was massive. I started to think maybe I could do this. I was getting better, stronger and smarter. I was still getting hit – belly, arms, you name it – but I was surviving. More than that, I was growing into it.

That's when Lancashire started paying a bit more attention. And that's when Bumble came into it.

More about Bumble in a bit. First, I want to mention another bloke at Lancashire: John Stanworth. He was involved with the second team and played a huge role. He wasn't flash or loud about it. Just steady, experienced and always there. He'd played as a wicketkeeper for Lancashire in the 1980s and early '90s and then moved into coaching and development work. And as well as playing a bit, he captained the seconds and had this role where he'd play alongside the younger lads, help them adjust and give them confidence. He picked me when I was 15 and made sure I was looked after.

To be clear, that wasn't age-group stuff – it was the Second XI. Men's cricket. I was just a kid, still growing into my kit, and suddenly I was out there with full-grown pros, playing proper games. That was Stanworth's call. He captained the seconds at the time and also acted as a kind of on-field coach, helping lads like me find our feet. That was my first real step into senior cricket, and it meant a lot. He made it feel like I belonged – not by being soft, but by being steady, clear and always present.

That's what mattered, more than any single tip or drill – the confidence. When you're a shy kid, like I was, it means everything to have someone who says: 'You're good enough. You're in.' I've always questioned myself. Still do. Whatever I'm doing, I'm asking – is this working? Am I doing it right? What happens if I'm not? Imposter syndrome, they call it. That was my rhythm even back then. I'd go through patches of form, then drop off a cliff.

Up and down, over and over. I'd have a run where I looked the part, then suddenly feel like a fraud.

But having people like Stanworth steadying the ship – that was everything. You learn to trust their belief when you're struggling to find your own.

There were others, too. Unintentional mentors, let's say. Blokes like Mal Dyer, who played in my dad's side. He was a West Indian lad who had a proper presence about him. Everyone back then seemed to have a Mal Dyer story. He hit massive sixes, and wherever you went, someone would tell you about the time that Mal cleared the clubhouse roof or broke a window. Mal didn't say much to me directly, but I watched him and listened and took it all in. That's how I learned in those days. Sit quiet, pay attention, pick up what you can.

That's the thing with mentors. You need them to learn. I don't think there's any getting around that. Even if it's someone who doesn't realise they're having an impact.

Here's an example of how it can work the other way, too. Although I was always aware of Lancashire's history, I never went to watch them loads as a kid, but I remember one day when my dad and my brother went to see them play Middlesex at Blackpool. I didn't go. I ended up at Professor Peabody with my mum, a soft play place in the Tower. That was the choice. Ball game or ball pit. What can I say? I was young.

Anyway, my brother came back with a load of autographs. Got the lot – except one. There was a fella called Eddie Hemmings, a spinner for England, who was a tough old pro and, as it turned out, not the sort to hand out freebies.

'Not now,' he'd said, which proper annoyed my brother. It stuck with me too. Every other bugger had signed.

Fast-forward maybe eight years. Fewer, possibly. I'm playing for the Lancashire Second XI, and who's lining up for Sussex? Eddie Hemmings. Small world, cricket. That day I had a bit of a knock, got a few runs and was feeling good.

Hemmings came on to bowl. And I remembered how back in the day he wouldn't sign my brother's book. It was one of those moments where you realise you've been storing something up, and right then I knew: I wasn't letting it slide.

I benefitted from a short boundary on one side, to be fair, but still – I hit 30 off one over. Eddie wasn't enjoying it, not one bit, grumbling and making excuses, but I was loving it. I told him afterwards, in the bar. I said, 'You should've signed me brother's autograph book,' which took him aback.

CHAPTER 5

ALWAYS MEET YOUR HEROES

Not to be forgotten now we're plundering the heroes section of my memory banks. Steve Davis. Yes, *the* Steve Davis, who – after my dad – is one of the first proper heroes I ever had.

Now, for anyone who didn't grow up in Britain in the 1980s (best time to grow up – period), that name might not land quite right. You'll be like, Who? Or maybe, if you were around then, you'll hear it and think: Steve Davis, the snooker player? Boring Steve Davis? The guy who gets done by Dennis Taylor in old replays on BBC Four?

But that's not how I saw him. Not then, not now. He was precise. He was calm. He made it all look easy. And for a kid growing up in Preston in a box room, with a six-by-four snooker table balanced on the dining table, that was enough. That was magic.

Snooker was massive back then. It wasn't just something

your dad watched with a cup of tea, it was box office. You had the characters – Alex Higgins with the chaos, Canadian Kirk Stevens in the white suit – but then there was Davis. Methodical. Quiet. Just brilliant.

My mum's mate, Susan – we called her Auntie Susan, even though she wasn't – she worked at the Guild Hall, so we'd get tickets. Proper nights out: me, Mum, Auntie Ennis, watching the big names in real life. I remember seeing Davis play. I remember the feel of the room, the hush before a shot. It was like church, only everyone was drinking tea and trying not to cough.

I think Steve Davis was the first autograph I ever got. Proper moment. He was coming out of the Guild Hall, no fanfare, no security, just strolling out after a match, and we were there – me, Mum, Auntie Ennis. I went over, got the signature, and the local paper even took a photo. *Lancashire Evening Post*: Steve Davis meets young fan. I've still got it somewhere. Looking back, it probably felt more like we were groupies than fans – Davis just minding his business, and us, star-struck.

Years later, I got to meet him again. Properly this time. We were filming the Sky show *A League of Their Own* – on which I was a team captain – some snooker thing in Essex with Alan Carr, Jamie (Redknapp – the other captain) and Tom Davis – and I brought the photo along, mainly for Mum.

I walked in and told Steve Davis he was one of my heroes, and he thought I was taking the piss. But I meant it. That childhood feeling never really goes, does it? We recreated one of those famous black ball frame moments – him and Dennis Taylor – and he was a total gent from soup to nuts.

Honestly, I walked away thinking, *What a man*. Like, they say never meet your heroes, but sometimes they're wrong.

And then, there's Botham. Beefy. Sir Ian.

Botham was mischief. He didn't walk onto the field, he *strode*. He was the heartbeat of English cricket. Could change a game in a session and change a session in an over. And when you're a young lad from Preston watching that on telly, you think, *Maybe. Maybe I could have a bit of that, one day.*

Growing up, I watched him. Everyone did. You couldn't not. But it wasn't until later that I got to meet him properly. I'd just started playing for England at the time. We were down in Hampshire for a NatWest semi-final, and I took a decent catch (although what I mostly remember about it was the bloke behind me giving me dog's abuse, pint in hand, all game long), and after we won, me and Mike Atherton stayed on for dinner.

It was a strange table. Me, Athers, Rod Bransgrove – who went on to buy Hampshire – and a few music industry types, people I was meant to know but didn't.

And Ian Botham.

To be honest, I thought it'd be a quiet one with Beefy, bit of food, a few stories. But it turned into a proper boozy night. Not that I'm complaining – I was good at that then.

I remember walking down the street in Southampton with Ian Botham under my arm. Just the two of us, wobbling our way back. Went up to his room for a nightcap, and he was trying to get something out of the minibar, got the heavy head, knocked the telly off the stand, ended up marooned over the fridge. I left him like that, and thinking back, it still makes me laugh.

What a night. What a bloke.

Thing is, it's not just about the cricket or the personality. It's that when you're young and you watch someone like him, they seem untouchable. And then years later, there you are, walking him home, propping him up, and you're a part of the world you used to just observe. It's surreal. But lovely.

Another one: Viv Richards – possibly the coolest man ever to walk the earth.

Viv Richards didn't just play cricket. He was cricket. Cap on, gum-chewing, chest out, bat twiddling like it was part of him – it was theatre. No helmet, just swagger – and not the showy kind but the real thing. He hit fast bowlers like they were club trundlers, dismantled spin with a flick, and he did it all with this calm that never cracked. Ninety not out or nine for three – same look, same intent.

Viv scored over 8,500 Test runs, averaging over 50. Watch the old footage – the way he moves, the sound off the bat – and it still gives me goosebumps. Everyone copied his walk and tried the flick. But you couldn't *be* Viv. You could only watch and want.

I met him once. World Cup, 2003, South Africa. There was this big do in Cape Town before the tournament started – all the teams together, all the players milling around the hotel. I was talking to Wasim Akram – who, by the way, was a godsend to me at Lancs – when Viv walked in. And I swear to you, the room just parted. Like Moses turning up at a nightclub. Everyone clocked him. Everyone felt it.

And then he came over, said hello to Wasim, turned to me and said, 'Freddie, you all good?'

Freddie. He knew my name.

He told me he'd been watching me bat, and I'll never forget what he said. He said I had power. Destructive power. But I had to give myself time. Take a few balls. Let the game come to me. I nodded like a schoolkid. It wasn't just advice – it was a moment. I don't think I even heard the rest of the conversation. I was too busy floating.

I never get star-struck. Not really. But cricketers – the proper ones – that's different. Viv. Malcolm Marshall. Wasim. Men who had this aura. Who carried the game in their bones. That's when I got star-struck.

I had heroes closer to home, too.

Shane Warne – who I later got to know – redefining what spin could do. He made the ball talk. Made you believe in magic again.

There were also the blokes I played with, who became heroes of a different kind. Marcus Trescothick, calm and unflappable. Steve Harmison, my mate, my brother, who bowled with fire and felt everything. Michael Vaughan, who had a way of making you feel ten feet tall just by saying your name right. And, of course, a special mention for Rob Key, England's best captain who never was, a batter who played the world's best bowlers with ease and struggled against some of the worst. Rob's my closest friend, with whom I can share a dressing room, a game of golf... anything. He was there for the good times but – more importantly, as far as I'm concerned – has been there for the bad, and he has helped bring me back from the darkness.

These weren't just players. They were chapters in the story. And every one of them left a mark.

COMING HOME

Anyway. Where was I?

Oh yes – talking of heroes and mentors – Bumble.

CHAPTER 6

BUMBLE

There's a kind of hush that descends when something's about to go down. You wouldn't call it silence, exactly. More like a heavy stillness.

That's what it's like right now, as me, my mum and my dad sit in the 'best' room of our house – the front room that's never normally used – trying to keep calm and act like this is normal.

But it's not normal. It's anything but. Because David 'Bumble' Lloyd is in our living room, and the shape of my life is about to change.

Bumble's a cricketing legend who needs no introduction, but let's give him one anyway. Left-handed batter, part-time bowler, full-time presence. He wasn't just a character on the telly. He'd lived it. He'd played for Lancashire and England in the 1970s, coached both, knew the game inside out. He made 200 in Mumbai against India in 1974 and never looked back – carrying that same no-nonsense intent into coaching England, then lighting up the commentary box with that unmistakable Lancastrian lilt and a grin you could hear through the radio.

Right now he's in our Preston front room in his position as Lancashire's head coach, here to offer me a contract – though he's not exactly doing it like a job interview. More like a pint and a pie. He's chatting away with Mum and Dad like this is just another stop on his afternoon round. Outside, his Rover's parked just off the kerb, clean as a whistle with 'Lancashire' printed down the side in red letters. You couldn't miss it. And believe me, no one on our street did. Curtains twitching, neighbours peering out, trying to clock who the VIP visitor might be. It was like the Queen had popped round, only with a thick northern accent and a better batting average.

Bumble always called me Andrew. Even when everything else got louder and faster, Bumble never wavered on that. Not Fred, not Freddie. Just Andrew. Like he saw past all the noise and kept his eye on the person underneath.

'We've been keeping an eye on Andrew,' he says to my mum and dad, who are agog. Bumble's sitting on the sofa with Geoff Ogden, the Lancashire cricket chairman. 'We're very impressed,' he goes on, 'and would like to offer him a contract at Lancashire.'

Simple as that. One minute you're this. And then, with a few words from Bumble, you're that.

Sure enough, my heart thumps. Proper thumps – the kind you can hear in your ears. Because it's real now. This isn't a throwaway conversation at the edge of a net session or a well-meaning pat on the back. This is Bumble, the man who once captained and coached and carried the red rose of Lancashire, and he's offering me a way in.

I glance across at Mum. She's got her best teapot out and the good biscuits are on a tray. Dad's sitting a bit straighter than usual.

And me? I'm trying not to combust. Because on the outside I'm nodding along, trying to stay cool, but on the inside I'm practically levitating. Sixteen years old, still revising for GCSEs, and here's this bloke I've grown up watching on telly – now sitting ten feet away, telling my family that I've got what it takes. Telling me that I can make a living out of the thing I love most. It's bonkers.

Bumble's got a way of talking that makes everything sound clear, even the complicated stuff. Telling my parents how it all works, talking about how Lancashire is one big happy family and that 'Andrew will be well cared for.'

Next he talks about wages. 'Ian Austin,' he says, 'he's got a second-team cap, so he's on £16,500 a year.'

You should see my parents' faces. Sixteen and a half grand – they're floored. Then he goes on: 'Michael Atherton gets £28,000 a year.'

It's like he's reeling off lottery numbers. And then he drops mine: 'We'll start Andrew on £2,500 a year.' It feels huge. I don't care what the others are on – that's real money, and it's money for playing cricket.

What he doesn't say is that Phil Neville got offered that contract first. This is Phil – brother of Gary – who goes on to win everything with Manchester United and play for England. He's a year older than me and already a star, totally eclipsing me in the juniors. He opens the batting, opens the bowling, does everything. Then Manchester United come in for him – five grand a week, not five grand a year – and that's that. I'm the new golden boy for Lancashire.

The next morning, I run into Bumble at the club. 'You've decided, haven't you?' he says. I nod. 'One last thing,' he adds, and the grin gives it away. 'All that stuff I told your mum and dad yesterday, about Lancashire being one big happy family – absolute rubbish. Truth is, it's hard here. And it's going to be hard for you.'

That's Bumble, right there. Warm, funny and full of mischief – but never pretending it's going to be easy.

*   *   *

Being good at cricket wasn't something that came quickly. I was about nine when things started to change. A coach suggested I go for trials with Lancashire and sure enough, I went along. It wasn't a big deal at first – I was still just a kid, playing for fun. But that invitation opened doors, and suddenly, I was on the radar.

The first trial was for Lancashire Under-11s. But I wasn't 11 – I was nine. But I didn't let that stop me.

It worked out, and it wasn't long before I was playing regularly for the juniors. I was in the Under-15s before I knew it, scoring runs, taking wickets. But it wasn't just the cricket that was shaping me – it was the environment. Being around other players, learning from them, even watching them. The best way to get better was to play with those who were better than you, and that's exactly what I was doing.

Back then, you'd be playing for loads of teams, all the time, so I divided my time between Lancashire second team, Lancashire juniors, England Under-15s and St Anne's.

I had my moments playing for each of them, but what got a lot of attention was the day I scored 232 not out for St Anne's Under-15s against Fulwood and Broughton. As an event, it received a lot of press, but in truth I was practically a professional by then and probably shouldn't even have been on the pitch.

When I was 15, I was fast-tracked into Lancashire 2nd XI, and I suddenly felt very young playing with seasoned professionals and internationals. That was also when I first encountered Bumble. What struck me most about him was the way he carried himself. He wasn't just a great player – he was a character. Larger-than-life, full of confidence, and always approachable. He had this aura around him that made you respect him instantly.

But there was something else. He genuinely cared. One of the things about him is that he never does things half-hearted. When he backs someone, he really backs them. When he commits, it's total.

It was all moving quickly by then. Second XI matches, scouts around, a few good knocks under my belt. I could feel things shifting, even if I didn't know exactly where it was headed.

A contract was the answer. And Bumble turning up at the house just made it official. But the truth is, I'd already started living it. Cricket wasn't a dream any more – it was just what I did. Every day. No fuss.

A few years on, when I walked into the England dressing

room for the first time, there he was again. Not just in my memory, but physically there – Bumble, now the England coach, still calling me Andrew, still offering that same directness, that same support. He'd seen me start out, and now he was helping me take the next step. There's a symmetry to that I'll never forget.

It's funny. I've had quite a few mentors, all told – a lot who shaped my journey. But Bumble? He was the one who handed me the pen and pointed to the contract. He made it real.

And that day in our front room, with the teapot steaming and the Rover outside, was the moment the dream became a job. It was the moment that everything changed.

CHAPTER 7

CATCHING PIGEONS

I'm 19, I'm in a hotel in Pakistan and I've just declared myself an alcoholic.

It's true, this. No word of a lie. But it's not quite what you think . . . see, I'm in Pakistan with the England Under-19s and – as is common in a cricketer's life – I'm away for Christmas.

Now, Pakistan back then had strict laws around alcohol, and for us, that means no drinks over the festive period. We're all missing our families, missing home, wanting to kick back and relax, and what better way to do that than with a beer?

But we can't. Because it's the law.

However, it turns out there's a loophole: if you declare yourself an alcoholic, you can buy beer from the hotel. And if that makes sense to you, great, because it certainly doesn't make sense to me, but I'm not about to look that gift horse in the mouth. And so, as team captain – and already by then one of the thirstier members of the squad – it falls to me to go down to hotel reception on Christmas Eve and declare myself an alcoholic.

I do it the proper way. Give them the shame-faced look, like I'm putting my hand up at a meeting, and say, 'My name is Andrew Flintoff and I am an alcoholic.'

Do they know I'm full of it? Do I care? Not sure on either count. What I *do* know is that they take me out the back and get me to fill in a form. And the next thing you know I'm buying 250 bottles of beer, which I cart up to my room and dump in a bath of ice, before phoning round the team to let them know there's a meeting in my room.

That night the whole squad crams in – laughing, drinking, making the best of it. It's chaos, the good kind. The next day there are enough beers left over for Christmas Day, and we have a meal together. It's not home, but it does the job.

* * *

Rewind a bit.

After Bumble offered me the contract, things started moving fast. I made my Lancashire First XI debut at Portsmouth at 16 and Bumble was all over me from the start.

I mean that in a good way. It was almost like having a second dad. At that time – just three short years before declaring myself an alcoholic in Pakistan – I didn't drink, didn't go out with the lads, didn't do much at all. My main aim in life was 'don't let Bumble down'.

Prior to my debut, Bumble had told the captain I had to field in the slips.

'He catches everything, he's brilliant, he catches pigeons,' was what he'd apparently said. (I can't claim to have ever caught a pigeon by the way.) Thing is, the slips were normally for the pros – the old hands. Neil Fairbrother got bumped out to third slip so I could go second. First over from Wasim Akram, and I dropped one. No – I didn't even drop it. I didn't get near it. Hit me square in the chest. Then I dropped two more. Wasim was fuming. He boomed, 'Get that boy out of the slips. Or I'll throw him a fuckin' pigeon.'

I wasn't one of them yet – not in my head, anyway. I kept quiet. Spoke when I was spoken to. Some of the older players were suspicious of any young lad with a bit of attention, always thinking about their own spots. But the big names like Fairbrother, Watkinson, Wasim: they backed me. I wasn't quite part of it yet, but I wanted to be. That feeling – aspiring to belong – stayed with me.

In the Second XI, though, it was different. Toxic, at times. I remember playing against them when I was 15 – an academy game, I think it was – alongside my best mate Paddy McKeown, and the abuse from their players was ridiculous. Then I turned up a year later, suddenly playing for them, and they expected it to be fine. I did well in one game, and one of the older lads said I'd been 'accepted' now. Mate, you're 30, still playing seconds, and I'm meant to earn your approval?

In the winters, I worked for the club. At 16, my back was already a problem which meant I couldn't do manual labour or go overseas to play. So Lancashire gave me a job in the office. I started in accounts. That didn't last long. I'm not a numbers lad. They moved me down to the ticket office.

That was better. Connie, Val and Kath took me in. Made me meals. Looked out for me. Meanwhile, I lived with Pete Marron, the head groundsman. His house was on the ground. First time we met, he said, 'You'll be good?' I nodded. 'Right then.'

At first, I was too polite to even go downstairs. Didn't watch telly. Then, one Sunday, Pete said, 'We're going to the pub. Get your coat.'

It was a rough place. When I said I'd have a Coke, he looked at me like I'd asked for a milkshake. 'It's bitter or lager. You can't have Coke.' So I had a lager that I nursed for an age and hated. Even so, I loved being there.

One week I went without him – just turned up and waited. I sat there for two hours and had five or six pints before he came in and found me. From then on, we were sound. His mates reckoned I was all right, and that was enough.

Eventually, I got sacked from the ticket office and sent to the club shop. Best thing ever. Why? No one ever came in. We'd chat all day, and what I soon discovered was that for the other workers in the ticket office, it wasn't just a job – it was a way of life. These people weren't chasing pay rises or transfers. They loved the club. Planned coach trips to away games. Talked about Lancashire like it was a family member. That changed the way I saw it all. At the same time, I got a job in retail on the side, stacking shelves at Woolworths, putting out the CDs for the album chart, to try and get some cash in.

While all that was going on, I was hoping for a call-up to the England Under-19s winter tour to the West Indies, but it didn't happen. Then one of the lads had passport trouble and I got called up at the last minute. Just like that, I went from putting up decorations at Woolworths to flying to Barbados.

That West Indies trip blew my head off. I mean, I'd just turned 16, and there I was staying at the Caribbean Beach Hotel in St Lawrence Gap. I remember coming down for breakfast that first morning, still half asleep, opened a little barrier by the foyer and there it was: bright blue sea, palm trees, sun like I'd never seen. Until then, the only beach I'd ever known was Blackpool. I stood there thinking, *What the hell is this?*

I roomed with Neil Killeen. He was three years older. We work together now with England, but back then I was just a wind-up merchant. I'd line up his toiletries, just to do his head in, mess about with his kit. One day I pushed it too far and he went to dive on me – but forgot about the ceiling fan. Sliced his fingers open. Even now he brings it up.

That tour set something off in me. I was just batting – my back still wasn't right – but I was playing well, and I knew I could hold my own. That was the start of people noticing what I was capable of, and although I was only bowling now and then as my back allowed, I was starting to make noise. Once you're noticed at that level, things start to move.

By then I was 19 and captain. John Abrahams – my coach from Lancashire – had asked me to lead the side, which was incredible. I'd captained most of my junior teams, club cricket, too, (although they never gave me the Under-15s captaincy, which still annoys me), but never anything at this level. This was proper. I was proud.

COMING HOME

Here's the thing about being a captain. It's not like football. As a cricket captain, you do everything: pick the bowlers, set the fields, run the meetings, talk to coaches, shape the culture. The coach helps, of course, but it's your team out there, and you've got to read the game, read people, set the tone. It's not just about tactics. It's about how a dressing room feels.

That tour was tough. We played in places I'd never heard of, trained in heat I wasn't ready for. The only place you could get a sense of home was the High Commission, where you could get sausages and the occasional pint.

We won matches, had a good side – Ben Hollioake and Alex Tudor were with us. A bunch of us went on to play for England. Some didn't. That's how it goes. Some end up at Lord's, others in retail. But for me, it was clear: this was what I wanted. I felt like I belonged.

Somewhere in the middle of it all – on the way out to Pakistan, I think – was the Guinness incident. Gareth Batty, Zac Morris and me were flying down to London ahead of the team dinner, and we got to the airport early to find there was a Guinness promotion on. So of course, we got stuck in prior to our internal flight.

Five pints deep, we landed at Heathrow and still had hours to kill so we kept going – Guinness, then Guinness and port. As we were flying out the next morning, we had to get to our hotel, and we were falling over each other, loud, dropping bags.

Next thing you know, the police got involved. I gave them a fake name – Daryl Newman, a lad from school (sorry, mate) – and an old address in Preston, all the time forgetting that my kit had my real name stitched on. We blagged our way out, just about.

It's funny. That trip sounds like madness now. But it made sense at the time. It was cricket, chaos, leadership – even a bit of lying about being an alcoholic. Deep down I knew: if I could get my bowling going, I'd become the cricketer I wanted to be.

CHAPTER 8

CHIRPING AT HAYDEN

Hampshire away. County Championship in 1997. Day three. I'm 19 years old, playing for Lancashire and itching to prove something.

The County Ground in Southampton is one of those proper grounds – a sense of occasion, a good crowd, a decent wicket – and Hampshire have got some serious players. Robin Smith's out there – the Judge himself. South African-born, Smith played for England in the 1990s and was known for his courage against fast bowling. I grew up watching him crack shots through the covers in the West Indies. Square jaw, serious eyes, high collar and of course the hair that resembles a judge's wig, hence the nickname. The kind of bloke who made you sit a bit straighter just watching him. And now he's on the other team.

But he's not the problem.

The problem is Hayden.

Matthew Hayden – big, left-handed, full-chested, chest out. One of the great Aussie openers, brutal at the top of the order, with a reputation for walking the line between intimidation and flair. Hayden walks like he's ten foot tall and owns the postcode. Australians called him Buzz Lightyear, because that's the way he looks, like he's ready to fly into battle, armed with huge biceps, comparatively thin legs and ego. He's their overseas, and he's absolutely creaming it. Ninety not out overnight. He's dominating us, plain and simple.

Next morning, we gather for the usual pre-play huddle on the outfield.

One thing we all know: we're going nowhere in the game unless we get Hayden out.

So there's a plan – get in his ear, rattle him. Classic Aussie tactic reversed. Remember, I'm just the young lad listening, nodding along, thinking that whatever goes off won't really involve me, when all of a sudden I feel the shift. Everyone starts looking at me.

Come on. Not my job, this. It's never the kid's job, right?

But next thing I know, I'm fielding at silly point, helmet on, box in, standing close enough to see the stitching on his bat. Gary Yates is tossing down his offies, and I'm there, practically under Hayden's nose. No hiding place.

He plays a shot and I chirp up. Not rude, just cheeky.

'Shot, son,' I say to him. Just like that.

You have to realise. This is a no-no. International player, senior pro. And here's me calling him 'son'. Hayden glares at me.

'What are you looking at?' I say.

He looks genuinely puzzled by the turn of events but says nothing.

Next ball, he swings and misses.

I pipe up, 'Keep your eye on it, lad.'

That does it.

He turns, full snarl. 'You fucking what?'

I just shrug. 'Calm down, son. You'll be all right.'

And that's it. The switch has flipped. I'm in. He's rattled. Swings hard at the next one, nicks it, and he's gone. Caught behind. Massive wicket.

We go wild. Hayden storms off. Their dressing room's on stilts and I can hear him up there, fuming. Doors banging. He's not taking it well.

Lunchtime comes and I'm heading for the pavilion, thinking job done, but I spot Hayden on the boundary, waiting. Just waiting. Not moving. I clock him, clock the size of him, and then clock my teammates disappearing quick, like smoke. No back-up. Cheers, lads.

I don't fancy it, so I loop back to the dressing room and give the lunch room a miss. But I know this isn't over.

We go out to bat second innings. I'm coming in at five, and sure enough, Hayden's still burning. I walk out – no helmet on – and he starts striding towards me, halfway to the middle. Big man, full of intent. I'm thinking, right, I'll put the helmet on now.

He gets close, lowers his voice. 'You know what, son?'

'What?'

'This game's got a funny way of biting you on the arse.'

I nod. Fine. Let's see, eh?

After that, he's in my ear the whole time. Bouncer first

ball, then the verbals, just trying to get inside my head. Part of me is listening, thinking, *Maybe he's right. Maybe this'll be the day it all goes wrong.*

But it isn't.

I bat. And I bat. And I get my first first-class hundred (and will go on to knock 117).

As I raise the bat, I look over to him. 'Still waiting for that bite, Matty. Only it's not bitten yet, has it?'

He doesn't say a word.

After that, he's as good as gold. Fair play to him. Maybe he respected it or saw something of himself. Maybe he just appreciated the scrap.

Whatever it was, this is the day I learn a couple of things. One, I can play at this level, and two, sledging's a funny old game. Sometimes it's poison. But sometimes, it's fuel. If you can take it as well as you give it, you start to realise you're not just surviving out here. You belong.

Saying all that, I wasn't built for sledging. Some of the guys loved it – thrived on it, even. They'd walk onto a pitch already mouthing off, full of pre-rehearsed zingers and with all the confidence of a northern stand-up. I never had that. What I had was a sense of when to go, when to pull back, and – maybe most importantly – what not to say. Not everyone shared that.

The thing is, I grew up on the edge of four council estates in Preston. At our school, you played football all year round – two jumpers, a ball, and off you went. Cricket was for 'posh' lads, so playing it was a risk. At school, just making it through the day with all your teeth felt like an achievement. The idea that a few sledges from a slip cordon could unnerve me? No chance. I'd already been through harder things.

Still, that didn't mean I was innocent. I gave it out, now and then, and there are a few moments I still think about when I crossed a line or said something that makes me wince to think back on it.

There are also times when I've had things said to me that crossed the line. My England Test debut in July 1998, for example, when I walked out to bat against South Africa at Trent Bridge, full of nerves and expectation, heart thumping, unsure how it would go.

Before I'd even taken guard, I was getting it in the neck. Daryll Cullinan was chirping away, a proper batter, decent record. Next to him was Jonty Rhodes, the best fielder in the world at the time. Brilliant players both, but the stuff they came out with? It wasn't clever, it wasn't funny; it was just vile. 'Fat cunt' was the phrase that came my way more than once. I'd never even heard some of the terms they used. But I've never forgotten them. And I'll remember that one to my dying day.

To me that kind of stuff was just abuse – personal, nasty and unnecessary – and when I brought it up later and it appeared in the press, years down the line, Cullinan responded by trying to claim it was all attention-seeking on my part. He said I was chasing headlines. As if I needed to bring up a name barely anyone remembered for clout. It wasn't about that, mate. It was about calling it for what it was: bang out of order.

Compare that to someone like Hayden – and I know that might sound strange, considering the bust-up we had early on – but honestly, I never felt like he crossed the line. He was in your face, sure. He'd let you know he was there. But there was a craft to it. An intent. He was trying to rattle you in the moment, not destroy you. There's a difference.

I played with Hayden later, in 2005, and got to know the man behind the presence. Big, bold, brash, yes, but also one of the good ones. We'd joke about that early game, when I got under his skin and he waited for me at the boundary rope like some action movie villain. But even then, even in the middle of it, he never made it personal. It was all part of the contest. And that's the way it should be.

The thing about sledging – when it's done right – is that it adds something to the game. It's not just you versus the ball. It's you versus the bowler, the fielders, the conditions, and now, the noise. If you can make a batter play against you, mentally, you've got a real edge. The Aussies were brilliant at that. They understood the psychology. They pushed you, prodded, waited for cracks. But they didn't need to get dirty to do it. That's the difference.

CHAPTER 9

WHEN THE FINGER GOES UP

Getting out. No matter how many times it happens, the feeling's always the same. A feeling that begins in the pit of your stomach and seems to sink lower from there.

Even if you've scored runs, it feels crap. But if you've got nothing it's brutal. It feels like you've embarrassed yourself. Publicly. Visibly.

You feel it in your chest. And then there's the long walk. Past spectators, past murmurs, sometimes boos. Sometimes worse. You try not to look, but you see the faces in the crowd, some silent, some shaking their heads, others blank with disappointment.

Flashing forward a bit, but there was one time playing for England at Lord's. West Indies, last over before lunch. Classic situation: just survive till the break. Block it out, regroup. But this bowler – they'd thrown on some part-timer – he's rubbish.

First ball, I block. Second, he lobs up another pie, and I send it for six straight into the sight screen. Bit of a murmur from the crowd. Bit of theatre. So now I'm thinking, Right, shut up shop. Next ball, same delivery. I try to block it but miss. Bowled.

It's the indignity. Last ball before lunch, and I'm the idiot trudging back while everyone else walks in behind me. I take my helmet off and start up the stairs towards the Long Room with the Lord's members lining either side. And that's when it happens.

A rolled-up *Telegraph* hits me square on the back of the head.

I turn around, and there's this old fellow, scuttling quickly off, leaving a rolled-up newspaper and a parting shot that he calls back over a tweedy shoulder. 'It was fun while it lasted, Flintoff.'

Ouch.

I mean, it could be worse, but still.

Oof.

Back in the dressing room, you sit with it. Rewind. Replay. *If I could just do that again . . .* you say it to yourself on a loop. Not just that shot, but the whole thing. You dissect it till it's nothing but pieces. And it doesn't leave you that day. Or the next.

Sometimes, not even years later.

The thing is that you go out there with so much hope, but at the end of it all, it's the hope that kills you, and that's what people don't understand – you step onto the field full of possibility. You're thinking, *This might be the day.* And you imagine it all: the shots, the runs, the applause.

It builds before you've even taken guard.

But then, when it doesn't happen – when you get nothing – the drop is brutal. The embarrassment of it. The silence. The walking off in front of thousands who've just watched you do absolutely fuck all. And even if they say nothing, you can feel it. You can feel the disappointment, and the judgement.

* * *

Getting out is bad. But dropping a catch? That might be worse. I didn't drop many, thankfully, but when I did, I'd spend the next hour praying for the batter to get out. Not just hoping – properly *praying*. If he went on to make a double hundred, you felt like such a dick. No one would say it, but you knew they were thinking it.

There are 'acceptable' ways to get out – at least that's how it feels. Play a defensive shot, get a thin nick to the keeper – that's forgivable. Play a wild shot, caught on the boundary with fielders out there? That's not.

Even so, I much preferred the second way. I'd rather have a go than just nudge and prod and fart about. That's not how I saw the game.

It wasn't just on the pitch, either. Cricket is one of the few places where grown men act like kids and no one blinks. Dressing rooms are part playground, part therapy session. The chat, the pranks, the tantrums. You see some of the most accomplished blokes in the country throwing helmets, smashing bats, breaking stuff, proper toddler energy. I was no different.

The worst (or maybe just the first) of it came in 1997,

when I was just 19. Although I was making appearances for the firsts, I was playing for the Second XI against Yorkshire, and I wasn't playing well. I was frustrated, got out and came off fuming, threw my helmet, launched my gloves, and then, for some stupid reason known only to my teenage ego, punched the wall.

I sat on the toilet afterwards, head in hands, feeling sorry for myself. When I looked down, there it was – a lump on my hand, swelling fast. I'd busted it. Proper 'boxer's break'.

So now I had to go and tell the coach, Peter Sleep, an Aussie. I liked him and didn't want to lie to him, but I panicked and told him I got hit while batting. He raised an eyebrow, said nothing, and sent me for an X-ray. Hand pinned. Eight weeks out.

Later, guilt got the better of me. I went to Pete's hotel room, knocked on the door, and said, 'I didn't really get hit. I punched the wall.'

He didn't look surprised. Said, 'I know. I just wanted you to tell me.'

Then came the bit I was dreading. He told me I'd have to inform the first-team coach.

Bumble.

I was terrified. The next day, I was at Old Trafford, post-scan, towel round my waist after a shower, walking back from the old changing room.

Bumble's coming the other way.

'Andrew,' he says – always Andrew, never Fred – 'How are you?'

'I've broken my hand,' I say.

'How did you do that?'

And now I'm bracing for it – the full bollocking. I tell him: 'I punched a wall.'

He just looks at me and says, 'That's stupid, Andrew, isn't it?'

Then he walks off.

And somehow, that's worse than anything he could have shouted. It kills me. I want a bollocking. I want to be punished. But instead, I just feel like I've let him down. Still do, when I think about it.

But weirdly, it turns out to be one of the best things that ever happens. I miss eight weeks, true – but something shifts. It gives me a line not to cross again. Not with my body. Not with my game.

And then I got picked to go on an England A tour.

CHAPTER 10

MY FIRST CAP FOR ENGLAND

I walk into the dressing room. Right away, I know I don't belong.

No one says it, but it's not like they need to. It's in the way no one shifts to make space, or says anything, or looks at me.

So, no, the England dressing room at Trent Bridge isn't exactly what you'd call welcoming, and right away I work out that there's no space for me.

I look around the room and what I see are blokes I've grown up watching. Michael Atherton, the stoic former captain. Alec Stewart, sharp behind the stumps and sharper in conversation. Darren Gough, the Yorkshire spearhead with a grin as wide as his action. I've seen them on TV since I was a kid. Now I'm sharing a room with them, but I'm not part of it. Not really. I'm just there.

Instead, I sidle across to what looks like a utility room, complete with washing machines, towel rails and an aroma of Persil and jockstrap. I drop my bag and try not to look fazed. But I'm changing next to a Hotpoint on my Test debut. It's not exactly what I'd pictured.

Changed, I go back out to the main dressing room, where Goughy's the first to speak. 'All right, Fred?' he says, and I nod.

'Everyone calls me Rhino,' he says. 'Know why?'

'No.'

'Because I'm as strong as an ox.'

I laugh nervously.

Next I'm handed my England cap. No ceremony, no team huddle, family on the boundary. Just David Graveney, the chairman of selectors, shaking my hand and a quick photo. I put the cap down by the dryers, back in my little laundry corner.

I never see it again.

I've no idea where it went. Might've been nicked, might've been lost. If you're reading this and you know what happened to my first-ever England cap, well, answers on a postcard, please.

Anyway, back to the pre-match atmosphere, and the room's quiet, but not calm. It's full of fear. People are nervous, uptight. No one's talking about the game, but everyone's talking about South Africa. Allan Donald, the great fast bowler they call 'White Lightning'. Jacques Kallis, a rising all-rounder who already looks the part. Daryll Cullinan, elegant but edgy. There's a sense that we're already beaten. I can feel it in the air. I don't understand it. If we're scared of them, what are we doing here?

I bowl first. I'm not that quick – not with my back the way

it is – but I take Jacques Kallis for my first Test wicket, and it doesn't feel real. None of it does, if I'm honest.

Then I'm in, my turn to bat at number seven, and as I walk out, the South Africans give me both barrels. Donald especially. The sledging I mentioned before.

Anyway, the barrage begins and his first ball hits me on the arse. I finally hit one straight past him for four. Then one through the covers. These are proper shots, and I feel all right. Then Kallis comes on and I launch one over extra cover for six. Ridiculous. Next one, I try it again. Caught behind. Gone.

We go on to win the Test match and level the series. I get picked again to play at Headingley in the final Test of the series. I score no runs in the match or take any wickets, although we go on to claim a historic win. (Darren Gough took the last wicket, caught by sub-fielder and my mate Matthew Wood. In those days the crowd used to run onto the pitch. Absolute euphoria.)

Back in the dressing room the celebrations start and the beer is flowing, but I don't feel a part of it. Not just down to the fact that I've done nothing in the game, but I don't feel part of the team. It's a feeling solidified when one of the production crew from Sky Sports came and interview everyone in the side apart from me, Graeme Hick, and Ian Salisbury – who I have a sneaky suspicion feels exactly the same as I do.

I'm dropped from the final Test of the summer against Sri Lanka, which I expect, but it also comes with a strange sense of relief.

Next morning, I'm on a flight to Southampton. Lancashire

have got a quarter-final. I've gone from Test cricket to the C&G Trophy overnight. And weirdly, I can't wait. Because at least there, in the Lancashire dressing room, I know someone's going to notice I've turned up.

*   *   *

Prior to that, I'd been playing well for Lancashire, getting some wickets, feeling good. There was a buzz about the place. We were playing Worcestershire, and I knew the England selectors were sniffing around. David Graveney and the others had been popping up at games. I'd started to believe something might happen, but still didn't expect it.

We were on the team bus, heading back from Worcester. I'd taken a few wickets that day – decent players too – even though I was half-knackered, waddling in off a short run, part-injured but still getting them down. Then Mike Watkinson, our captain at Lancashire, got a call. He turned round and said it was for me. David Graveney, chairman of selectors. I thought it was a wind-up. Phones weren't what they are now. This was 1998, and I had a mobile, just about, but barely used it. Orange pay-as-you-go, never charged, never answered. I remembered my dad saying it was a waste of money, that they'd never catch on.

So anyway, I took the call, all polite, thinking it was a joke and that I was being so cool not falling for it.

'Cheers, David, I've been picked, have I? Yeah, sounds lovely, see you there.'

Handed the phone back like it was nothing.

Mike just looked at me and said, 'No, you are. You've

been picked.' I still didn't believe it until Graveney rang again.

The call came out of the blue, but being rung up was a rarity. Back then, there weren't emails or big announcements. Players would sit refreshing Ceefax – page 340 for the cricket, 341 for the England team – hoping your name showed up. That time, though, I got the call. I was 20, just about finding my voice in the dressing room, and suddenly I was heading to Trent Bridge. Proper Test cricket. Still wet behind the ears. But there I was.

After that, the whole laundry room situation was a bit of a let-down, if I'm honest. I tried not to let it get to me. Just focus on what you can control, I'd thought. Bowling. Batting. Fielding. I mean, I'd been used to the Lancashire lot – warm, rowdy, proper team spirit. But England was the opposite. It was a cold, distant clique, and I felt like an outsider the whole week.

And then there was the cap. That bloody cap. You don't forget your first England cap. You treasure it. Or at least you try to, if someone doesn't nick it first.

Looking back, I can't say it was a dream debut. I mean, it wasn't a disaster, but it wasn't special either. It was just . . . weird. No sense of being part of something. You'd think playing for your country would be the peak. For me, it just felt like a warning. Like, if this is what international cricket's going to be, you'd better toughen up fast.

I was too young to understand it then, but that debut told me something about the game – about the levels of it. Domestic cricket was about mates, banter, shared graft. International cricket was about survival. About pecking orders. You had to earn your place, not just in the side, but in the room.

That lesson took a long time to sink in. But Trent Bridge, 1998 – that's where it started.

CHAPTER 11

CONTROL

Two years since I made my Test debut for England, and I'm now a regular, though you might say 'struggling for consistency' and getting a bit of a press battering for it. It's now the year 2000 – July, to be more precise – and here I am standing on the balcony at Old Trafford with a mic in my face, heart still hammering, sweat sticking to my back. We've beaten Zimbabwe, I've been named man of the match, and the crowd's behind me, cheering, clapping, singing my name.

But none of it quite lands the way it should, and instead I feel like I'm floating above it all, watching myself from somewhere else. Could be because the bloke asking the questions is Paul Allott of Sky Sports, who's among those who've been hammering me.

Everyone's had a dig. Commentary, columns, studio panels – they've joined in. Too fat. Unfit. A joke. My name's been dragged through it every week. And now here I am on the balcony having to front up, do an interview, like nothing's been said.

I mean, I'm hurting. I'm embarrassed. I'm questioning my very existence. But I'm supposed to stand there, answer their questions like a good boy, when I've got all this going through my head.

Allott asks me something about the game. I answer. Then he says something else, and I don't even hear it; instead I just look at him and say, 'Yeah, I did all right for a fat lad.'

I don't plan it, like. It just comes out. I don't intend the venom. It's just there.

My answer catches him off guard. He goes pale. 'We've never said that,' he says, but that's not strictly true, and anyway, so many *have* been saying it.

It should be a good moment. Redemption. Vindication. Sticking it to those who have been sticking it to me. But it isn't and instead I feel flat, like the game's over, yet I'm still stuck in the mess of everything else. There's a reason for that, and the reason is that I'm not right and haven't been for a while.

Why? I've been making myself sick.

Started with booze. Nights out where I'd drink too much and then want to undo it. Get it out of me before it turned to fat, minimise the hangover. A quick trip to the loo, finger down the throat, get it all out.

And then it moved to food. I'd eat late, or eat badly, and feel the panic set in. Like I'd done something wrong. Like I had to fix it.

So I'd fix it.

Finger down the throat. Eyes watering. Chest heaving. Get it all up. Feel better. At least for a bit.

Then again.

The scary-weird part is that it's working. I feel lighter. I look thinner. I'm moving and playing better and the press have stopped going in quite so hard. I start thinking that maybe this is how it has to be. Maybe the whole being sick deal is the price I have to pay, and perhaps it's a price worth paying.

No one knows about it. I'm sitting in dressing rooms with blokes I've played with for years, and no one has a clue. I'm the one cracking jokes, flicking towels, being the clown. Then I nip off for five minutes, empty my stomach into a toilet bowl and look in the mirror afterwards and feel disgusted. Red eyes, sweat down my neck, bits of food on my chin. It's gross and at some level I know that it's unsustainable, but at the same time, I feel like I've got away with something. As though I've taken back control.

And now here I am, back in front of the crowd, being cheered again. Holding a bottle of champagne I don't want, wearing a shirt that sticks to me in all the wrong places, talking to a man who's helped make me feel ashamed of myself for months, saying, 'All right for a fat lad.'

It's not just for Allott. It's for all of them. All the papers, all the pundits, all the people who made me feel like I wasn't enough. And also for me. Because I've said it now. I've put it out there. That's what they think. That's what I've been called. And it's what I've been calling myself, quietly, every single day.

Later, I'll go home and throw up my dinner. I'll feel my

throat burn and my ribs ache. I'll look in the mirror again and feel like shit. But for now, on that balcony, I've said it out loud.

I've said it before anyone else could.

* * *

Let's call it what it is. No point in being coy about it. I made a TV documentary about it, after all.

Bulimia. It had started quietly.

I mean, I'd always been tall. But now I was what you'd call *heavy*. And the world let me know it. I'd pick up a paper and see headlines about my size. One compared me to Lennox Lewis. We were the same weight, apparently, except he was world champ and I was eating pies. That stung. And I wouldn't see this kind of thing just once, it was every week. Every outlet. People who'd never met me deciding I was lazy, unprofessional, a joke.

I started feeling ashamed in my own skin. Going to the supermarket became an ordeal. I'd walk the aisles and feel like everyone was watching. Judging me. I'd reach for a pack of Hobnobs and hear the comments in my head. So I changed how I did the shop. Healthy stuff only. Nothing indulgent. Always aware of who might be watching.

And when I wasn't careful, when I did let go, the guilt would hit me hard. I started drinking more. Nights out, pints, fast food on the way home. And then the regret. That's how the cycle began, and how it went on.

It became a habit. A routine. I didn't call it bulimia. I didn't call it anything. I just thought I was keeping control. I saw it as a way of dealing with a situation. You know you shouldn't do it, but it gets the job done. Maybe you'll make this one the last time. Start afresh tomorrow. You've got it under control.

But it wasn't control. It was panic. It was fear. It was shame pretending to be discipline.

That summer, I kept playing. Still on the edge of the England side, I was putting in some good performances. From the outside, it probably looked like progress.

Meanwhile, inside, I was lost.

Then came India in 2001. That's when it *really* took hold.

I was called back up to the senior squad and I should have felt thrilled, but wasn't because I was panicking about how I'd look and what I'd eat. About how I could keep the weight off. On tour, it was constant food – hotels, buffets, late dinners – and I couldn't handle it. It felt like every meal came with a side order of guilt. I'd go through the motions of eating, smile through it, then excuse myself. Back to the toilet. Get rid of it all.

And it wasn't clean. It wasn't neat. It was violent. Messy. My throat would burn. The food would come back spicy and sharp, sometimes through my nose. My eyes would water. My heart would pound. I'd look in the mirror and see someone I didn't recognise. And then I'd wipe my face, pull myself together, and go back out there like nothing had happened.

No one knew. Not the lads. Not the coaches. Not even Rachael, who was my girlfriend at that time, noticed at first. I was good at hiding things. Jokes, banter, bit of noise – it kept people looking the other way.

In India, it got worse. I was throwing up during lunch breaks in games. Play a session, eat, vomit, have a smoke, go again. It was routine. I lost ten kilos on that tour and everyone said I looked great. Said I was fit again. Ready. No one asked how.

At the same time, I trained obsessively. Gym sessions every day. Long runs. I'd punish myself for eating. My relationship with exercise got all turned around. It wasn't about getting strong or healthy, it was about earning or undoing food. I saw food as the enemy and exercise as atonement. I'd wake up thinking about what I had to burn off. If I'd had a takeaway the night before, it wasn't just guilt I felt – it was urgency. Punishing myself, I'd hammer the treadmill until I was dizzy. I'd lift weights until my arms were shaking. Food had to be earned, and if I hadn't sweated enough that day, I'd either skip meals or find another way to get rid of them. The worst part? People thought I was finally taking things seriously. They praised my work ethic. The transformation. No one saw that I was flogging myself to bits just to feel okay in my own skin.

The lads probably thought I was just serious about my fitness. Maybe even dedicated. They didn't know I was timing my meals so I could be sick between sessions. That I was picking what to eat based on how easy it was to bring it back up. Curry was a nightmare. You don't want that coming back up through your nose. Chinese was simple. Ice cream helped. Water was essential. I had a system.

I hid it effectively. I didn't want to lie, but I couldn't tell the truth. I didn't have the language. I thought eating disorders were something teenage girls got. I didn't see it as something a bloke like me could have. I didn't want to be seen as weak. I didn't want pity.

So I kept it quiet.

Looking back, I'm not even sure when it tipped from habit into compulsion. One minute it was a thing I did now and again to feel in control, the next it was just . . . my life, something I structured my days around: timing meals to make sure I had space to be sick, avoiding certain foods because they were harder to get rid of. Didn't matter if I was home, on the road, in a hotel or a stadium – it was always with me. Find a bathroom, lock the door, go through the same motions every time. It was physical – retching, heaving, burning in my throat – but it was emotional too. That sense of relief. Of having corrected something. And then the crash, the shame, the regret.

Rachael noticed I wasn't myself. I looked thinner but seemed more distant. She saw me obsessing over training, getting edgy about food. There were moments where she'd ask questions and I'd just deflect them with tales of being dog-tired and worn out by a punishing work schedule. And to be honest, part of me believed that too. That it was just stress, just me pushing myself. I wasn't ready to face what it really was.

Because that's the thing – bulimia isn't just about what you do, it's about what you tell yourself. For years I convinced myself that this wasn't an eating disorder – that it couldn't be. After all, I was a bloke. I played cricket. I hit sixes, took wickets, went out with the lads. I wasn't some kid in a health textbook. I thought bulimia was something fragile people had. Something dramatic. Not something I could be part of. Making the documentary in 2020 really helped on that score. I began to see that what I had was at the lower end of the scale, but even so, it was still a disorder. I also realised that real strength isn't in hiding something – it's in admitting it.

Meanwhile, I told myself it was fine. That I had it under control. That it was temporary. That it was working. And in some twisted way, it was. I was getting fitter. Playing better. Losing weight. Getting picked. The same media that had torn into me for being overweight were now calling it a comeback. They said I looked sharp. They said I looked like an athlete again.

No one ever asked what the cost was.

When you're the big lad, the joker, you learn how to deflect. You control the narrative before anyone else can. I'd take the piss out of myself in interviews – laugh about my size, make the fat jokes before the press could – and people thought I was comfortable. They thought I was bulletproof. But I wasn't. I was drowning in it, and I couldn't tell a soul.

My throat would be raw, my eyes bloodshot, and my skin looked grey. And all I could think was, *I hope no one ever finds out.*

The documentary told the whole story – or as much of it as I could – and as I say, helped me to understand why it had taken hold the way it had. I went back over the timelines, looked at the photos, spoke to experts, even sat in group therapy sessions with others who'd lived through it. And the thing that struck me most was how common it actually was – how many people were living with it, silently, just like I had.

It wasn't about food. Not really. It was about pressure. About control. About punishment. About trying to meet expectations that were never clear and never achievable. I thought I had to look a certain way to be accepted. I thought I had to be leaner, meaner, sharper – that the cricket world only had space for one version of me, and it wasn't the one I saw in the mirror.

The documentary was tough to make. Reliving it, talking about it, seeing old footage of myself in those years – it opened up wounds I didn't realise were still sore. But it helped, too. It let me talk to my kids about it. Let me be honest with them about what I'd been through. Let me show that it's okay to struggle, and it's brave to speak up.

I don't think in terms of cures. That's not how it works for me. I've not been sick in years, but I still feel it sometimes – that urge, that old voice in my head. It's quieter now, but it's still there. And I've learned that managing it is about kindness, not control. About accepting that I'll never be perfect, but I can still be all right.

I train now because I want to feel good, not because I need to undo anything. I eat what I like, within reason. I don't obsess over scales or mirrors. And if I have a rough day, I talk about it. That's the biggest shift – I don't hide any more. I don't need to.

Bulimia took a chunk out of me, but it didn't finish me. It changed the way I saw myself, and for a long time, it nearly broke me. But it also taught me something. About pressure. About identity. About what matters. And maybe, weirdly, it made me stronger.

Not in the gym. Not on the scales. But inside.

CHAPTER 12

ME AND GANGULY

The little battles like me and Matthew Hayden were often the best bit of a match. That's where the real fun was: the ego stuff, the one-on-one contests, you versus them. And sometimes, if you were lucky – or unlucky – one of those little battles would run for years. That's how it was with me and Ganguly.

Sourav Ganguly. He and I went back. We had our first round at Lancashire, 2000, when he came in as our overseas player that season, and I won't lie, it was hard work from the start.

The club were trying to replace Wasim Akram – which, let's be honest, is not an easy gig for anyone – and Sourav was the man they went for. Great player, but let's just say we weren't exactly a match made in heaven.

The thing was, Sourav wasn't really bothered about fitting in. He wasn't one for sitting in the bar after play, having a pint and chewing the fat. He'd get his runs, take his catches, do his job – and then do one back to the hotel, back to his own world. No offence meant, like. No real attempt to be part of things either.

I remember early on thinking, *This is going to be a long season*. And it was. Sourav did fine on the pitch. He scored his runs. But you could feel the disconnect. Lancashire's always been a pretty tight dressing room – a few beers, bit of chat, plenty of piss-take – but he was never really in it with us.

And that stuck with me. It lodged itself somewhere. Not in a nasty way, but as a little needle. Something to file away for the future.

So when we faced India not long after, I already had a bit of extra spice for the contest. Now it wasn't just England against India – it was me against him.

Before I talk about me and Sourav, quick sidebar, a digression, if you will, because I really need to mention that this tour was the one where I got shot.

Actually shot.

With an air rifle. But still.

* * *

Picture it. It's January 2002 and I'm standing on the boundary in Delhi, fielding in front of a wall of noise. It's not like anywhere else. Football back home? Multiply that by ten and you're getting close to how they feel about cricket here. It's not just a game; it's everywhere. You drive through the streets, you see kids playing on every patch of land, cricket on every billboard, every advert fronted by an

Indian superstar. Turn on the telly – cricket. Walk through the airport – cricket.

It's in the air, in the culture. It's incredible.

And of course the grounds are packed. There are 20,000 people in here today, but it feels like double that. And unlike a football crowd, where they surge and fall depending on what's happening, this is just constant. Constant noise. Constant energy. It never dips. The whole ground hums, like a live current running through it.

When you first arrive on tour in India, nobody really knows who you are. But as soon as the matches start getting televised and you put in a few performances, it all changes. The crowds still want India to win – of course they do – but there's an appreciation, too, even if you're the bloke trying to beat them. They're partisan, but they appreciate good cricket. It's one of the things I love most about playing there.

I'm young, still trying to find my place, but I'm doing all right on this tour. The crowd have started to get to know me, and I'm getting to know them. It's all part of it – a bit of toing and froing, a bit of fun. There's a slight pantomime villain thing going on with me, but it's in good spirits. They like having a go, I like giving it back. It's brilliant.

But today, something happens that I'm not ready for.

I feel it first as a little sting in my back. A sharp, sudden jab. Then another. Then another.

I spin round, confused. What the hell was that? I look down and see them lying there on the grass – little metal pellets. Air rifle pellets.

Someone's shooting at me.

I walk in from the boundary, waving to the umpire. I'm

holding the pellets in my hand. 'I'm getting shot out here,' I say. The umpire looks at me, half-confused, half-disbelieving.

'You what?' he says.

'Seriously, look – they're shooting me. These are air rifle pellets.'

I hold them up, and he stares at them for a second, like he can't quite believe it either. The game pauses while they try and figure out what to do. Eventually, we carry on. What else can you do? It's bonkers, really. Absolutely bonkers. But it doesn't change how I feel about playing here. This isn't India. This is just one idiot with an airgun.

(Incidentally, when I first went public with this story, Delhi cricket officials claimed it was a fib, saying that a gun would never have got through ground security. Hm. Maybe it was someone spitting those pellets at me, then.)

None of which matters. I've got way too many good memories of India to let a few pellets ruin it, although in many ways the experience sums up my relationship with India – a bit of a roller coaster. Some success, some frustration. What really strikes you is the way they revere their own players.

For instance, the master technician Sachin Tendulkar, who made the genius look routine. Weirdly, I always believed I could get him out. Even before I played against him, I had this feeling.

I remember when he made his Test debut at 16. I was 14 at the time, playing for Lancashire Under-15s, coming back from a game, listening to the radio. This kid with the big hair, scoring runs for India against England at Old Trafford. And now here I am, bowling at him. Full circle stuff.

One day I'm bowling well, and I see him call for an arm

guard. And I think to myself, *You're not enjoying this, are you?* That's respect. That's the little win within the contest. And he always brought the best out of me. Not because I disliked him – far from it – but because I revered him. I never wanted to get him out just to say I'd done it. I just wanted to prove to myself that I was good enough to be out there.

I never spoke to him. I wouldn't have known what to say. What do you say to Sachin Tendulkar? Better to keep that little distance.

Then there was Yuvraj Singh. Left-hander. Fantastic player. Me and Yuvraj had a bit of a running battle, but in a good way. We'd wind each other up, a bit of needle between us. I'd try to get in his head, and he'd give it back, sometimes just ignoring me with a little smirk, like he was pretending not to hear me. But it was fun. I always felt like it sharpened both of us. He was another one I respected massively – still do.

Which brings me back to Sourav. And Mumbai. Wankhede Stadium, 2002. Final ODI of the series, England needing a win to make it all square and salvage pride. It came down to the last over. India needed 11. I was bowling. The place was heaving, noise ricocheting off every concrete surface. First ball – Srinath on strike. I found a bit extra, a touch of shape, and bang – stumps everywhere. Game over. England win by five runs. Series drawn 3-3.

I don't know what came over me. One second I was roaring, fists clenched, adrenaline spiking like never before. The next, I'd ripped my shirt off and was swinging it above my head, running like a lunatic across the Wankhede outfield.

Total chaos. The crowd were stunned, then furious, and I was loving every second. Ten seconds of madness, I called it later. Bit embarrassing, if I'm honest. But in the moment? It felt right. Pure, reckless release. Shirt off, heart thumping, living every ounce of it.

I remember Goughy coming over afterwards, shaking his head. 'You pasty farmer. What have you done now?' he said.

Classic Goughy. Always ready with a line.

Of course, Sourav got his moment back at Lord's. The following year, same scenario – another one-dayer, another tight finish. This time, they got over the line, and off comes his shirt. He ripped it off, waved it around on the Lord's balcony, a brilliant fuck you in shirt-waving form. I mean, you're not really supposed to do that at Lord's – not the done thing – but fair play to him. It was brilliant, actually. I laughed. He got his revenge.

By that point, the whole thing had turned almost into pantomime. We both knew what we were doing. Bit of a show for the crowd, bit of edge, bit of theatre. The fans lapped it up.

Mind you, the Indian fans never really forgave me for the earlier stuff. Even now, years on, I'll still get abuse on social media – 'You disrespected Ganguly!' – like I've insulted a family member. That's how they feel about Sourav. He's cricketing royalty over there. You don't mess with Dad.

Over time, me and him mellowed. You do, don't you? And lots of people say what a great bloke he is. And the thing is, you enjoy those battles. You need them. Although at Lancs we might not have got the best of him, he was a completely different animal when he played for India. Proud, fierce, never took a backward step. Could take you apart in the blink of an eye.

Hopefully, at some point in the future we can sit down and have dinner and smile about what, at the time, was war. And that was what made him such a good opponent. That edge. That needle. He was tough. He played with a chip on his shoulder, and he captained India at a time when they were starting to shed that nice-guy image and become genuinely hard-nosed.

You could see it in how India changed under him. Before, they were always stronger at home than away. Under Sourav's captaincy, they started winning everywhere. He backed his players fiercely – especially his young lads – and they repaid him.

And that's why, deep down, I always respected him. He was fighting for his team, the same as I was for mine. That's what made the tussle so good. It was never cheap. It was proper cricket.

I do sometimes wonder how different it would've been if we'd got off on a better foot at Lancashire. If we'd had a few pints, if he'd bought into the dressing room a bit more, maybe we'd have been mates from the start. But then again, maybe that tension is what made it so compelling. Maybe we needed that little bit of needle to sharpen the edge.

Because that's what sport is, really. You don't remember the easy wins, the games where everything flows. You remember the battles. The days when you had to dig in, when someone was coming for you and you stood your ground. Me and Sourav? We gave each other that.

The South Africans, though? They were another level.

CHAPTER 13

THE HANGOVER

It's July 2003 and I'm walking back into the hotel after another long, draining day at Lord's. I know exactly where this is heading: in the second Test of the series, South Africa have just declared on 682 for six – Smith's made 259, Gibbs chipped in with 49, and they've batted for almost three days without letting up. In reply, we've been bowled out for 173, and now we're three or four down again, following on and still miles behind. Technically, there's another day left in the game, but let's be honest – this one's already cooked.

Me and Harmy head through reception, past the bar. We can see the lads already dotted about – a few sitting having a beer, a few heading out for food. I pause. The bar looks inviting. It always does. Condensation glistens on the beer taps . . .

I turn to Harmison.

'Fancy a pint?'

'Yeah, go on then.'

And that's how it starts.

First pint of Stella goes down easy. *Another? Be rude not to.* We sit there chatting, putting the world to rights. Second one goes down even easier. Then a third. No big deal – nothing crazy – just two mates winding down after another long day of Test cricket. The game's gone, after all. Might as well enjoy the evening.

It's a different time back then, by the way. Drinking like this isn't exactly encouraged, but it's not unheard of either. The culture's looser. Not reckless, but not as tightly managed as it is now. You get a bit of latitude. Enough to go unnoticed. Or so we think.

A few pints turn into five. Five turns into eight. By the time we're hitting 12 or 13, we've completely parked any thoughts of tomorrow's batting. We've been buried under a mountain of runs, it's stinking hot, and the pitch has gone flat. In our heads, the game's done. The only thing still in play is the bar tab.

Then Vaughan walks in.

He's been out with his wife – gone for dinner, doing things properly – and now he's come back to find me and Harmy 12 deep on the hotel bar sofas, looking like two lads on a stag do. He stops in front of us, eyebrows up.

'What the hell are you two doing?'

'Just having a couple, mate. Unwinding. Nothing heavy.'

He's not buying it. You can see the manager in him fighting with the mate.

'I've got to say, Fred – not impressed. You're batting tomorrow.'

I grin. 'Yeah, I know. But let's see how tomorrow goes first, eh?'

He scowls. 'You what?'

'I'll get a hundred tomorrow. Go on, back me. Give me odds.'

Now he's properly wound up. He knows I've barely got any Test hundreds at this point. It's a big ask.

He says, 'I'll give you a thousand to one.'

I don't blink. 'Right – £100 then. That's £100,000 if I pull it off.'

He panics. 'No chance. Tenner. You can have a tenner on it.'

So that's the bet. Tenner at 1,000/1. If I make a hundred tomorrow, he owes me ten grand.

Vaughan shakes his head, muttering as he disappears into the lift. Me and Harmy look at each other and – because we are deeply professional athletes – order one more for the road.

Eventually, I stagger up to my room, way past the sensible cut-off point. But that's for tomorrow's Freddie to deal with.

*　　*　　*

As if I didn't have enough to deal with. This five-Test series against South Africa was being played at a tempo. Makhaya Ntini – South Africa's first black Test cricketer, and one of the most relentless fast bowlers I ever faced – was on his mark, plus it was hot, the sun beating down on us like it hated us, drying out the pitch.

Added to which, I was being given the evil eye.

It had started with a stare. First Test of the series at

Edgbaston, and I was already being sized up like I was the weak link by their captain, Graeme Smith, only 22, barely settled in the job, and already full of intent. I hadn't even faced a ball and he was in my ear, throwing jibes from slip like he'd been leading that side for years. 'Oh, you think you're a batsman now, do you? You're not that good, mate.' Proper getting into me.

I stared back at him. *You want a battle? Fine*. I love this stuff.

That's how the series had started – full of needle, from ball one. They wanted to assert themselves. Smith's only young, new in the job, still trying to stamp his authority. But I've been around long enough to know how this works. The trick is to give a bit back, but not too much. Don't let them smell blood in the water. Keep smiling. Keep swinging.

The thing is, I've got previous with South Africa. I know these lads. Boucher's always got something to say. Herschelle Gibbs – very talented, but he's got a mouth on him too.

Ntini, though – he's different. He doesn't say much. He just bowls. Relentless. The kind of bowler you admire even while you're facing him. He comes in hard every time. Nothing half-arsed about him. The more you hit him, the more he wants to bowl. Hit him for six? He just runs back to his mark and goes again. It's actually quite something to watch. Except, of course, I'm the one getting peppered with it.

From the first ball of that series, it was on. You could feel it – that extra edge. Michael Vaughan had just taken over for us, still settling in as skipper, while Smith was trying to stamp his authority on a dressing room full of strong characters. He wasn't easing his way in either. He'd decided, for whatever reason, that I was the pressure point. That if he could get at me, the rest would follow. And I didn't mind that. In fact, I quite enjoyed it. I've always liked a bit of fire in a series. Makes you sharper, more alive.

That first Test was a draw.

Then came Lord's for the second Test. And that drunken bet . . .

* * *

Morning hits like a hammer.

I wake up drenched in sweat, head thudding, stomach upside down. The hotel room's doing slow pirouettes around me. I sit on the edge of the bed for a full minute, trying to remember how cricket works. Pads, bat, helmet. Something like that.

I shuffle down to breakfast in a state. The staff clock me instantly. Why? Because I've got that *look*. I grab a bacon butty, scalding coffee, and a big bottle of water. I sit as close to a window as I can without falling out of it. I need light. I need sleep, at the very least a blood transfusion.

Most of all, I need not to have spent the previous night sinking pints of Stella.

When I make it to the dressing room at Lord's, I park myself in my usual spot – end seat by the door. Always sat there. Creature of habit, even when I'm half-cut. I call one of the attendants over.

'Mate, get us another bacon butty, will you? And some Lucozade.'

Jimmy Anderson's nearby, checking his gear. He looks over.

COMING HOME

'You all right, Fred?'

'I'm in a pickle here, Jimmy. I've overdone it. Vaughany's on my case. And I've got that bloody bet to deal with.'

Everyone already knew about the bet, of course.

He smiles. Doesn't say much else. What can you say? It is what it is.

The wickets start falling. Not in clumps, just steadily enough that I know my time's coming. I put on my pads. It's like armouring up with bricks. Every buckle feels like a mission.

When my name's called, I take a last sip of coffee, wipe the sweat off my neck, and step out into the sunlight. Lord's is packed. Humid air, no breeze. And I can feel every pint I drank. My stomach's in a slow churn, and my head's still foggy.

I walk to the crease trying to breathe through it.

Deep in, deep out.

Breathe, you twat, breathe.

It's not nerves – it's maintenance. Keep the engine running long enough to get moving.

First few deliveries come in. I leave one, prod at another. Then I find a gap – nice crisp drive through mid-off. Crowd lifts. I hear it, but I don't let it in. Next ball, short – I hook. Clean. Boundary. That helps.

Then something shifts.

I stop thinking about the hangover. I stop hearing the dressing room. I find rhythm. They pitch it up – I drive. They drop short – I pull. It's starting to flow. The ball starts looking bigger. The bat feels lighter. I start trusting the instincts.

Fifty comes up quicker than I expect. It's noisy now. The scoreboard's ticking. I'm losing track of the runs, which is always a good sign. I'm in the matrix now – that headspace where the body just knows what to do.

And then the bat goes. It's during an intense over of facing Ntini, when mid-swing, I feel it – crack – clean through the handle. It splits in two like something out of a cartoon. I look down at it in disbelief. The bottom half's in my hand, the top half's somewhere near square leg. The crowd erupts. Even I laugh.

New bat, fresh gloves. Bit of a reset. Still going.

Harmy's out there with me at some point.

'You all right?' he says.

'Yeah.'

And I am. I really am.

I edge into the nineties, and this is usually where I start to wobble. That old instinct kicks in – try to finish it with a big one, go for the six, sky it, and end up walking off shaking my head. But not today. Today I keep it simple. Just nudge it around. Pick up ones, twos, keep the scoreboard moving. Bit of patience, bit of rhythm. The hangover's gone now – burned off in the heat and the adrenaline.

Then comes the moment. It's a full ball, and I clip it through midwicket and set off. The crowd knows before I do. I hear the roar, glance up, and there it is on the board – three figures.

Hundred.

I lift the bat. Helmet off. Give it the wave with a mix of elation and relief. And somewhere behind me, up on the balcony, I know Vaughan's watching. I can't see him, but I don't need to. I can picture the look on his face.

Afterwards – with my final tally 142 – he comes over in the dressing room.

'Well played. But don't you fucking do that again.'

I grin. 'Where's my ten grand?'

He grumbles. And you know what? Never pays it.

I mean, I knew he wouldn't. But the point wasn't the money – it was the moment. That weird, glorious, ridiculous morning after the night before. The bet. The hangover. The hundred.

It's only later, when I'm watching the highlights back, that I realise how significant it was. That knock changed things. Something clicked that day. I stopped playing safe. Stopped worrying about what people expected. I just played. Free. Honest.

Vaughan had to face the media afterwards – and they were all over it. Not just the innings, but the whole story. We were lucky, really – this was just before phones were smart enough to catch us in the act. No video. Just word of mouth. That helped.

But I know it stung him a bit. Not the hundred (ahem, 142) – he was proud of that. But the idea that the story became mine instead of his. He was the captain, after all.

Still, we laughed about it later. I'd scored a few runs against the odds and realised I'd got away with it. But at the same time, that wasn't the way I wanted to play, moving forward, and I owed it to the new captain, the team and myself to be better and more professional.

And that's cricket, isn't it? Some days you train for, prep for, visualise. Others just happen. You wake up sweating Stella, chew a bacon butty, and walk into one of the best innings of your life.

All off the back of a stupid tenner bet in a hotel bar.

* * *

We won the third Test. By the time we reached the Oval for the fourth and final Test, we needed to win to level the series.

It didn't start well. South Africa were 362 for 4 at the end of day one, and it felt like the kind of pitch where you could bat forever. Bookies had England at 40–1 to win. You don't need odds that long to know the vibe around the ground – tight-lipped press guys, arms folded, the crowd already half-resigned. But the next morning, something shifted. We clawed our way back with five wickets before lunch. Giles deflected a run-out off his own bowling, Mark Butcher threw one in from the deep, and suddenly there was a spark. It still felt like a mountain, but at least now we had climbing boots on.

The atmosphere went from resigned to electric. Tresco was outrageous: 219 runs, calm as you like, nine and a half hours at the crease. Thorpe chipped in with a hundred and then it was my turn.

By the time I came in, batting late on, the heat had properly kicked in and the crowd were buzzing. I fed off the atmosphere and the big shots were coming off, the noise rising with every swing, everything feeling connected. That whole innings felt like one long release. The pressure had been building all summer, and suddenly I had this stretch where I couldn't miss. For a few overs, it was just fun. No plans, no calculations – just swing hard and trust it. I smacked 85 off 72. Final tally: 95 off 104.

That match said a lot about where we were as a team.

COMING HOME

The series wasn't going our way at that point. South Africa had taken control early and were playing some strong stuff. Graeme Smith had been monstrous with the bat – he made 277 at Edgbaston and followed it with 259 at Lord's. Back-to-back double hundreds. That's no accident. That's a young bloke announcing himself, and doing it in England, where the ball does plenty early doors, makes it even more impressive. But behind all the runs and numbers, what I remember is the feel of the contest – loud, abrasive, full-on from both sides. It wasn't cricket for the polite or the passive.

In all, one of the best team wins I've ever been involved with.

And in the middle of all that was Ntini. A proper fast bowler in every sense – strong action, long spells, never seemed to flag. He was one of the most committed bowlers I ever faced. There were spells where he bowled at me for what felt like hours, and his effort never dropped. The more I hit him, the more he came at me. That relentlessness – you can't teach that. It's built into a player's bones. I'd hit him for six, and he'd turn round and jog back to his mark like nothing had happened. That sort of stuff earns respect, even when you're on the receiving end.

Then there was Gibbs. Herschelle Gibbs was electric with the bat, but he also had a habit of letting his mouth run.

Which brings me to the Oval. Final Test of the series, and with South Africa leading 2-1, it really was a must-win for us.

As I say, that knock at the Oval ended on 95 from 104 balls. No century, but it was one of my favourites – raw, reactive, and right in the middle of the storm. We made 604 for nine declared in that innings, and I was happy with how I'd played. Twelve boundaries, four sixes, and every run felt like it mattered.

All of which meant that we went on to defy the odds and break South African hearts by winning the match and levelling the series 2-2. Smith ended with 714 runs for the series, Ntini topped the wickets with 23, and I finished with over 400 runs and a handful of key breakthroughs with the ball. But the stats only tell part of the story. The bigger picture was how it felt. Every Test was a scrap, and the edge never dulled.

After that final game – and with the series a draw – the South Africans came into our dressing room. That's the tradition – you battle it out, then sit together and share a drink. At first, it's stiff. People are still bruised, physically and mentally. But it's a good tradition, because it reminds you that even after all the noise, it's still a game.

Smith walked in and sat next to me. Not across the room – right next to me. We'd been going at each other all series, and now we were thigh to thigh on the same bench.

I had a bottle of Jack Daniel's on the go, and I looked at him and said, 'Fancy a drink?'

He didn't hesitate. 'Yeah.'

We passed the bottle back and forth, no mixers, just straight whiskey. At first, it was civil but tight. The kind of chat where you're both watching for signals, still half in battle mode. But a few swigs in, something loosened. We started laughing. Proper laughing. Talking about pressure, about leadership, about how the game pulls you in all directions when you care about it too much to let go.

That drink changed something between us. There was still tension, still the edge, but it wasn't personal any more. The next time we saw each other was in South Africa, later that year, when the rivalry was still alive, but the anger had shifted. I came out to bat in the first Test with sun cream slapped all round my mouth to protect some cold sores. Smith looked at me and grinned. 'Who do you think you are – Andrew Symonds?' One of those 'if you know, you know' jokes just for cricketers.

I laughed and gave it back, told him he was the worst captain South Africa had ever had and half his team didn't want him in charge. He didn't bite. He just said, 'Go easy.'

Later that day I passed him between overs and said, 'Graeme, do you fancy a pint tonight?'

He gave me a look.

'Come on,' I said, 'We've done all this before – the aggro, the shouting – might as well skip to the drink this time.'

He nodded. 'Yeah, all right.'

He told me, eventually, that his plan had always been to come for me during that series in the summer. He reckoned if he could knock me off my stride, he'd knock England off ours. I didn't know how to take that at first – sounded like a dig – but I understood it. I wasn't always the best player, but I was central to how that team felt. If I played well, we usually lifted. If I got rattled, the dressing room got twitchy. He'd spotted that and gone after it. And if the roles were reversed, I'd have done exactly the same.

Graeme Smith didn't inherit an easy squad. He was 22, captaining senior players and trying to earn their respect while also earning his own place. That's not a cushy job. But he did it. He went hard. He made it his. And I respect that.

It's funny how these things go. You start out snarling at each other across the pitch, and by the end you're sharing a bottle, trading stories, and actually hoping the other lad does all right. I wouldn't have said we were mates then, not quite, but we weren't enemies any more either. Somewhere in between. Opponents with a shared past and a grudging sort of admiration. Maybe even a bit of fondness, if we're being honest.

That series gave me a lot – not just stats or highlights, but something deeper. It showed me who I was when tested, and it showed me who Smith was too. And once all the noise had settled, what was left wasn't bitterness or regret, but respect. And maybe something that lasted.

Looking back, I respect that from Smith. Not just the tactic, but the guts. He wasn't handed an easy dressing room when he took the job. Some big names, big egos. And there he was, 22, still getting his own game together, leading the lot. That takes something. You don't always have to like a rival to admire them. But sometimes, if you stick around long enough, you find yourself liking them anyway.

That was us. Two strong-willed blokes, each trying to get one over on the other, and in doing so finding a kind of odd camaraderie buried underneath the aggro. Because once the dust settled, what was left wasn't bitterness or regret, but something closer to respect. And maybe even something that lasted.

Funny how cricket does that.

CHAPTER 14

BATTING

In 2002, I scored my maiden Test century for England: 137 vs New Zealand in Christchurch, batting with Graham Thorpe (who knocked a clean 200). The following year I scored a century and three 50s in the home Test series vs South Africa, including the one already mentioned, where I broke a bat smashing Makhaya Ntini at Lord's.

But in answer to the question I'm often asked, none of these are my favourite innings, nor any of the really *big* moments you may think of.

Before we go into which innings takes that honour, let's talk about batting for a bit, because alongside 'What's your favourite innings?' I often get asked questions like, 'How do you bat?' or words to that effect.

You know what I say?

Just this. I say, 'Hit the ball.'

Which sounds simple, I know, and it sort of is. People

expect some technical answer, something profound or complicated (from me? God knows why, but there you go), but at its heart, it really is that straightforward. Hit the ball. That's your job. Don't overthink it.

That said, to coach batting is a different beast entirely, especially with kids just starting out. As I'm sure you know if you've got this far, I do a show called *Field of Dreams*, where I've taken young lads who know fuck all about cricket and kind of moulded them into a half-decent cricket team. I've done some TV work I'm very proud of – the documentary about bulimia, for example – and *Field of Dreams* is way up there.

Anyway, when I worked with the lads on *Field of Dreams*, I found that batting isn't about technique as much as it is about confidence, about stripping back all the fear that comes with trying something new. Coaching the lads, we weren't talking about high-end technique or match strategies; we were talking about showing them how to hold a bat, where to stand, dropping balls and placing them onto tees and just getting them used to hitting the thing. And even that was hard enough. Half of them were terrified of looking daft in front of their mates. My job was to make them enjoy it. To get them coming back. Because if they didn't enjoy it, they wouldn't keep doing it.

The only real non-negotiable I had for them was simple: if you're here, you're all in. For these two hours, you give it everything you've got. And that doesn't mean you've got to be good. It just means you've got to give a shit. We can't guarantee performances. We can't guarantee outcomes. But you can guarantee effort.

That was something that took me a long time to fully understand in my own career too. Because at the higher levels – professional, international – everyone's that good. Everyone can bat; everyone can bowl. The margins become so fine that it stops being about technique and becomes almost entirely about confidence. A head game, in other words. When you're on it, you feel like you can do anything. When you're not, you feel like you can do nothing.

Confidence is everything. And fear of failure is the killer. I'd sit in endless team meetings where people would plaster buzzwords up on boards – 'honesty', 'integrity', 'bravery' – as if that sorted it. But fear of failure? You never truly get rid of that. You just find ways of dealing with it. And when you're properly on, when you hit that sweet spot, it's like playing inside The Matrix. You see everything. The ball looks massive, you spot all the gaps, your body feels smooth, like it knows what to do before you've even asked it to.

Those days were rare, but when they came, they were magic. And yes, they did happen on the big stages too. Even under the lights, even with 25,000 people watching, there were times when I walked out there, looked around and thought, *Yeah, I've got this*.

Other days? Completely different. I'd walk out and instead of seeing gaps, I'd see fielders everywhere, like the ground was full of people with no room left to hit a shot anywhere. I'd stand there thinking, *Jesus, how many blokes have they got out here?* and that's when the anxiety would kick in.

But the thing is – nobody else cares. Your teammates don't care because they need you to get runs. The crowd don't care; they just want to be entertained. The opposition certainly don't care; they want to bury you. So you have to put on a front. You act. You walk out there like you're in control. You pretend to be calm and collected, while inside you're just hoping you can survive the first few overs and find your rhythm.

That's when the mental side really kicked in for me. I realised that most of the battle wasn't against the bowler at all – it was against myself. All those battles I thought I was having with opposition players – really, they were happening inside my own head.

I tried to play on my ego, too. People always talk about ego like it's a bad thing, but it isn't necessarily. It depends how you use it. For me, especially early in my career, ego was what helped me survive. I was a 15-year-old fuckwit trying to make it in professional cricket. You need something extra to make you stand out. So I built up this version of me – Fred – who was tough, confident and never backed down. And it worked. On the field, I carried myself like someone who was always on the front foot, someone who gave nothing away.

That's the thing with me and the nickname. There's me, Andrew, and then there's him, Freddie. And funnily enough, the nickname came before the fame, when I was 15, still a kid. My brother had been called Fred at school (the Flintstone connection, just in case you're one of those people who sometimes come up to me who never made the connection and have that open-mouthed, penny-dropping moment), then one day, at a Lancashire Under-15s match against Yorkshire, John Stanworth, the coach, called me Fred. It was a bit of a laugh – but it stuck. After that, I was Fred. Not Andrew. Not Flintoff. Just Fred.

Funny how names work. Only my mum and dad, my wife, Rachael, and a few close mates still call me Andrew. Everyone else calls me Fred, even people I barely know. But here's the weird thing: I introduced myself to Rachael as Andrew. And that stuck with her. She asked me once if I had a pet name for her – I said, no, your name's Rachael. I'm not into 'babe' or anything like that. Same with me. I'm Andrew. Except I'm not.

See, Fred became a sort of character. A version of me that people could hang things on. The big lad, the confident one, the one cracking jokes and smacking sixes and lighting up dressing rooms. But the real me – quiet, introverted, happiest at home or with a small group of mates – he stayed Andrew. There's always been a tension between the two. When I wrote about bulimia or depression, I used Andrew. That felt right. More honest. When it's telly or cricket, it's Fred. That feels like performance. Acting. The version of me I thought I had to be.

Even now, when someone calls me Andrew and they're not close to me, I sometimes correct them. 'No, it's Fred.' Not to be rude. Just to say, *Andrew's not for you. That's the inner circle. That's the bloke behind the name.*

It's strange how a throwaway nickname from a coach ends up shaping your life. But that's how it happens. You play a game, you get a name, and the world takes it from there. Fred's fine. I like Fred. But deep down, I'm still Andrew. And only a few people get to see him.

* * *

Anyway, back to batting, and there were times, especially when I was flying, where it almost didn't matter who the bowler was. I could go out there and feel like I was walking on air. But on the flip side, when I was out of form, it didn't matter who was bowling either: Anil Kumble – one of the best spinners the game's ever seen – or some nobody on his debut. It wasn't them, it was me.

I always loved walking out to bat, though. Especially in front of a big crowd. I'd get out of my chair, trot down the steps, hear the announcer call my name, hear the crowd roar in response. And it's a buzz like nothing else. You're putting on a show. You feel good. You hit a four or a six and the place erupts. Some players say they don't hear the crowd. I heard everything. Why wouldn't you? It's brilliant.

Of course, if you got out for a duck, the same crowd could turn on you. Especially when you're young, you're hyper-aware of that. You play a shot and you're already wondering what the commentators are saying. But you grow out of that pretty quickly. After a while, it's just another game. Another crowd. You learn to detach yourself from it.

What I never liked, though, was people speculating about what I was thinking out there. The commentators trying to guess my mental state.

'Oh, Freddie's looking nervous here.'

'He doesn't look comfortable.'

They had no idea what was going on in my head. Sometimes, I was probably thinking about what I was having for tea. I didn't need anyone dissecting my mood or pretending they could read my mind.

As for facing different kinds of bowlers – that was

always interesting. Spin bowlers didn't scare me, but they got me out. Fast? Yeah, I probably played them better. Not because I wasn't scared – I was. Anyone who says they're not frightened facing quick bowling is lying, if you ask me. Don't forget, I started in the days before helmets – the pre-helmet era, as scientists now call it – and I've been hit in the face plenty of times. All the same, there's something about the challenge of facing real pace that's addictive.

A lot of it depends on where you're sitting before you go in. At some grounds, you sit behind the bowler's arm in the dressing room, so the ball looks slower. At other grounds, like Old Trafford, you sit side-on and watch the ball fly past the batter so fast you can barely see it. I remember sitting there as a kid, watching the keeper standing miles back, and thinking: 'Fucking hell, I'm not sure about this.'

But when it's your turn, you just get up, grab your bat and walk out. No idea what's going to happen. That was half the fun of it. And sometimes, when you're on, you see it like a beach ball. Other days, you see nothing.

So to bring us full circle, what about that thing I'm often asked: 'What's your favourite innings?'

Not the 2002 maiden Test century or the hundreds against South Africa. No, it's my first ever hundred, when I was with the Lancashire Under-11s, playing at the Dartford Festival, miles away from home.

I got 125 not out against Kent, and I can still see every ball now.

Walking off that pitch, raising my bat, taking my cap off – it felt like the best day ever. I even hit a six over midwicket, which at 11 years old felt like launching it into orbit.

You never forget moments like that, because that's when cricket first truly hooked me. The day the game planted its flag in my heart and went, 'You're mine now. You belong to me.'

Of course, I've had other innings along the way. I got 100 for Lancashire in a one-day game against Surrey when I was still pretty young. Played nicely that day. Getting a century at Lord's is good, because when you get a hundred, you go up on the honours board. They write your name up there forever. Test on the board, one-dayers on the wall. Your name's there. And every time I walk into that dressing room and look up, I still feel that little buzz of pride.

(But it wasn't a win, which leaves a bit of a sour taste. Like, I always feel that if you're going up on that board, it should be for winning contributions. Same with my five-wicket haul there – which I'm even prouder of, because we actually won that one.)

Then there were the near-misses. I had this habit, for a while, of getting into the nineties and then deciding to try and bring up the hundred with a six. It sounds daft, but that was just how I was wired. I'd be going well, seeing it like a football, feeling brilliant, and then I'd get to 95 or 96 and think, *Sod it, let's go big*, after which, more often than not, I'd sky it. I got out for 99 once doing that in a one-dayer – tried to hit it into the stands, it went straight up in the air instead, and got caught. I walked off laughing, because I mean, what else can you do?

You always know, by the way, the moment it leaves the bat. You know whether you've got hold of it or not. Occasionally you get away with one, when it just creeps over the fielder's head, but usually, you know your fate instantly. The ball's up, the fielder's under it, and you're standing there thinking, *Drop it, you dickhead, drop it, drop it.* You do that half-run, pretending you're interested, but really you're just watching, hoping.

And most times? They catch it. That's cricket. You play your shot and you know your fate before anyone else does.

It's the same with whole matches, actually. In a Test, you usually know by the end of day two or three which way it's going. You might have two more days officially scheduled, but everyone knows how it's going to finish. That sense of inevitability is part of cricket's weird charm.

As for shots, people used to ask if I had a trademark. I suppose I did. I always loved hitting straight back over the bowler's head. Just a little check drive – not a full-blooded follow-through, more controlled – but when you middle one like that, it's a great feeling.

And then, of course, the pull shot. I played that a lot. Because I bowled a lot of short stuff myself, people naturally came at me with the same. So, I had to get good at pulling. If they came at my head, I'd get in first. If they pitched it up, I'd have a go regardless, even if there were men out on the boundary waiting for the catch. That was my ego again, part of that little battle I always had with myself as much as with the bowler.

That was (is) cricket for me. Those little moments of pure joy and utter madness, all wrapped into one.

CHAPTER 15

ALL IN MY HEAD

Leading up to the 2005 Ashes, I was still searching for rhythm. I wasn't quite right, and I knew it. My head was foggy, the form patchy, and that old familiar enemy – consistency – was nowhere to be seen.

I'd picked up a decent haul of man of the match and man of the series awards over the years. I always liked those. They meant I'd turned up, done something meaningful, helped the team when it counted. But while the moments were there, stringing them together was a different story. That kind of week-in, week-out reliability? I never had it. Not properly. Maybe for a spell here and there, but never the long haul. I wasn't the bloke who quietly racked up his 35, chipped in with a few tidy overs, and did the job every time. I was boom or bust. And when it boomed, it was bloody brilliant.

That said, the thing that still gnaws at me – quietly, and only sometimes – is how much better I could have been. Not in a self-pitying way, just the facts. I can see it clearly now: the shortcuts, the missed sessions, the things I let slide thinking they didn't matter. They did. I mean, I retired at 31, and I've often thought about those lost years between then and 35. That should have been my prime.

As a bowler especially, I was just starting to figure it out. The art of it. The tempo, the tactics, the way to play cat and mouse with a batter. And mentally, I felt sharp – calmer, clearer, more able to block out the noise. I wasn't trying to be everything any more. I was just being what the team needed. But by then, my body had started waving the white flag. That's what hurt most. I'd finally got my head around it, just as the rest started falling apart.

I still think about that. Not all the time, but enough. The cricket I didn't get to play – the games, the series, the final stretch of what could've been a more complete career. And not because I coasted. I gave everything. I just didn't always know how to give it in the right way.

It's different now, with a bit of space and a different angle on it all. I look back and wonder why I was so hard on myself. Every innings felt like judgement day. Every failure stuck in the bones. That kind of pressure – some of it real, some of it self-made – gets heavy after a while. That's why I tell young players now: don't lose touch with the joy. Don't forget that kid in the nets or the garden or the alleyway who just loved to hit a ball or bowl a bouncer. That's where it all starts. That's where your best self lives.

These days, as a coach, that's what I'm chasing. Not just better technique or stronger bodies. I want to help them rediscover that joy, that playfulness. I've made enough mistakes for all of us – blown enough chances, ignored enough warnings – to know what not to do. That makes me useful now. When I speak, they know I've lived it.

And they can't pull the wool over my eyes. I've tried every excuse, every trick, every lazy option. Didn't work. Still doesn't. So now, I don't care what the stat sheet says. I care about how they're feeling. What's on their mind. Where they're struggling. Because the answers are always in there – not on a whiteboard.

Back then – we're talking the early to mid-2000s – I didn't buy into sports psychology. Thought it was fluff. Or worse, a sign you'd gone soft. That word – 'psychologist' – made it sound like you were broken. But that's not what the good ones do. They help you figure yourself out. They don't fix you, they walk alongside you. I got there in the end, but nowadays, I wish I'd taken sports psychology more seriously earlier in my career.

Steve Peters, as psychiatrist/psychologist is a well-known name in this field, especially in cycling where he'd worked with Chris Hoy and Victoria Pendleton. When I first got sent to him, I wasn't ready. I drove over to his place in Disley, walked into a room with a Chesterfield sofa and, worryingly, a flip chart. Never been a fan of flip charts.

Steve started strong – CV, achievements, medals. I thought, *Nice one, this guy's done it all.* Then he told me they weren't his medals. He just worked with the people who won them. Right. Conversation medals, then.

Next came the science bit. He drew a big head on the chart and said, 'You've got a chimp in there.' I wanted to laugh. Apparently, your chimp lives in the back of your brain and causes havoc, while your rational self lives in the front. The trick was to quieten the chimp.

All I could think was, *Let this end.*

I nodded through the hour, never went back. Not because he was wrong. I just wasn't in the right place to hear it. I wasn't ready to change. I wanted out. Not answers.

People asked how it went and I'd say, 'Great. Turns out I've got a chimp in my head.' Then I'd get out next match to a terrible shot and blame the chimp.

There was another bloke, too – one of those 'smile through the storm' types. He told me, 'Every day above ground's a good day.'

I thought, *No it's not. Some of them are shockers.*

He'd try to find positives in every disaster. Hit a four? Yeah!

Oh, but I was out for seven.

The psychologist Dr Steve Bull was a bit different. Lovely guy. We got on well. He never pushed too hard. But even then, there were moments. I remember him saying, 'Next time you eat a carrot, imagine it's a Mars bar.'

I mean, come on. It's still a carrot. Crunchy. Orange. A carrot.

The point is that none of it really worked for me. Not then. Not in the middle of it all. The proper change would come later, when I stopped thinking of the mental side as a soft option and started treating it like the engine room. The thing that drives everything else.

And I guess you'd have to say that it was around the 2005 Ashes that it really clicked. For a start, it came at a time when I'd been playing well. Also, the dressing room had changed under Vaughan. There was more trust, more freedom, and Vaughany let me be me.

Meanwhile, the stakes were massive. After all, this was Australia. Peak Australia. Langer. Ponting. McGrath. Warne. A team of giants. And I wanted them. I wanted to beat them. And to do that, I had to be all in – body, yes, but also head and heart.

It must have been around that time that Jamie Lawrence came in. He worked with Red Bull athletes and was a different thinker who talked in pictures, shapes, concepts. We spoke about presence. About stature. About walking tall, literally. Under his guidance, I started visualising it all: the run-up, the grip, the release, the reaction. Not just seeing it, but feeling it. Sounds, smells, everything.

At home, I'd bowl in the garden, dodging the kids' toys. I'd rehearse it in the car, in the dressing room. And it worked. Even when I couldn't train properly – because of the pain – I'd already bowled the spells in my mind. I was match-fit in my head, even when my body disagreed.

The pain never left, mind you. It became normal. The cortisones, the surgeries, the injections. I stopped counting after a hundred jabs. But in a strange way, I welcomed it. It became a test. Could I still do it, still push, still fight? Because the opponent was never just the batter at the other end. It was always me. My own demons, doubts, distractions. That's who I played against. Not only that, but I was about to enter the most intense, dramatic, exhilarating stretch of my career. *The Ashes*. The biggest series of my life. And somehow, despite all the setbacks, all the pain, I felt ready.

CHAPTER 16

PRESSURE

It's 2005, the first Test of the Ashes, and I can feel the hum of Lord's before I've even stepped through the Long Room. I'm practically levitating.

It's not noise exactly – not yet – but something sharper. A kind of tension, low and crackling, settling into my skin like static before a storm. I'm in the belly of the pavilion now, moving past the stewards and the old paintings on the walls, feeling the weight of all that history pressing against the back of my neck.

And when I finally step out into the sunlight, there it is – that gleaming outfield, the hush of 25,000 people holding their breath.

And beyond that?

The Aussies.

McGrath stretching, Warne with that little grin on his face, Hayden standing arms folded like he owns the postcode.

Glenn McGrath moves like an old-school sci-fi android – tall, pale, tidy – hitting the same spot over and over like it's programmed into him. A metronome in boots. You know what's coming, and still can't lay a bat on it. Seam upright, bounce nagging, patience limitless.

Shane Warne has the lion's mane, the sunblock and a grin full of menace. But behind the theatre is genius – drift, dip, rip. He doesn't bowl leg spin. He conjures it. You watch it leave his hand and still misread it three seconds later. Like, what? Mischief winding up to explode.

Adam Gilchrist looks like someone's just told him a joke, always grinning – and then he swings that bat like he's trying to end the match in half an hour. A keeper who bats like a storm. Comes in at seven, walks off with games.

And Ricky Ponting, all purpose and precision. That squared jaw, yes, but more than that – the compact technique, the ruthless footwork, the pull shot that cracks like gunfire. He doesn't just lead. He inflicts.

Legends. The lot of them.

They know it, too. And why not? For 16 long years, Australia have ruled the Ashes, winning eight straight series since 1989. England haven't even managed a close contest, let alone a victory. This isn't just a team riding a hot streak – it's a dynasty. You're not just seeing players – you're staring at something that feels nailed on. Winning has become their routine. England are still chasing memories.

I feel the eyes. Not just theirs – everyone's. The punters, the press, the lads in the dressing room. They're all watching. Because this is it. The Ashes. My first proper one. And I'm meant to be the difference. The lad who can shift a game, hit it miles, swing it both ways, put Warne onto the pavilion roof. I'm Fred Flintoff, England's great white hope.

But something's off.

I walk out, bat in my right hand, helmet in my left, as always, gloves tight, trying to play it cool – but inside I'm a mess. I'm still levitating, buzzing with nervous energy. There's no rhythm in my stride, no ease in my body. Just adrenaline, twitchy and sharp.

I grip the bat harder than I should. Try to swallow that rising nausea. Glance up at the big screen and instantly regret it. This is supposed to be the moment, the lift-off. But all I can think is – what if I stuff it? These aren't just big names – they're serial tormentors. McGrath and Warne dismantled England almost single-handedly in 2001 – 63 wickets between them, and not a hint of mercy. Gilchrist and Ponting pile on runs for fun. Every time someone thinks maybe the Aussies are slipping, they just wipe the floor again. They're just . . . inevitable.

Added to which, everyone's watching. This will be one of the last Ashes to be shown live on terrestrial telly – Channel 4 – so it's not behind a paywall. Not highlights late at night. It's on every TV in the country. Back gardens, barbers, corner shops – people stop what they're doing and watch. You don't have to like cricket to get caught up in this. It's England against the machine, and everyone wants to know if we've finally got something that can dent it.

As far as I'm concerned at that very moment, the answer is no. I'm out for a duck.

*   *   *

Building up to the Ashes, it had been a different story. You couldn't move for optimism, and everyone was at it. The papers were full of it, Vaughany was full of it, and I'd just about made it back from ankle surgery, so I was full of it too. Fit – or at least close enough to pretend. The ankle was still howling on some days. The op had left bits of bone and gristle floating about, and I was managing it with injections, tape and stubbornness. But that wasn't the version anyone wanted. The story was already written. I was the engine. The game-changer. The one they thought could go toe to toe with the Aussies.

And I got it. I'd been around the team for the worst of it – '01, '03 – watching from the outside while we got taken apart. I never played in those Ashes. Didn't even really know most of their squad. And maybe that helped. No baggage. No bruises. Just this little window of belief.

The summer series against South Africa had been a turning point. I'd scored a hundred – felt every bit of it. Didn't feel like luck, didn't feel like one of those days that just happens. It felt earned. Felt real. And the ball had been coming out well too – round the wicket, decent wheels, a bit of swing. People started talking. Saying maybe this was my time.

So yes, the build-up had been mad. There was energy everywhere. Streets buzzing, kids in replica shirts with my name on the back. The one-dayers ended level, but we left our mark. I hit Brett Lee with a short one, sharp and loud – felt like a message. KP was batting like a lad on a trampoline, bouncing around, flaying McGrath, telling everyone he was going to do it again in the Tests. And for once, we weren't backing away. We were front-footing it.

But belief and pressure? They were twins. And by the time we reached Lord's, I was alight – but, as it turned out, not quite in the way I needed to be, because leading into that match, the mood around us was pure energy. Maybe too much. We'd just come off a strong run, beating South Africa, beating West Indies, and everyone was talking us up. This was England's time. And inside the dressing room, it felt like we believed it.

But belief can be a fragile thing, especially when it's fuelled by hype. I remember saying to Michael Vaughan before the series, 'You're going to get pelted in this one, you know. Media, press – there'll be times when they'll come for you.' And he just looked at me and smiled: 'You too, mate. Especially you.'

He wasn't wrong.

There was a lot flying around about me in the build-up. Best all-rounder in the world. Match-winner. England's danger man. And I was proud of that, yeah – but it also messes with your head. You start thinking about the headlines before the game's even begun. You start wanting to live up to the billing rather than just playing your game.

Anyway, we got to Lord's. Packed house. The noise was different. This wasn't just cricket now, it was theatre. Or war. We won the toss and elected to bowl first – and it started like a dream.

First spell – Steve Harmison. And what a start he made. Hit Justin Langer on the elbow, cut Ricky Ponting's cheek open. Blood. Ashes blood. You don't forget that image.

We were up. I came on, all fire, charging in – but something was off. My action was there, the pace was there, but my eyes had gone. Tunnel vision. I was running on fumes, aggressive to the point of distraction. I couldn't hit a length. Couldn't calm down. I was just steaming in, trying to make something happen. Not bowling – just sort of *flinging*.

Gilchrist was at the crease – the danger man. Him and Ponting, always the two. Gilchrist was the kind of player who turned a crisis into a lead. And he was doing that again. He knocked a couple of fours, edged one over the slips, then belted another. I was close to going back over the wicket, and if I had, it could have changed the entire series. I decide to back my skill against his. Round the wicket to a left-hander was something I'd had great success with, and in a moment of doubt, I backed myself, resulting in getting Gilchrist out and having the wood over him for the rest of the series.

I can still see the photo – arms spread, roaring like it meant everything.

At the break, Australia had posted 190. Not huge, but enough. Especially at Lord's. Especially with that attack.

Then it was our turn, or innings. And it didn't last.

The collapse came fast.

McGrath did us. All that build-up, all that talk – and then I was in, and I froze. Just froze. Couldn't move. Couldn't see. I walked out like always, bat in right hand, helmet in left, but I was trembling. I was standing there, helmet off, heart racing, looking around and thinking, I don't belong here. And McGrath – fuck me – he looked like a giant. He bowled one that nipped and hit the top of off. I didn't even see it. Even if I'd known exactly what was coming,

I wouldn't have hit it. Ten goes at that ball, and I'd have missed it ten times. It was just perfect. Or maybe I was just completely gone.

And when I got out – out for a duck – I walked off, head down, the weight of it all pressing me into the turf.

And sitting in that dressing room after – Christ. I was gone. Properly gone. I didn't hear a word Vaughan said. Couldn't even feel my limbs. I was just a lump in a chair, wanting the ground to open up and swallow me.

The second innings wasn't much better.

I got out to Warne. I was partnering KP. We shared a bat sponsor, and Ricky Ponting had said, 'Hope they're getting their money's worth from you two fuckwits.' I tried to fight it, tried to feel something. But the next ball, delivered by Warne, nicked off and I was caught by Adam Gilchrist. I was gone for three.

Next thing, I was sitting in that dressing room again, and I'd gone blank. To be honest, I don't remember anything about what happened after that innings. Not a word. Could've been a funeral. I'd disappeared.

So I legged it.

I didn't want to go home. I didn't want to see people and pretend everything was okay. So me and Rachael – and baby Holly – went down to Bovey Castle, Devon. It was quiet and warm and green, and I drank wine, smoked cigars, sat in little pubs and let the days blur. Not mashed, not wild – just numb. I sat with Chubby Chandler, my agent, in an old wine cellar beneath the hotel.

He said, 'What are you going to do?'

And I said, 'Fuck knows.'

But somewhere down there – in that quiet, in that haze – something moved.

Not a grand plan. Not a light bulb. Just a decision.

Fuck it. This is the Ashes. Fuck the pressure, fuck the hype, fuck injury, fuck all y'all telling me I'm this and that. This is the Ashes, and next time I go out there, I'm going out there not as a talisman but as me; I'm going out there and I'm going to bloody well enjoy myself.

CHAPTER 17

THE SECOND TEST

It's just under a fortnight later. We're at Edgbaston for the second Test, it's match morning and something's stirring before a ball's even bowled. We're in the middle of our usual knockabout warm-up – bit of keepy-uppy, some throw-downs, usual messing about – and the Aussies are over the other side of the square, stretching, skipping, looking casual as they always do.

Then there's a noise. A shout, maybe, or just a change in energy. Something's happened. No one says anything directly, not at first. But heads start to turn.

And there he is: Glenn McGrath, on the turf. Flat out. No fuss, no drama, just this strange little tableau – one of the game's greats lying like he's been dropped from the sky, ankle twisted, pain writ across his face. You're not supposed to cheer a bloke getting injured, obviously. But in that moment, watching their spearhead being carried off with a rolled ankle, I'll be honest: something in me lifted. Not in a cruel way. Just relief. He'd destroyed us at Lord's, had our numbers, and now he was gone. A freak accident in the warm-up, of all things – he'd trodden on a stray ball – and just like that, the whole mood shifts.

When Ponting won the toss and stuck us in to bat, it felt like a statement – an alpha move, as they say. Like he was saying: we've battered you once, we'll do it again. But inside our dressing room, something had shifted too. We didn't mind batting. We liked the look of it. And without McGrath, they weren't quite the same. The emperor had taken a knock, and suddenly the robes looked a bit threadbare. Out we went.

Marcus Trescothick was first to spark. He laced three through the covers in the opening over, like he was laying down a challenge. And KP, of course, was already fizzing – all confidence and wrists and swagger. He wasn't waiting around. Never did. He'd told us pre-match that he was going to take McGrath down, which felt a bit daft when McGrath went down by himself – but still, the intent was there. Kev always had that in him – that 'I'm here now' energy. It rubbed off.

When my turn came to bat, I wasn't totally settled. To be frank – and despite my refreshing Devon break – I was still carrying some nerves from Lord's. But I'd made a decision over cider and cigars and long afternoons doing nothing, that this time I'd have a proper go and enjoy myself doing it. My terms.

So when I faced Warne – and he tossed one up, classic flight, tempting – I thought, *Sod it. I'm going.*

COMING HOME

Big swing. Mid-off's lurking, and I didn't quite get all of it, thought I might be out, thought Kasprowicz might grab it – but it sailed just over his reach – *just* – and dropped for four. Sliding doors moment, that. If he'd taken it, who knows? I'd have been back in the shed, all at sea again, and maybe, just maybe, I wouldn't even be sitting here telling you this story. But it landed, and something in me clicked. Right, I'm off.

From then on, it was fun. Proper fun.

Kev was still going full throttle, and we found this rhythm – not just runs, but joy. I was hitting shots I didn't even know I had, taking Warne for six over midwicket, and instead of second-guessing, I just let go. The ball looked big, time seemed slower. I could see the angles, feel the gaps. I was even singing to myself – little tunes running through my head as I played. Can't remember what exactly, might've been Oasis or something daft. But it was there. A sort of soundtrack to being in the zone.

You don't always know when you're in it – but I knew. I wasn't thinking about scoreboards or averages or head-lines. Just playing. Present. I scored 68 and overall we made 407 in a day. Against Australia. Let that sink in. The press still moaned, as they do, about not kicking on for 500, but they missed the point. We were back in the series. That was the statement. That was the line in the sand.

Me? I couldn't wait to bowl.

CHAPTER 18

BOWLING

Batting or bowling? That's another one I'm often asked, and to be honest, the answer can change on any given Sunday. But since I've already covered batting. I'm going to talk about bowling for a bit.

Bowling came later for me. I'd always been an all-rounder when I was a kid, but there was a stretch – during those early back injuries – when I couldn't bowl at all, so I focused on batting. That worked in my favour for a while. Like, if I'd been fit and bowling, maybe I wouldn't have batted as high. But I got my reps in. I ended up signing pro as a batter, even played for England just as a batter. In 2004, I was ICC ODI Player of the Year – I've got the trophy on the shelf at home.

So yes, I could bat. But bowling? That came a bit later, and because I had so few options with the ball, it weirdly worked for me.

I wasn't one of those bowlers with a toolbox of tricks. I had three balls. That was it. I could bowl a heavy length,

COMING HOME

I had a bouncer, and when I got older, I got really good at reverse swing. That became my weapon. I didn't move it like some of the great swing bowlers, but I could hit the seam hard, and I was quick – high 80s, early 90s, even touching 97 mph at one point.

Towards the end of my career, before the knees gave in, I was bowling quicker than ever – over 90 regularly. I only had two gears, fast and faster, but I knew where it was going. That was my real strength. Accuracy and aggression. Lots of bouncers, trying to hit people. That was part of the job. And when I batted, I expected them to do the same to me. I never enjoyed it – nobody likes a ball flying past your ears – but I felt equipped to deal with it. It's not often I got out playing short balls.

Technically, my weakness was probably the fuller ball around off stump. If they pitched it up there, there was every chance I'd nick off to slip. But people often got dragged into playing me in the wrong way. They wanted to test me with the short stuff, and that played into my hands.

I learned that approach from watching others too. Shane Warne, for example – he was brilliant at dragging you into playing him. It wasn't that he bowled mystery deliveries – he just bowled with relentless accuracy and made you think you had to take him on. I tried to do the same, whether I was bowling or batting. Get them playing my game.

Reverse swing was my favourite. It was the Pakistani bowling legend Wasim Akram who showed me how to do it properly, and it's a thing of beauty when it comes off. You look after the ball, get one side rough and keep the other one shiny. The drag from the rough side pulls the ball in that direction, and unlike conventional swing, which comes early in the delivery, reverse happens late – just before the batter plays the shot. That's what makes it so dangerous. It's only legal if the ball gets roughed up naturally, but back in the day, people would rough the ball up however they could. Bottle tops, sandpaper, you name it.

But reverse swing done right – with just sweat, patience and proper technique – that was where I did my best work.

What people maybe don't realise is that being a bowler is agony. It just is. There's no getting away from it. I never had a day bowling where something didn't hurt. My knees, my ankles, my toe – Jesus, the toe. Your big toe turns black from slamming it down all day, and you keep going. Getting jabbed in the knees, injections in the ankles. Nine out of ten days, it felt stiff, sore and just plain awful. Your body's not built to do that – 15 times your body weight goes through your front foot when you bowl. I was 106 kilos, so every delivery, that's over one and a half tonnes crashing down on my ankle. And my action – it wasn't pretty. In my head, I was smooth and graceful. In reality? I looked like a T. rex with tied shoelaces. But it worked. It got the ball down the other end quickly, and that was all I cared about.

And yet, some days, it would just click. You'd bowl fast and not even feel it. Adrenaline carries you.

I wasn't technical. I didn't think too hard about grip or angle. I'd stand at the end of my mark, head down, ball in hand, and I'd know what I was going to bowl. I'd picture it in my head – the exact delivery – and then I'd just go. I could probably have done it with my eyes shut. It was all about simplicity for me. And mindset.

COMING HOME

I loved bowling when the game was on the line. When things were tough and everyone else looked tired or fed up, I'd get this weird little spark. A buzz. Like, 'Right, give me the ball. I'll make something happen.' I loved being that guy – the one who'd step in when no one else fancied it.

And there was always a bit of theatre to it. Always eye contact with the batter. Always a bit of presence. You want them to know you're there; you want to disrupt them. Not always with words – in fact, with the Aussies, I barely said anything. I'd just stand in front of them, move fielders around unnecessarily, smile, laugh, make it look like I was having the time of my life. Get into their heads. You want them to feel like you're not going anywhere, like they're going to have to deal with you all day.

Now some batters you don't mess with. The great South African Jacques Kallis, for example. Phenomenal player, probably the best all-rounder I played against. But a bit sleepy at the crease – big, dozy lad. And that worked in your favour. I didn't want to wake him up. Didn't want to poke the bear. So with him, I left him be. But most others, I'd engage.

And the best days? The days when your body's screaming, when the game's going nowhere and you're out there trying to drag something out of it. Then you finish, back in the dressing room, you sit in the shower, light a cig, and you can't move. That's the good stuff. That's the real satisfaction.

People think bowling's mostly physical. It is, sure, but it's also mental. When the pitch is flat, the batters are on top, and there's no movement – that's when you've got to find something extra. That's when you want the captain to look at you. That's when I wanted to be the one to change the game.

And funnily enough, the older I got, the more I enjoyed it. Early on, I'd have said batting all day long. But later, when I understood bowling better – when I got more control and could feel the ball coming out how I wanted – I started to love it.

Bowling's got its stories too. One I always go back to is watching that old drama, *Bodyline*. Douglas Jardine and Harold Larwood taking on Bradman and the Aussies in the early 1930s. It changed the game. They used bouncers – which wasn't done back then – and set these aggressive fields with men crowding the leg side. It was deemed unsporting, ungentlemanly, and it led to rule changes. But I loved it. Thought it was genius. Proper game-changer, that.

These days, you can only have two men behind square on the leg side. That's a direct response to what Jardine and Larwood did. It's amazing how those tactical innovations can shift the sport forever. They came home to criticism, but I'd have been clapping them off the plane. Brave, bold, effective.

It's stuff like that – the history, the evolution – that reminds me why I love cricket so much. I don't bang on about it often, but I'm a bit of a student of the game, deep down. Always have been.

So, batting or bowling? I still don't know. But by the end, I reckon Flintoff the bowler might just have had the edge.

Next question: what do I consider my best-ever over?

That would be . . .

CHAPTER 19

THAT EDGBASTON OVER

It's been called the greatest over ever bowled – not by me, I'd never say that – but by pundits, writers, players. One of those cricketing moments that keeps popping up in highlight reels and pub chats, 20 years on. And I get it. Not just because of the wickets – though they were big ones – but because of what it did. The shift. The mood swing. The way it grabbed the game by the throat and changed the feel of everything.

It happened during Australia's second innings at Edgbaston, in the second Test of the 2005 Ashes. To recap, we'd already lost the first Test at Lord's – badly – and we knew we had to hit back. In our first innings we'd posted 407, and they had hit back with 308 in their first innings.

Our second innings had notched 182 (73 of which were mine), so they had to knock off 282 in their second innings in order to post a win – a win that would have seen them leading the series 2-0.

Their innings began, and the Aussies settled in. Langer and Hayden cruising, crowd restless, panic just starting to creep in.

Then I got the ball.

What followed next were seven balls of raw adrenaline.

Ball one. I'm coming in hot. The ball's reversing now – late, sharp – and not to forget, I was on a hat-trick ball having taken the last two Australian wickets in the first innings with successive deliveries. I send it full and fast at Langer, just to feel things out. He pushes forward and it hits the middle safely enough, but there's a noise from the crowd, a rising 'ooh'. They can feel it. Something's happening.

Ball two. This is the one. Langer's set, on 28, looking his usual gritty self – squat, still, always working an angle. I aim to hit top of off stump and try to take it away from him, maybe sneak an edge. But it doesn't; it bounces sharply and nips back, hits him on the elbow and deflects onto the stumps. Langer doesn't move. Not even a flinch. He turns slowly, looks at the wreckage, then walks. He knows he's done. No tantrum. No protest. Just silence. That's the way with great players – they know when they've been had.

Langer walks off. I celebrate with the finger in the air mobbed by players.

In comes Ponting to replace Langer.

Ball three. Ricky Ponting. Captain. Opponent. Ruler of the crease. There's no one harder to bowl to when he's on. He struts out, bat tucked under his arm, jaw clenched. I know he's dangerous – pulls anything short, drives anything full. He's the guy who turns tricky chases into cakewalks. And I've been thinking about him. At Lord's, he'd given me a bit – sledged me, made some sponsor joke about me and KP. So this isn't just a new batter. It's personal.

I go full again, fast and jagging in. It hits him on the thigh pad, thuds hard, and I give it a shout – more out of instinct than hope.

Not out – umpire shakes his head – but it lands a message. He doesn't like it. You can tell. He hasn't settled. And now I've got him thinking. Seeing Ponting jumping makes me realise the importance of the next few balls. My tail's up, the crowd's up, the ball's reversing. Everything's in my favour.

Me, I always bowled aggressively. Bouncers, hostile lines, trying to hit people. That was the job, wasn't it? You're not out there to be liked. Same with Warney – he always made you think you had to do something. I tried to be like that. Get the batter playing my game, not theirs. In this over, that's what I was doing to Ponting. Short one, then a fuller one, then one angled in. Make him guess.

Make him twitch. And then – when the time's right – land the one that counts.

Ball four. I know the ball is reverse-swinging in, but I want to see if it'll swing away, too. That's the holy grail for me – if I can reverse it away. So I stand at the top of my mark and turn the ball around, rough side on the inside. If I pull this off, the game changes. I run in, clear in my head, visualising the ball nipping away, the keeper taking it cleanly – and hoping that's exactly what will happen.

It so nearly does what I want. Nearly. Instead, it squirts off the thick outside edge of his bat and drops short of gully, where Ashley Giles is waiting. Ponting still looks uncomfortable. He fiddles with his gloves, walks a couple of paces, then back again. I can see him thinking now, adjusting. And that's when you know you've got a window. I've dragged him across his stumps defending outside off, and the window is closing fast. It's got to be this over.

Ball five. I've decided I'm bringing it back in – going for the stumps or his front pad. I nearly hold up my side of the bargain. The ball swings back in at 90mph and thuds into his pad, but unfortunately he's just outside the line.

Ball six. Ian Bell comes into short leg, the idea being to make Ponting think I'm bringing this one back in. Hopefully he'll stay on leg stump. But I've already decided: this ball's going away, looking for that edge again. I let it go a little wider. He leaves it. But it's a no-ball. A wasted chance.

Ball seven. So I get another go. The one. The moment. I keep the seam upright, trying to swing it away. Same angle, same pace – but this one holds its line. Doesn't swing back in. He's expecting it to come at him again, sets up for that. But it doesn't. It shapes away just enough, and he feels for it, early, hopeful. Thick edge. Gone. Straight to Geraint Jones behind the stumps. Big nick. Big reaction. Possibly the best ball I've ever bowled.

I don't even think. I just explode. Arms out, face up, chest heaving. It's not about showing off – I barely even know what I'm doing – it's just that everything inside me has to get out. All the noise, all the pressure, all the build-up. That's the release. That's the over. That's the moment I'll remember.

And Ponting? He walks off like he's in a trance. He knows it too. A duck. Gone in four balls. Later he'll be nice enough to say that it's the best over he's ever faced. But as for now, we're up. Every England shirt on the field piles in – hugging, shouting, clapping me on the back. The ground is bouncing. Actually bouncing. You can feel it through your boots.

Those six balls don't just change the session – they change the match. Australia go from 47-0 to 48-2. We've got their openers. We've got their captain. We've cracked the door open. And the belief that floods in after that – from the stands, from the dressing room, from the country – it's unreal.

People still ask me what I was thinking during that over. Truth is, I wasn't thinking. I was having fun. Feeling. Reading the batters. Holding the seam just so. Using the slope. Letting the crowd fill my lungs. There's no plan you can write on a whiteboard for that over. It's instinct. Pressure. Timing.

Afterwards, in the dressing room, someone says, 'That might be the best over I've ever seen.' And I just laugh. Not because I disagree. But because I'm still catching my breath.

But it wasn't over yet. We were back in it, but we hadn't won it. And now it was a simple equation: they needed runs, we needed wickets.

Warne, somehow, was still standing, still scrapping. Brett Lee, their other deadly quick bowler, was batting like Botham. Kasprowicz, of all people, was hanging in. The crowd were buzzing, roaring, dying inside. Every ball felt like a movie moment.

And with every passing over, the panic built. It had started as belief – we're going to win this, easy. But once the runs target dropped below 60, then 50, it began to twist. Brett Lee was still there, playing like a man possessed. Brave as anything. Shane Warne had been out – he'd stood on his stumps, off me – but even then, it didn't end. Michael Kasprowicz, who looked like he couldn't buy a run earlier in the series, suddenly found a rhythm. And as their target shrank, the feeling started to shift – from excitement to dread. We'd had them. We *had* them. And now?

Now I could see it slipping.

You don't script games like that. Not really. The plan was always to finish them off, get the win, get out of there. But by the time Harmy came in to bowl that final over, I'd lost all sense of the script. I remember pushing too hard, willing something to happen. And then suddenly, Brett Lee smacked one, and they were down to two or three needed.

I honestly thought, *This is it. This is going to be the worst defeat of my life.*

And then came that last over. Harmy was bowling. Partnering Lee, Kasprowicz was ducking and swiping, every ball an event.

On the board: 'Runs to win: 3'.

Then it happened. Harmy bowled a short ball, which climbed, took the glove, and looped into the air. Kasprowicz was caught by keeper Geraint Jones. Game over. England won by two runs.

We mobbed each other like kids, tearing across the outfield as if we'd already won the whole series.

And in the middle of all that chaos, I looked up and there was Brett Lee, still at the crease, bat in hand, completely spent. He'd fought like hell and come up just short, and so I went over to console him.

Everyone remembers the photo of me shaking his hand – me, reaching out, him bent over, wrecked but still standing. It looked like a big gesture, but honestly? It's just what you do, isn't it? I mean, that's what we got taught at Lancs as kids – if someone's given their everything, you acknowledge it. In point of fact, Harmy had actually got to him first and shook his hand before I did. But there were no cameras on Harmy. No photo, so it didn't get the same publicity.

I find it a bit sad, to be honest, that something so basic – shaking someone's hand, showing a bit of respect – became headline news. Has sportsmanship slipped that far that this is now the image everyone remembers? For me, it was just 'Unlucky, Brett. See you next week.' That's all it needed to be. We'd been part of something massive, and he deserved that.

Later that evening, I was back on my mate's garden path for his daughter's second birthday party, kids playing at the back, sat with a can of Strongbow, and the quiet thud of it all starting to settle. The adrenaline was still fizzing, but the crash had begun to arrive. I sat there, done in, but proud. I didn't know where the series would go from there. But I knew I was in it now. Not quite fit but present. Committed. Playing like a kid again. And it had made all the difference.

CHAPTER 20

IN THE LEAD

The break after Edgbaston should have been a chance to exhale, to catch my breath, but I did nothing. Literally nothing. Maybe had a quiet word with the sports psychologist again, but nothing more. It was different now. There was a sense we'd found something, that we weren't just part of the series any more – we were driving it.

Next up was Old Trafford. My home ground. The place I grew up going to as a kid, where I'd watched my heroes and once imagined myself in their shoes. Now I was in them myself, and they were pinching a bit.

The feeling in the squad was positive. The public were buzzing. The press were everywhere. But there was still space to think. I stayed at home. Didn't go to the team hotel. Just kept it low key. I don't remember much about the days before, but what I do remember is the sense of occasion.

We batted first, and Michael Vaughan notched 166.

Could've been out three times, but they were all no-balls. It was one of those matches where, for a while, everything went our way. I chipped in with 46 before trying to launch Warne into the next postcode because the crowd were shouting. Gave in to the moment. Caught in the slipstream of it all. And caught by Langer. Our innings ended with us on 444.

As a bowling unit, we were on it again. Simon Jones picked up six wickets. Everything felt sharp. I was fit now, moving all right and loving it. There was pressure, of course, but it felt right. Felt like we belonged. Aussies: 302.

In our second innings, Andrew Strauss scored 106, and we declared on 280-6, but then came the Aussie reply, and Ricky Ponting did what Ricky Ponting does. He dug in. Grounded himself and built an innings that was hard to shift.

By the end of day four, Australia needed 399 to win, while England still needed to take all ten Australian second innings wickets.

The atmosphere on the fifth day was like nothing I'd experienced. Queues down the road. Thousands standing outside from early morning. I was late and tried to drive past the traffic. Got stopped by police. Told them who I was and they let me through. Even then I had to walk the last bit because the ground was at capacity. Walking in, I could feel it.

All day we pushed. The crowd roared through every appeal, every edge, every block. We chipped away. Wickets fell. The belief kept growing. And by the time we reached the final over, it was down to this:

One wicket needed. Six balls. Everyone on their feet. You could feel it in your bones.

But they held on. Time ran out. That's the thing about Test cricket – it's not enough to be ahead on runs. You've got to bowl the other team out twice, and we didn't quite manage it. One more wicket and we'd have taken the match, but they survived.

Australia celebrated a draw like it was a win. They were jumping up and down on the balcony and punching the air – which told us something. We had them. They were relieved, clinging on. We weren't gutted. Just moved on.

Nottingham next.

After that third Test at Old Trafford, I went down to see Pete Marron, the groundsman at Old Trafford. Lovely bloke, but sadly not with us any more. If you recall, I'd lived with him when I was younger, so I took a case of beer to the sheds, sat with the ground staff into the night, just chatting, drinking. The kind of debrief I needed. No headlines, no pressure. Just people who love the game.

Then I disappeared to the South of France. A mate had a house near St Tropez. We flew out and got a helicopter to the place. Big house on a hill, pool, quiet. A couple of drinks with lunch, a bit of rosé in the evening. No cricket, no training, just switching off, playing with my daughter in the pool, going out for food. Proper reset. I had no idea what was going on back home. The country was apparently losing its mind, but I was miles away from it all.

By the time we got to Trent Bridge for the fourth Test, I was refreshed. I turned up in this ridiculous American pick-up truck I'd just bought – Ford F-150, Harley Davidson edition. It took up two spaces, but I didn't care, I felt invincible.

The only problem was that my ankle had gone again.

There were whispers about whether I'd play, but nothing was going to stop me and I ended up getting jabbed up through the game. Just wanted to be out there.

During our first innings, Vaughany went to Ricky Ponting's little dibbly-dobblies – absolute phantoms – my worst nightmare. I walked out expecting to face the same, but Ponting took himself off and Brett Lee came on. I felt sharp. Geraint Jones was with me and we had a laugh. He got 85, I got a hundred – my fifth in Tests. Then, as ever, I got carried away. Tried to hit Shaun Tait into next week, changed my mind halfway through and missed it. Still, it was a good score. 477.

For their innings, we bowled them out for 218, and Strauss took an unreal catch to get Gilchrist off my bowling. But because they didn't get within 200 of our score, we made them follow on. We were bullish. Let's get them back out. Simon Jones was up for it, but then suddenly, he's injured. Just like that, down a bowler. Still, we kept going. Then Ricky Ponting got run out. Classic Ashes moment, that. Because Simon was off, we had a sub – Gary Pratt from Durham. Proper young gun in the field. Ponting nudged one and Gary swooped and threw down the stumps. Ran him out. And Ponting lost it. Absolutely lost it. Shouting up at Duncan Fletcher on the balcony, fuming. It was glorious. We were all pissing ourselves.

Then came the chase. We needed 129. Should've been simple, but the nerves kicked in. Wickets started falling. I got 20-odd and felt great, just wanted to see it through. But Brett Lee got me. Fast, nipped back, did me. Celebrated with my own move. Couldn't even be angry. Fair play.

It got tight at the end. Giles and Hoggard out there, needing 20-odd. Tense doesn't cover it. We were counting runs on the balcony, barely breathing. Nobody spoke. KP was pacing. Vaughany had this fixed stare, not blinking, like if he looked away we'd lose a wicket. Collingwood, not even playing, had his head in his hands. Every run felt like a mile. Then the moment came – Giles threaded one through the covers, we all surged to our feet. Game done. Relief, joy, disbelief. We'd done it.

Now here we were, 2-1 up going to the final Test at The Oval. First time we'd led a home Ashes series in nearly two decades. The dressing room had a weird energy afterwards – part joy, part relief, part sheer exhaustion. Some lads were grinning, others just slumped in their seats, drained. Not much was said at first. Just that sense of: we've done something here. And me? I just kept thinking: we've got one more shot. One game to finish it. One last push.

CHAPTER 21

THE URN

By the time we got to the fifth Test, you could feel it everywhere. The series had taken on a life of its own. England 2-1 up, Oval looming, and for Australia, it was must-win territory. A draw wouldn't be enough. Because here's the thing – if a Test series ends level, the team who already holds the trophy keeps it. And Australia were the holders. They'd dominated us for 16 years. If we drew this match, we'd win the Ashes. If they won it, they'd keep them. That was the line. No shared glory. No middle ground. All or nothing.

But more than that, we could feel it. You'd walk into a petrol station and there we were on the front pages. Turn on the telly, and it was wall-to-wall Ashes. You couldn't get away from it even if you tried. Not that I did. But still – I couldn't tell you what I actually did that week. I didn't practise. I don't remember doing anything in particular, other than shutting the door and staying with Rachael and Holly.

We always stayed at the same hotel by Tower Hill. Only this time it wasn't quiet. Far from it. The reception was packed. People crowding around, lining the pavement, cheering when the players arrived. Every lad checking in was met with applause, like rock stars arriving at a gig. And that courtyard – there's a sushi restaurant and a bar where the after-work crowd gather – well, it was heaving. Everyone there hoping to buy you a drink, have a chat. It was bonkers. And brilliant.

Was I feeling pressure? I don't think so. I just didn't want it to end. I'd been through tough patches in my career, long spells of doubt and injury, and here I was, playing my best cricket, in the biggest series of them all, in front of a public that actually seemed to care. Properly care. Millions watching. On terrestrial telly. Everyone talking about it. This wasn't just sport – it was something more. And The Oval was always a favourite. Big boundaries, good wickets, crowd right on top of you. We went in with belief, not just hope. And that changes everything.

We batted first. Strauss, again, was class – another century (129, to be precise). I came in and couldn't miss. It was the best I'd batted all series. One shot off Brett Lee stands out. Good ball, but I got hold of it, cracked it so cleanly it flew to the sweeper and I heard Matthew Hayden behind me go, 'Fuck.' I thought, *There's more where that came from.* Next ball, same again, four more. I should've got a hundred. Played so well, but McGrath got me in the end, out for 72. Still, we racked up 373. Great total.

With the ball, we had them rattled. And it felt like they were in unfamiliar territory. This was a side full of winners – blokes who'd been the best at every level. Always winning, always dominant. But now they were behind in an Ashes series and you could see it. Not heads down, exactly, but unsettled. Shell-shocked. We were on top, and for the first time, they looked unsure.

We got wickets, I picked up five, and felt in a rhythm. But they didn't roll over. They fought. That's the thing about great sides – they don't just crumble. They find that extra something.

I remember that night I'd bowled a heap of overs, so I went out to dinner with Rachael, Neil Fairbrother – who was my manager – and his wife. We'd booked a table at The Ivy. I ate loads and Neil laughed when I ordered dessert.

'You having that?' he said.

And I said, 'Yeah, I'm bowling till they're out tomorrow, so I need it.'

Back at the hotel, I made a call. I don't usually get in early, always one of the last through the door, but that morning I wanted to be first. I wanted to be there when they turned up. Set the tone. So I got in early, had a cigarette by the entrance where the team buses pull in, and just waited. One by one, the Aussies got off. 'Morning,' I said. They nodded. Then I nipped round the back, where the dressing rooms are, and got them again. 'Morning, lads.'

Later, just before warm-ups, I sat at the top of the steps in front of the dressing rooms – coffee in hand, another fag on – and watched them come out. Clink, clink, clink went the spikes. 'Morning,' I said again. Third time. Just letting them know – I'm here. We're ready. And then I went and got my kit, dragged myself out. My body was stiff, swollen, aching. But I wasn't letting on. They were bowling through – McGrath and Lee were warming up – so I walked over and asked if I could join. Marked my full run-up, let one go. Gilchrist took it. I nodded, said thanks, walked off. McGrath looked at me and asked, 'Do you not get stiff?' I said, 'Stiff? What's that?' and carried on walking. Inside, I collapsed in a heap.

Then we bowled them out for 367 – seven short of our total. And at that point, we thought we'd done it. Maybe not won the game, but we'd done enough. All we had to do was bat well once. Just hold it together.

But this was England – it's never that easy. During our second innings, wickets started falling. I sat there, waiting to bat, not showing anything, but nervous. I can't remember much about the card. Vaughan and Trescothick got a few, maybe others chipped in, but what I do remember – what we all remember – is Kevin.

Kevin Pietersen played an innings only he could play. He did things no one else could do. Played on fear, in a good way. The faster they bowled, the quicker his bat came through. Pull shots, hooks, top edges flying for six, into the stands, everywhere. It was remarkable. Just sitting there, on the balcony, watching this madness unfold. Every time the crowd roared, he gave them more. It was like he was feeding off it, pushing the tempo. Ashley Giles stuck around too. Kev just kept going, scoring 158 in the end. Incredible.

That burst changed the game. Suddenly, it was out of reach for them. And yet, even then, we weren't done. We wanted to drive it home, go at them hard, even in a draw. We came out, ready to give it a burst, wanting to take some more wickets. But the light was fading, and they wanted off. We were still pushing. They weren't. Then came this moment – a strange one – the umpires walking out and ceremoniously knocking off the bails to end the match. All a bit theatrical. But it was done.

And that meant we'd drawn the game.

Which in turn meant that we'd won the series. 2-1. The Ashes were ours. And that's when it really hit me – what we'd done. The crowd went wild. I'd been protected from it a bit – keeping my head down, going away when I could – but now I was in it. Hugs, handshakes, seeing family and mates in the stands. Ian Botham bounding over, throwing his arms round everyone. And then the presentation. The Ashes urn – this tiny little thing – passed around like a pint glass at a wedding. Not even the real one. Still, we batted it around like it was a football. The crowd lapped it up.

Back in the dressing room, the drinks started flowing. And as is tradition, the Aussies came in about nine. We stayed there until half eleven, everyone buzzing, talking about where to head next. The kind of night you'd bottle if you could.

That was it. The end of the series. The end of a summer that changed everything. And deep down, I didn't want it to end.

CHAPTER 22

THE AFTERPARTY

It's early, and the bar's quiet, apart from the gentle clink of glasses and the low hum of post-midnight conversation. I'm still in my kit. Pads off, but shirt unbuttoned, boots scuffed, one sock half on. I'm sitting on a high stool, elbows on the counter, pint in hand. I've barely moved since we got back from the Oval.

We've done it. Ashes won. The urn, the moment, the madness – it's all happened. And I'm just sitting here, trying to take it in. It doesn't feel real. Not yet. Not fully.

I'm not even drunk. Tired, yeah. Heavy. But not drunk. Just staring ahead, trying to make sense of the last six weeks – the build-up, the battles, the bruises. What it took. What it cost.

People are coming in now. More of the lads. A couple of Aussies, even. Hayden's chatting away to someone near the bar. Harmy's laughing with Geraint Jones. The mood's shifting – creeping from disbelief to celebration. I sip my pint and breathe it in.

* * *

The celebrations start in the dressing room, of course. Standard stuff. Champagne flying, shirts off, whooping, hugging, all the usual carnage. But even in that moment, it's different. This isn't a win – this is a release. The pressure, the years of build-up, the expectation – it's all gone in one massive whoosh.

We've beaten Australia in an Ashes series. For the first time in 18 years. At home. It's the thing people said we couldn't do. The thing we'd built our careers around. And now it's done.

I remember sitting on the balcony at The Oval, a beer in one hand, arm around Vaughany, and just staring out at the crowd. Thousands of them still there, hours after the game. Singing. Chanting. Waving flags and shirts and homemade signs. One of them just says: 'Thank you.' That one sticks with me.

Back inside, the noise is deafening. Music's on, cans of lager being handed out like sweets. There's food somewhere, I think. I don't eat any. Just keep sipping.

The Aussies filter in slowly. Hayden, Langer, even Ponting. That's the thing with Ashes cricket – you go to war, but once the final ball's bowled, it's done. They shake our hands. They drink with us. There's respect. That's not always the case in sport, but it is here.

I end up at the bar in the hotel. Don't move for hours. Just sit there, talking to whoever comes by. Not a clue what time it is. I remember thinking: *Don't fall asleep. Just stay upright.*

I wasn't steaming. I was wired. Like my body wouldn't let me switch off.

At half-eight the next morning, I'm still downstairs, still going. A few drinks at breakfast. The team manager starts panicking about me getting on the victory parade bus, so I get delivered back to my room. Rachael opens the door to find me in the same clothes, eyes like saucers. She runs me a bath, helps me into it. I sit there like a pensioner, soaking in the steam, feeling every ache and bruise from the last six weeks. Rachael gets me dressed and then puts me on the bus like she's my carer.

Then comes the parade.

The bus. The route. The roar.

London's never looked like that before. Every bridge, every balcony, every lamp post is packed. People spilling out of buildings, climbing trees, waving shirts. Flags everywhere. Noise like I've never heard – not at a cricket match, not anywhere.

We're on the top deck, open air, crawling through the streets like royalty. Someone's handed me a gin and tonic – no idea where it came from.

Someone says Elton John's sent us cases of champagne. And a note. Something about being proud of us, and the spirit of cricket. Legend. 'Rocket Man' becomes our unofficial anthem that day. Every time it comes on, we belt it out like it's the national anthem.

First stop: the Mayor's office. Ken Livingstone's there. Big grin, full of chat. Shakes our hands, gives a speech. I compliment him on his mayoral necklace.

Next stop: Trafalgar Square.

Now, this is madness. Full-blown Beatlemania. People everywhere. Thousands of them. The bus pulls in, and I suddenly get shy. Duck behind the side panel. It's too much. The noise, the eyes, the sheer scale of it.

Eventually I stand up, wave, puff my cigar, play the part. But I'm rattled. All I want is a dark pub and a pint.

Then someone says, 'Right, Downing Street next.'

But I wasn't up for meeting the PM, so I say, 'Not for me, lads. Cheers.'

Vaughany's not having it.

'You're coming.'

'No I'm not.'

Then Harmison, ever the diplomat, says: 'Come on, we'll go in together. Quick one. No fuss.'

So I cave and get off the bus and stumble through the gate, straight into Number 10.

It's surreal. There are staff everywhere, all grinning. Blair's son, Euan, came over – wanting to meet us and ends up offering us a beer. I blag a Beck's and neck it on the spot.

Then, somehow, we get lost.

Me and Harmy wander off down a corridor and end up in the Cabinet Room. The actual one. Big table, chairs, paintings. Harmy grabs the seat at the head, starts pretending to be prime minister. I'm pissing myself.

Eventually someone finds us – aide or security – and frogmarches us out. Politely, but firmly. Back to the bus.

We're wrecked now. The adrenaline's fading, booze hitting harder. Half the lads are slumped in their seats. Vaughany's trying to make a speech and can't get the words out. Gilo's asleep against the window.

Next thing I know, Harmy's drawing on my face with a Sharpie. Proper black marker job. Moustache, monobrow, the lot.

Somewhere there's a team photo of us all, taken on that bus. And I'm in it, head slumped, marker all over my face, still gripping a gin and tonic.

Perfect.

Next morning, I wake up in my hotel room. Head like a bin. Can barely see. I shuffle to the door, open it, and there it is – the photo. Me, on the front page, from the celebrations the day before. Marker pen still all over my face thanks to Harmy.

But I can't help smiling.

Because for all the chaos, all the mess, all the Sharpie and shoulder pain and cigar breath – we did it. We actually did it.

We won the Ashes. And for one wild, wonderful day, the whole country celebrated with us.

CHAPTER 23

FAMILY

I'm with England for the 2006 India tour. No one expects much. We've not won here in decades. You might say the air is thick with heat and possibility – or maybe it's just the heat, the kind that clings to your skin and makes your shirt damp within minutes. I'm looking at my phone. Rachael's voice echoes in my head.

'It's fine,' she said. 'You stay.'

The thing is, our captain – and my mate – Marcus Trescothick has had to fly home with stress-related illness, and I've been offered the captaincy in his place. This should be good news, but the problem is that Rachael is expecting. As in, expecting our baby.

Me, I'd been expecting to play the first Test and miss the second for the birth.

But now I've been offered the captaincy, and captains need to stay with their team – baby or no baby.

It's Rachael who makes the decision for me. 'Really,' she repeats, 'It's fine. You stay.'

And for a second, I let myself believe it. That it really is fine. That I can stay here, captain England, lead this group of young lads through the biggest Test series of their lives, and somehow not carry the guilt of missing the birth of my son.

Corey, we plan to name him.

I lean back against the wall of the dressing room. I can hear the others inside. After our first Test in Nagpur we have Mohali and then Mumbai. England have never won in Mumbai, not once, and I could be the captain who breaks that record.

Or I could be the dad who gets home in time.

But I can't be both.

So I ring Rachael and lay it all out – the captaincy, the timing, what it means. And she doesn't even flinch. 'You stay,' she says. 'It's fine.'

She means it, too. She knows what this means to me – the chance to lead England, to do something with this young team. I think she thinks we'll both be proud of that, years down the line. And maybe we are. But even as I'm saying goodbye, something in me knows I'll be replaying this choice for a long time to come.

Though we lose in Mohali, the Mumbai Test is everything I hope it'll be. More on all that in a minute, but – spoiler alert – we achieve the impossible and draw the series.

That night, after the celebrations, I hire one of those little skiffs and sit out on the sea with some of the lads. Music on, beers flowing, just staring back at the lights of the city. It's perfect. And on top of that, I know I'm flying home soon to meet Corey for the first time – he's been born while I've been away.

At the airport I bump into Jack Simmons and Jack Bond – two Lancashire legends, out there on a supporters' tour. They see me half-cut and offer me a drink. We sit there knocking back Southern Comfort in departures. I board the plane completely hammered, order a brandy on take-off, conk out and wake up in England where my mate Nicey has arranged for a helicopter to meet me when I land – straight from the airport – and at last. At bloody last. I'm flown home to meet my son.

Holding Corey for the first time is emotional, but not how I imagine. He doesn't want anything to do with me. When I pick him up, he stares past me. He doesn't want me. It's not personal – it's just that he doesn't know who I am.

And that's the moment. Not the winning, not the singing in the dressing room, not the wickets or the handshakes or the applause. It's here, in this living room, holding a baby who doesn't know me, that I realise I made the wrong call.

It takes weeks for him to warm to me. He's a slow burn, Corey. But we get there.

Eventually.

*   *   *

Corey wasn't our first, of course. Rachael and I had already had Holly – she came into the world in 2004, a little early, a little light, but full of life. I remember the moment she arrived like it was yesterday. She was born at the Royal London, four weeks early and weighing in at six pounds two ounces. It was one of those moments that rearranges everything in your head. I'd missed a match to be there – England against India, a one-dayer at Lord's – and I never once thought that was the wrong choice.

After Holly, something shifted in me. I've said this before, but it's worth repeating: becoming a dad didn't distract me from cricket. It did the opposite. It set me free. I used to go out there thinking every ball, every mistake, every dismissal was the end of the world. Then Holly arrived and I thought – hang on, I'm dressed in whites, I'm chucking a ball around and trying to hit it. That's what I'm doing for a job. And for all that cricket meant everything to me – and it really did – it suddenly wasn't *everything* any more.

That was the year before the Ashes in 2005. And if you look at what happened that summer – the runs I scored, the impact I had – well, some people said it shouldn't have worked like that. That becoming a parent would soften me up, make me lose that edge. But it did the opposite. I started scoring more runs because I stopped being so scared of getting out. I knew there was a world outside the dressing room. And it made the dressing room feel lighter, somehow. Less like a trap, more like a stage.

Looking back, that's probably why the decision around Corey hit harder. Because I knew what I was giving up. I'd felt it once already – that immediate bond, that flood of feeling when you hold your child for the first time. But I let that go the second time around. Not maliciously, not carelessly, but still . . . I let it go.

Corey and I found each other eventually, but it wasn't instant. With Holly, it was all there straight away – the connection, the shared rhythm. With Corey, it took time.

He was more reserved. More stubborn, maybe. Or maybe he was just cautious because he didn't quite know who this bloke was, suddenly turning up and calling himself Dad.

These days, he and I have a brilliant relationship, and I see so much of myself in him. In cricketing terms, he had a tough path – being the first Flintoff boy to come through, carrying all the weight of the name, the pressure, the expectation. That can't have been easy, but he wore it all with quiet grit, and in doing so, probably shielded his younger brother, Rocky, from some of it when his time came.

Corey came through the Lancashire junior ranks steadily, never flashy, but always improving. He's got talent to burn, no question, but it's his work ethic that stands out. He's grafted year after year, often without much fanfare. That's why it's especially satisfying to see him breaking through now – making his first-team debut at Kent, getting a proper crack at it. It hasn't come easy or quickly, but that makes it sweeter.

He's earned it. And I couldn't be prouder.

Then came Rocky. Born in April 2008, our third. The name suited him from the start – tough little thing, built for scrapping, and, as it turns out, for batting. From a young age, Rocky was into his cricket, but we never pushed him. Rachael and I made a decision early on that we weren't going to be those parents – the ones who hover and hustle and shout from the sidelines. If our kids wanted to play, great. If they didn't, also fine. But Rocky . . . he really wanted it.

You could see it. Not just the talent – though he had that, no question – but the hunger. The bit that can't be coached. In 2024, he made his first-class debut for Lancashire at just 16, becoming the youngest to do so. Then he went and scored a hundred for England Under-19s, the youngest ever to do it. He even notched a ton batting at nine for the Lions in Australia. It was mad watching it unfold. Part pride, part disbelief. I mean, the lad had actually broken one of *my* records. I didn't know whether to laugh or pretend I was annoyed.

There's something surreal about seeing your child in the same shirt you wore, walking out on to the same pitches, getting cheered by the same crowds. But it's different too. He's his own player, his own man. He doesn't need to be me – in fact, I'd prefer if he wasn't. He's got his own voice, his own story to write. I'm just lucky I get to watch.

And then, just when we thought our family was complete, along came Preston. Born around Christmas 2019, a proper little surprise. Rachael and I had thought we were done – three kids, good innings – and then out of nowhere, we were back in the nappies and night feeds. We named him Preston, after my home town, and I think deep down, that name carried a bit of everything – roots, history, sentiment.

Preston was different from the start. He arrived into a very different household – older siblings, a calmer pace, a mum and dad who had been round the block a few times and knew the drill. He slotted in quietly, didn't kick up much fuss, and brought this lovely sense of completeness. I don't know if we'll ever stop being surprised by him. He's got this way about him – observant, a bit cheeky, likes to watch before jumping in. Whether he ends up on a cricket field or not, who knows? But he's already got that glint in his eye that says: I'll do things my way.

COMING HOME

That's all any of us can hope for, really. That our kids grow up knowing they're loved, knowing they've got choices, and knowing that home is always there – whether you're scoring runs in Mumbai, changing nappies in Manchester, or just trying to work out where you fit in the chaos of it all.

And if I've learned anything from this gang of mine – Holly, Corey, Rocky and Preston – it's that family doesn't care about scorecards or series wins. It cares that you show up. That you listen. That you admit when you got it wrong, and keep showing up anyway.

*   *   *

It goes without saying that family begins with Rachael, who's had my back pretty much from day one. And when was that? That would be in 2002, when we first met.

I wasn't looking, to be honest. I'd just come out of a relationship that had gone badly and was quite enjoying the simplicity of being single. I was still sorting myself out, shedding weight, getting back on track with cricket, slowly starting to feel like I might be heading in the right direction. At the time, Rachael was running a company called Strawberry, which provided hospitality and promotional staff for events – one of those being the cricket.

We met at Edgbaston. We'd finished the day's play against Sri Lanka – a Saturday – and as was often the way, I wandered over to the hospitality box for a pint. It was my turn to fulfil some sponsor obligations, so I had a couple and that's where I saw her. Managed to get her number and sent a text. We ended up meeting for a drink that evening back at the hotel. I suggested we go for dinner the next day –

Sunday – because we were on track to finish the match off quickly. She said yes. I remember thinking: happy days.

What I didn't count on was waking up to a tabloid story that morning – my ex had sold a piece to the *News of the World*. The headline, ridiculous as it sounds, compared my bedroom performance to my bowling. I got to the ground early and straight away, I could tell the lads had seen it. Everyone in the dressing room had their shoulders bouncing, trying not to laugh outright, and then I walked in and it was all over. Vaughany, being Vaughany, decided I should field right in front of the Hollies Stand – give the crowd something to talk about. I took it in good humour, because what else can you do?

That night, I still went out with Rachael. We went to the Living Room in Birmingham – Broad Street – and I had a 30 per cent off card, which helped. We sat down and I asked her casually if she'd seen the press that day. She said yeah, there was a lovely write-up in *The Times*. I said, 'Great – anything else?' She said, 'Well, there was a thing in the *News of the World* too, but I've not read it.' And that was it. No drama. No big talk. She just handled it with a shrug and a smile. One of the lads, Simon Jones, happened to be in the same restaurant and joined us for a bit. We had a laugh, and from there it just sort of . . . unfolded.

It wasn't something I'd been chasing. I wasn't on the lookout for a relationship. But sometimes things have their own pace. She started spending more time around the team, checking in on the promo staff, and before I knew it, she'd moved up north, we were living together, just kind of doing life as a unit. There weren't grand declarations. You didn't ask, 'Are you my girlfriend?' back then. You just kind of knew.

We got married in March 2005. So yes – that was pre-Ashes. People often assume it was after, when everything went a bit mad, but no. We tied the knot before the summer that changed everything. Which is fitting, in a way, because she's been the one constant through it all – not just the big public highs but the quieter battles behind the scenes. When things have gone off the rails – physically, mentally – she's been there, steady as anything.

And I'll say this too: I've never known anyone with such a gift for letting you be who you are, even when you're struggling to be that person yourself. That's rare. It's one thing to love someone at their best. It's something else to love them through the mess.

CHAPTER 24

CAPTAINING

Going back to 2006, and that captaincy during the Indian tour was my first proper taste of the metaphorical armband. But really, I was never England captain. Like *England captain*. I mean, I captained England, yes, but I was never *the* captain, which is an important distinction.

Nasser Hussain. He was England captain. Vaughan. He was England captain. But me, I was never appointed long-term, never handed the keys. I was always filling in – the stand-in, the caretaker. I captained in India when Vaughany couldn't. I captained against Sri Lanka. I captained the Ashes in Australia. But I was never *the* captain. And that sits with me. Not bitterly – just a little bit of embarrassment, really. The five-nil in Australia especially – you carry that with you.

To be fair, I loved that spell in India. We had a young side, with lads who weren't weighed down by history and expectation. Young blokes like Alastair Cook and Monty

Panesar were there. Steve Harmison, my mate, was bowling well. And I was on my game, which helped massively. Because that's the thing with captaincy – when you're playing well, everything else feels manageable. You lead from the front. If something needs doing, you do it yourself.

The first Test was in Nagpur. Normally, I'd bat first every time, but I agonised over that decision. Still, we batted first, and we did well. Cookie got a hundred on debut. Monty got Sachin Tendulkar out – which, let's be honest, is not a bad scalp for your first match. I got some runs, bowled well. The match drifted to a draw, but we'd done more than anyone expected.

We lost the second Test – I played all right, but they outplayed us. Then came Mumbai.

England hadn't won in Mumbai for years. It was stacked against us – big Indian crowd, Wankhede Stadium buzzing, pressure everywhere. But something clicked. The atmosphere in the dressing room was brilliant. Everyone was relaxed. Even on that last day, with everything in the balance, it just felt . . . fun. This is what cricket should be.

There was this moment during lunch, fourth day, a pivotal point in the match. I'd bowled in the morning, came off, and everyone was sitting round eating – naan, tikka, whatever we'd had delivered to the back of the dressing room. I didn't know what to say. I'd done the team talks, said all the usual stuff. But this was different. I needed something else. So I bought myself some time and went for a shower. Standing under the water I thought, *Right, Flintoff, what now?*

Then I had it. In the dressing room we had one of those old iPods, with the wheel on it, hooked up to a speaker.

I came out of the shower, towel round my waist, stuck Johnny Cash's 'Ring of Fire' on full blast and started singing, swinging my towel over my head.

(Whenever I tell this story, people say, 'I wish I could have seen it.' Trust me, not a pretty sight.)

Sure enough, the assembled cream of England cricket just looked at me like I'd lost my marbles. But then, one by one, they joined in, the whole dressing room jumping up and down, singing along, smiling, laughing. That was it. I didn't need to say a word after that. The mood was right. We were good to go. Thank you, Mr Cash.

I opened the bowling after lunch and we got a couple of quick wickets. We ended up beating them – *India in Mumbai* – a massive result. The series was drawn 1-1, but that win was one of my proudest moments in an England shirt.

And then, well, you know what happened next. A mad dash to meet my son.

*   *   *

I'd been at home a few days – just getting to know Corey, reconnecting with Rachael and Holly – when the Batphone went. It was Duncan Fletcher, the coach.

'You all right?' he asked. 'Yeah, just at home with the family,' I said.

He offered me the chance to stay put. 'You don't need to come back for the one-dayers if you don't want to.'

Perfect, I thought.

Then, before I could get comfortable, he changed his mind: 'Actually, you'd better come back.'

Typical.

COMING HOME

Back to India I went. I think I had about three or four days off, all told.

The one-dayers were a disaster. We got battered, and I left with the feeling that I never fully owned my opportunity at captaincy. I was parachuted in, given a squad I hadn't picked, never really allowed to shape things.

I captained at Lord's against Sri Lanka that May, and we should've won. I bowled 25 overs in the first innings, enforced the follow-on, and then bowled another 50. Seventy-five overs in a match – unheard of for an all-rounder. But I was that angry. Angry at the dropped catches – 12 of them. Angry at how toothless we were. So I just kept bowling.

As a captain, I always defaulted to myself. I trusted me more than anyone. If I was playing well, I could carry it, but if I wasn't, I'd be in all kinds of knots. As a player, I could switch off at night. As captain? Fuhgeddaboutit.

I lay awake, questioning everything – my selections, my tactics, even why I was doing the job at all. I think, truthfully, I did it for others. Everyone wants to be England captain – I was no different. But deep down, I was happier as a player, being the right-hand man to someone like Vaughany.

I didn't get much help from our coach, Duncan Fletcher. It was never straightforward with him. When things went well, he was all smiles. On the other hand, when they didn't, suddenly it was all my fault – even if I'd had no say in picking the squad or shaping the team.

As a result, it was lonely at times. You realise very quickly that team spirit often disappears when you need it most. When you're winning, everyone's tight. Little conflicts get brushed aside. But when you're losing, lads retreat into cliques, into self-preservation mode. I saw it happen. And once it started unravelling, it went quickly.

Injuries didn't help either. Marcus Trescothick wasn't there – and if Tresco was scoring runs at the top of the order, my job at number six was always that much easier. Kevin Pietersen could be brilliant, and when Steve Harmison was on it with the ball, I could come on first change and pick up the pieces. But Harmy was struggling. He was the one player I went out on a limb for – out of loyalty, out of belief that he'd come good. He was still the best bowler in the world on his day. Sadly, those days were getting fewer.

The thing is, captaincy exposes you. Every weakness – technical, mental, physical – gets magnified. And then there's the stuff off the field.

There was a moment with Nasser Hussain, back in my early days with England, that probably says a lot about why I was never really captain material. Nasser was England captain then, of course, but we were never especially close. There was always a bit of an edge between us, but I respected him. He was intense, no question, but he fronted up to everything and never shied away. And on this occasion, I managed to push things a bit too far.

It happened during an England tour of Sri Lanka in 2002, when my mate Muttiah Muralitharan was in their side. I'd known Murali for years from his Lancashire days, and we'd stayed good friends. Before one of the matches, he told me he was short of bats. We shared a sponsor, so he asked if he could borrow one of mine. Seemed harmless enough. But Nasser had made it very clear: no contact. We were supposed to freeze him out completely.

COMING HOME

The next morning, Murali asked again. Nasser was watching me like a hawk. I leant in and said quietly, 'When we go out to field, nip into our dressing room and grab one of my bats. Keep it low key.'

The match got under way. Sri Lanka lost a few early wickets, and then Murali came walking to the crease, swinging one of my bats as he went. Nasser hadn't noticed yet. He was busy sorting the field and talking tactics.

Murali and I had a deal in the early days. I wouldn't bowl bouncers at him if he didn't bowl doosras. And although Nasser wanted me to go short at him, I was trying to hold up my side of the bargain.

'Go short at him, rough him up,' Nasser said. I still thought full and straight might've been the better option.

'I said short,' he barked.

I bowled full anyway. Murali knew what was coming and just blocked it back. That went on for an over or so, and you could feel Nasser's frustration rising. He took me off and brought on Gareth Batty, the off-spinner. Murali hit him clean out of the ground. Met it as sweet as you like – right out of the middle of the bat – and sent it flying.

At the end of the over, Murali hung around, knocked a few more, and as we passed each other in the middle, he grinned and said, loud enough for everyone:

'Good bat this, Freddie.'

It made me laugh, but at the same time, I knew I'd let Nasser down. Naughty really, and was part of why I'd always known I wasn't cut out for captaincy myself. Captaincy carried a weight. There was a distance you had to keep, a discipline that didn't come naturally to everyone.

Left: The first time I played for Lancashire at Old Trafford, aged nine.

Below: My first ever captaincy: the rugby team at primary school.

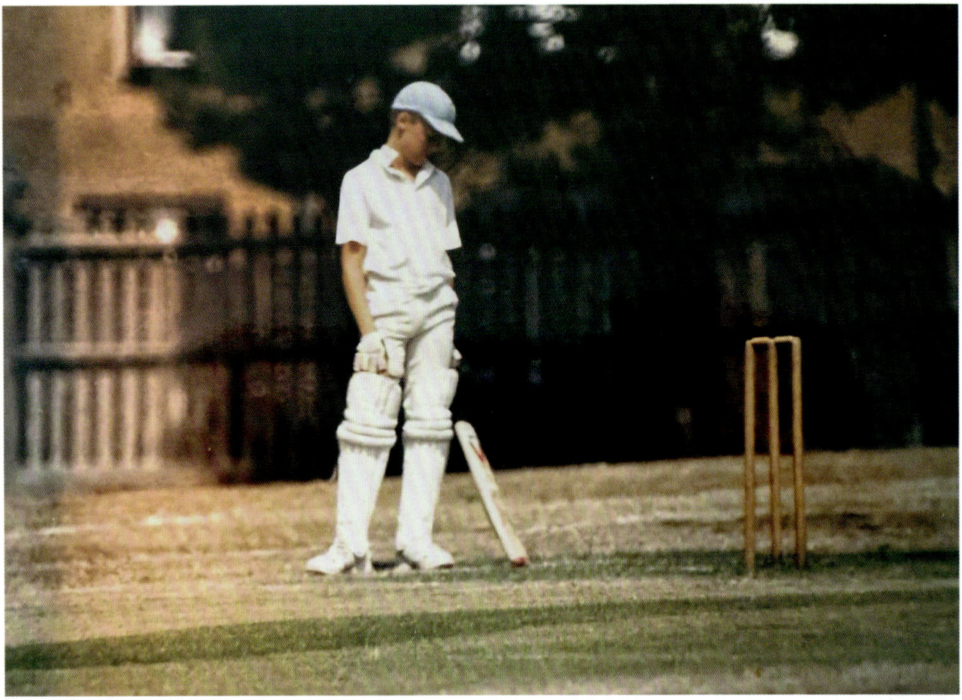

© Freddie Flintoff

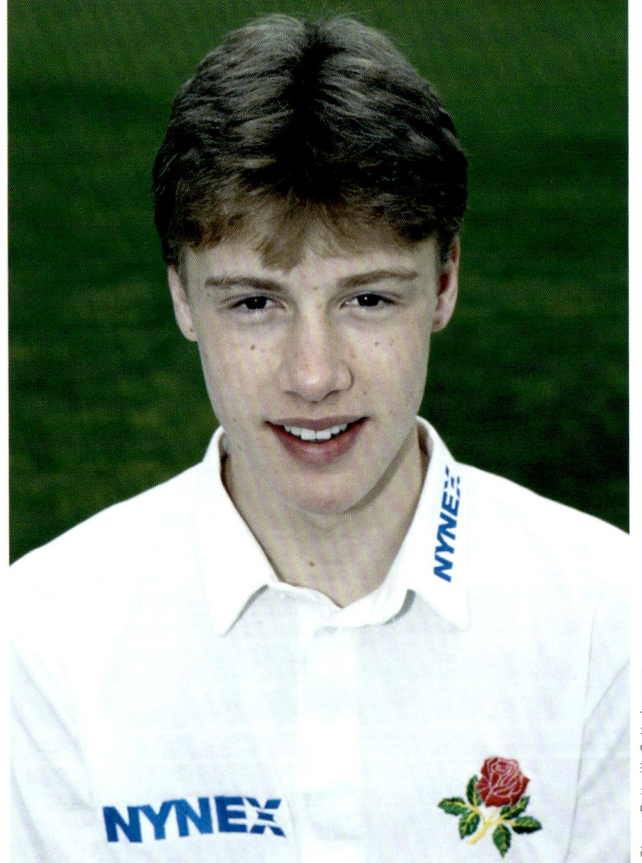

Above: My first century for Lancashire U11's – 125 not out against Kent at Dartford.

Right: My first year at Lancashire, aged 16.

© Shaun Botterill, Getty Images

© Stu Forster, Getty

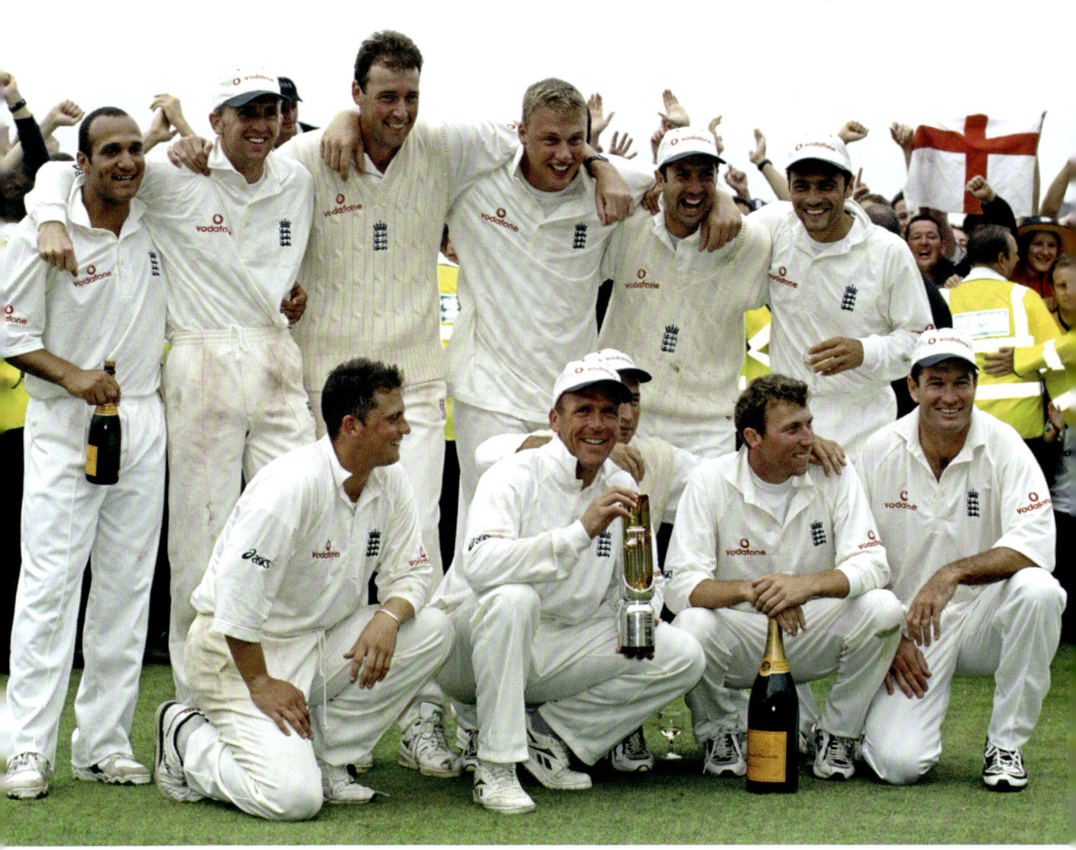

Above: Celebrating my first ever series win in the Test side against South Africa in 1998.

Left: A memorable moment: my maiden Test century in March 2002, against New Zealand.

Below: Me and Keysey celebrating our win against South Africa in January 2005.

© Ross Land, Getty

© Clive Mason, Getty

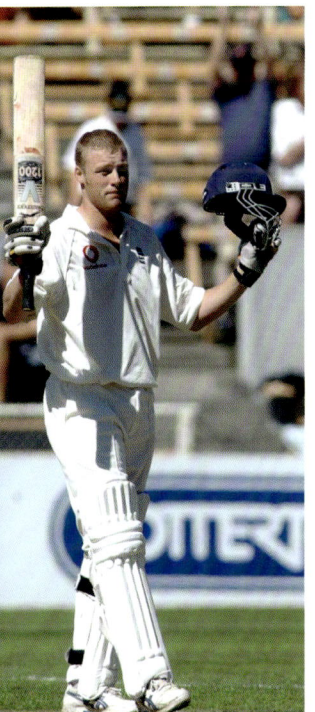

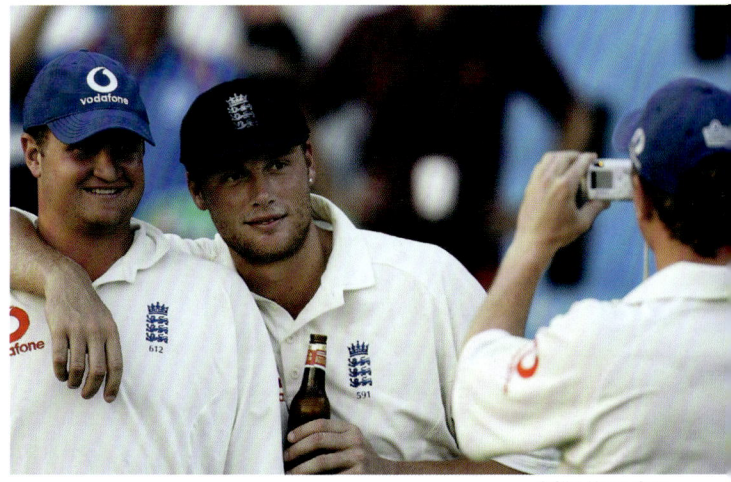

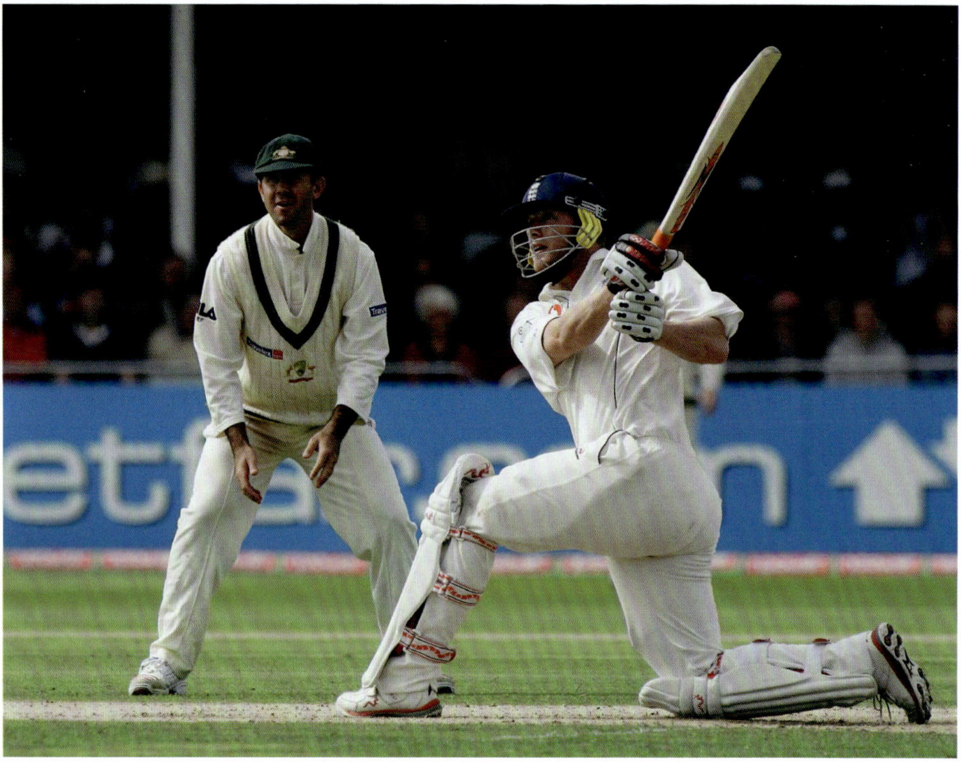

© Stu Forster, Getty

On my way to 100 at Trent Bridge in 2005.

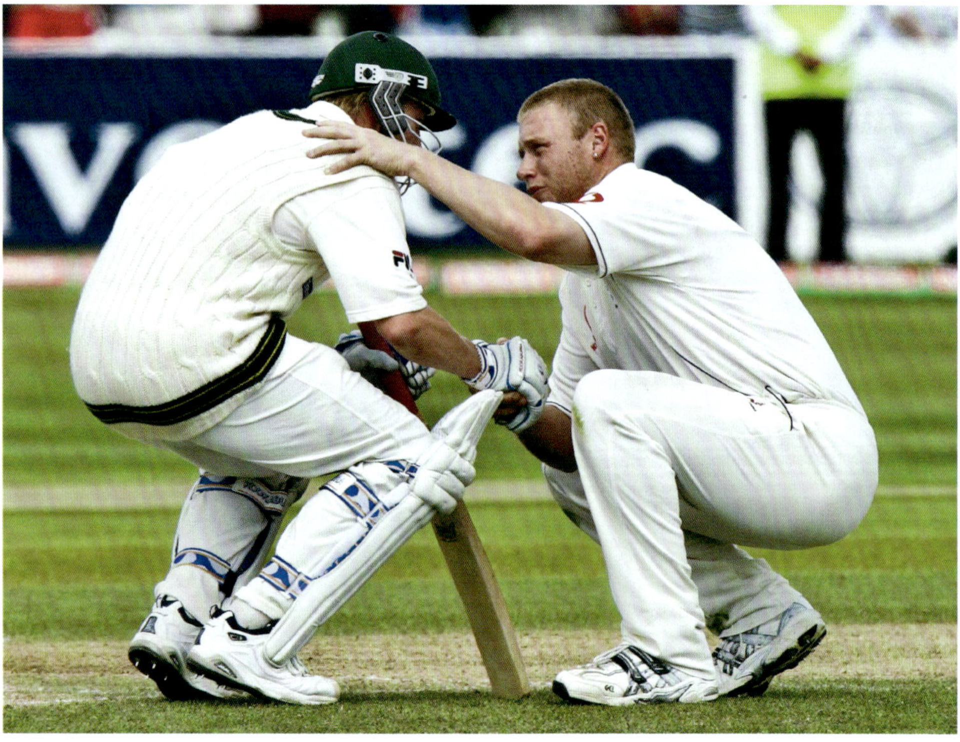

© Tom Jenkins, Getty

Consoling Brett Lee in the second Test at Edgbaston in 2005.

© Clive Rose, Getty

© Richard Sellers/Allstar, Getty

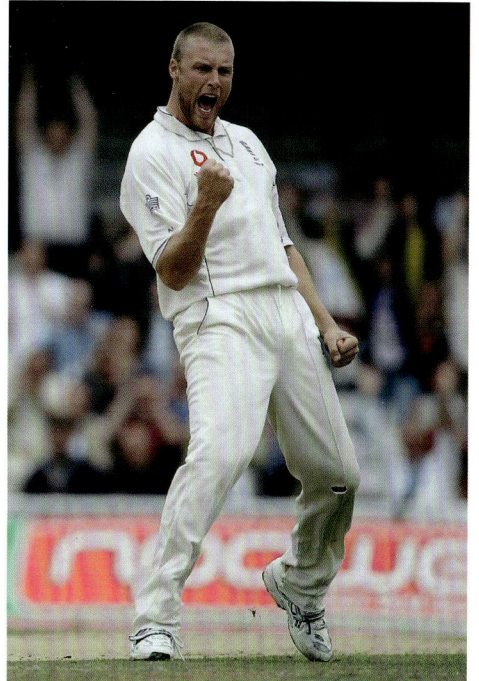

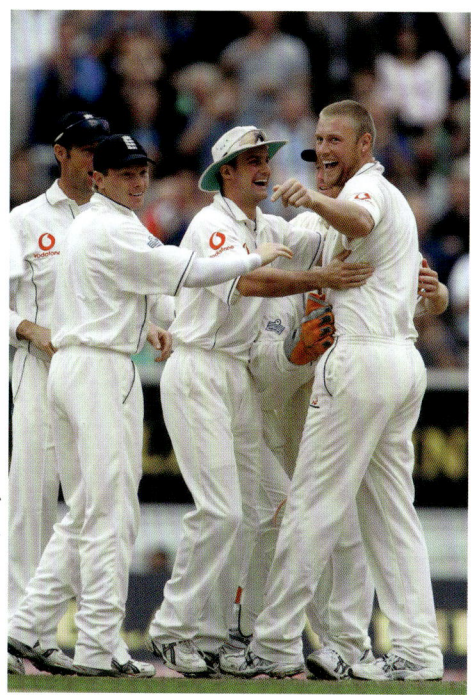

Celebrating wickets during the fifth Test of the 2005 Ashes – one of the proudest points of my career.

© Paul Gilham, Getty

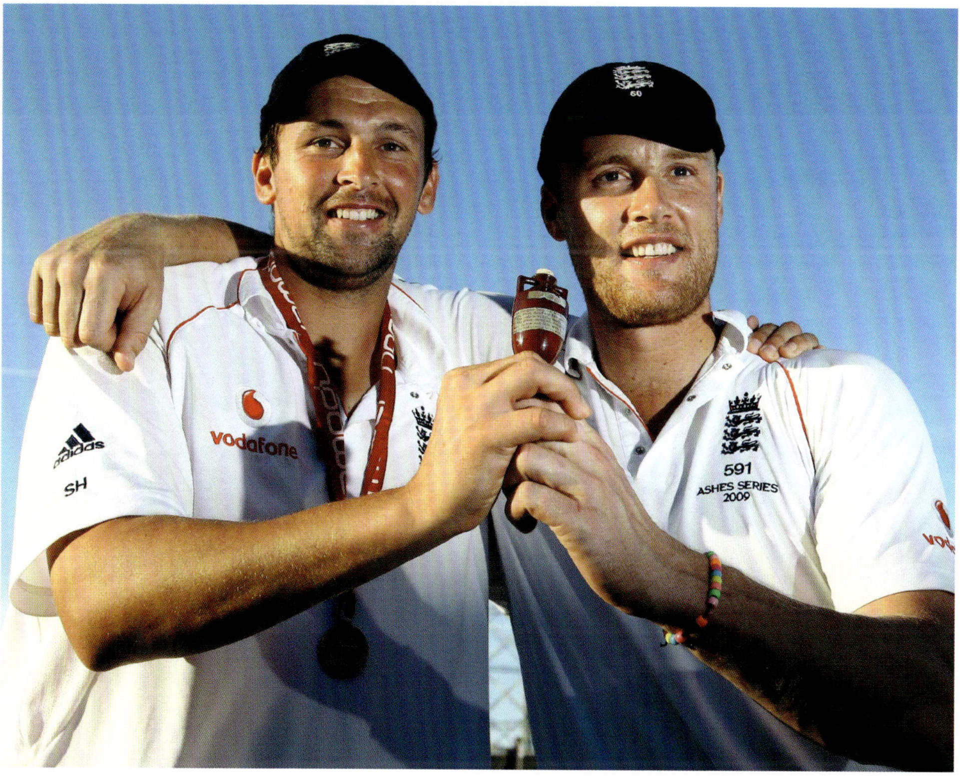

Me and Harmy with the Ashes, celebrating England's first Ashes win in 18 years.

© Philip Brown, Getty

Me and Bumble at the T20 Blast Final in 2017 – I'm Elvis, he's Johnny Cash.
Not how I imagined we'd end up when I was 17 …

© Shutterstock

© Laurence Griffiths, The FA, Getty

Below left: King of the Jungle! Celebrating a win in Australia for the first time in a while …

Below right: Me and James Corden on the football field at Wembley filming *A League of Their Own*.

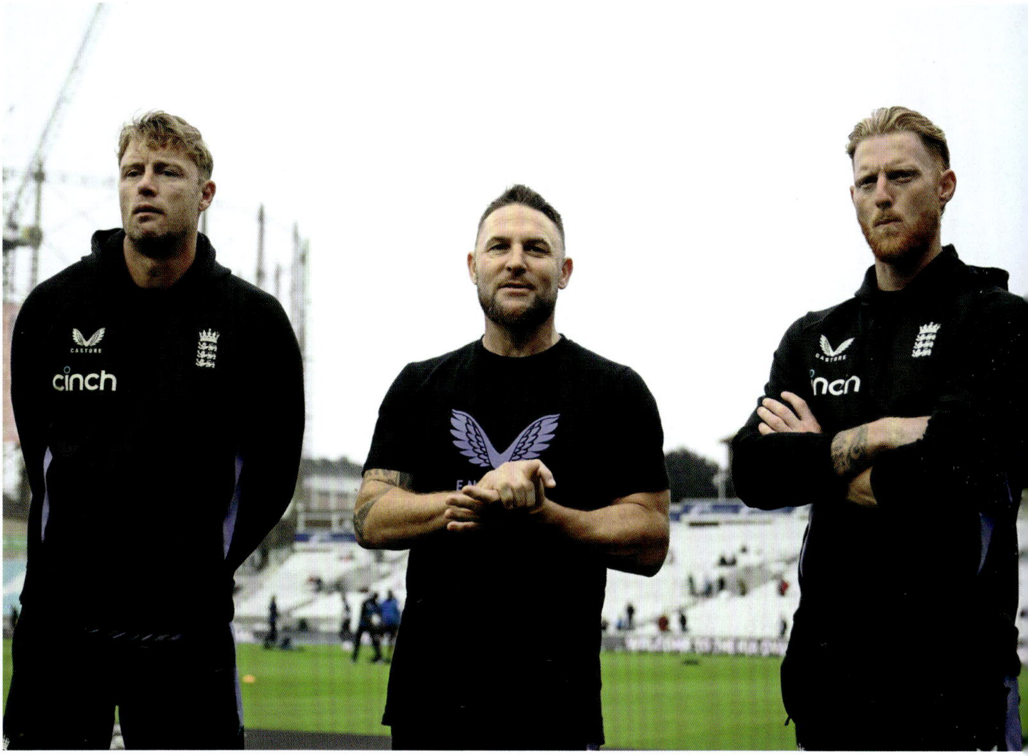

© Gareth Copley, Getty

Above: Me with Brendan McCullum and Ben Stokes, working with the England Team before the third Test against Sri Lanka in 2024.

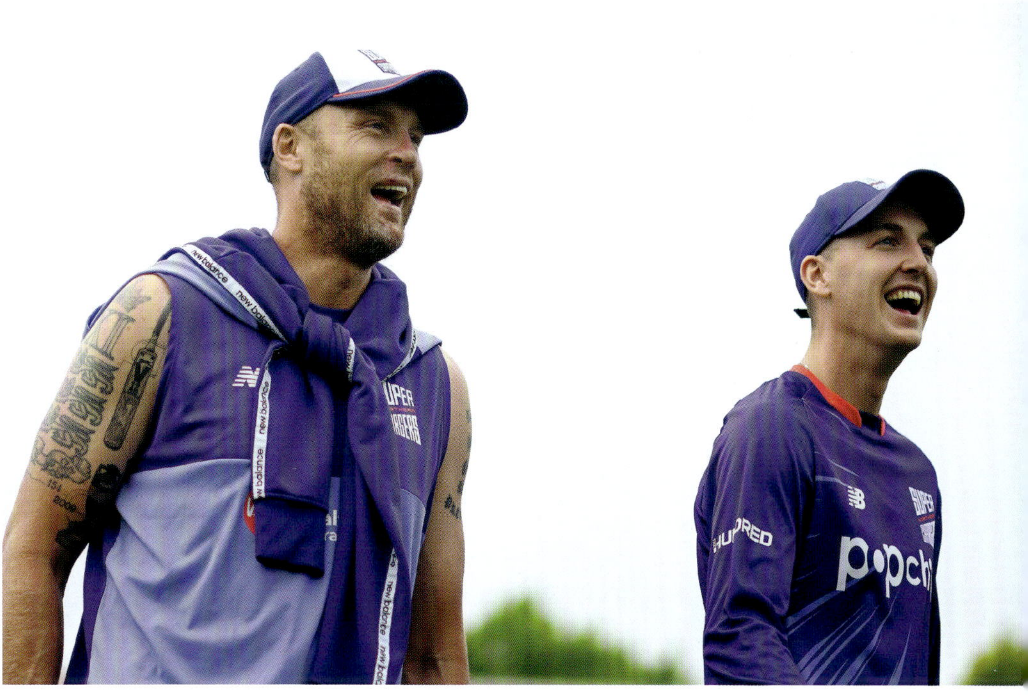

© Harry Trump – ECB, Getty

Right: Me and Harry Brook at a Northern Superchargers coaching session.

Certainly didn't to me.

Nasser's time in charge was hard going. He carried the fight and did his best to drag England forward, but it was intense, and you felt that in the dressing room. When Vaughany took over, it was like someone had finally opened a window and let a bit of air in. He understood people. He managed personalities rather than just players.

We were all wired differently. Gilo – Ashley Giles, our spinner – wasn't like me, and Tresco was different again, but Vaughany let us be ourselves, and that made all the difference.

By 2003, you could feel something building. The team felt like it belonged to us. When Graham Thorpe – one of our key batters – came back in, he just slotted into what we'd already created, rather than the whole thing having to shift around him.

We looked out for each other, whether it was me, Harmy, Hoggy – Matthew Hoggard, our devastating swing bowler – Gilo, Simon Jones – if one of us did well, we all shared it. Gilo, in particular, never got the credit he deserved. The press moaned about him bowling over the wicket, but he slowed things down and gave the seamers a breather when they needed it. He was massive for us.

It wasn't perfect, but it was ours. And I was always much more comfortable being part of that team than trying to run it.

Wait, I can hear you say. You've wanged on about captaincy but haven't mentioned the 2006 Ashes. Stay tuned . . .

CHAPTER 25

OFF OUR GAME

Second slip, and I'm frozen. I can feel the tension in my fingers, breath held without even realising, arms twitching up for a moment, then dropping back to my sides as the ball flies past. Not just wide – it's missed the pitch entirely. I mean, it's a good 15 feet off. No exaggeration. Like someone's bowled it from a trampoline.

We're at the Gabba – Brisbane's cricket fortress – baking sun, hard pitch, thick air, and nearly 40,000 Queenslanders already getting stuck in. It's the first ball of the 2006 Ashes series, and I'm standing there thinking, *What the fuck has just happened?*

Steve Harmison – who's not just one of our fast bowlers, but also one of my closest mates – has bowled it – and it's a disaster. He's run in, nervous as anything, and launched this absolute grenade that's veered so far off target it's ended up in another postcode. We've talked for weeks about setting the tone, about momentum, about how important it is to start well. Which, on reflection, probably puts too much pressure on one ball.

And then this.

I try not to react. Don't want to make it worse. Keep it calm, make it look like it was all part of the plan. I give him a nod and say, 'Bowled, Steve,' under my breath, like it's no big deal. The crowd makes that collective noise – sort of a *Wooooaah* – like they're not quite sure what they've just witnessed.

But inside? I'm already unravelling.

Because this is the moment it turns. In Australia for another Ashes series. The big rematch. We'd beaten them in 2005, one of the all-time great summers, and now they want blood. They're on home soil and every Aussie from Perth to Sydney wants payback. But back home, England expects. The whole country's looking at me now because Michael Vaughan's injured, and I'm the one standing there as captain.

And if I'm being honest – properly honest – I never really wanted the job in the first place.

*　　*　　*

To recap, my journey to the captaincy of the 2006 Ashes side had begun when Vaughany had his knee issues, pulled out of the Pakistan tour, and then Marcus Trescothick had to leave the India trip early for mental health reasons.

So I got the call.

You already know how that one went. Despite the Corey issue I stayed on in India, and despite everything, it went well. We drew the series. We were buzzing.

But then came that summer series against Sri Lanka.

We drew, but like I said, we should've won. My body was starting (I say 'starting', I mean 'continuing') to creak, and I had surgery on my knee afterwards.

And then came the build-up to the Ashes.

I was rushing to get fit, trying to ignore all the chat, which was mainly focused on whether it would be me or Strauss as captain at the Ashes. Who's it going to be? I was training hard, doing rehab with Rooster, trying to get my head right. I went to Portugal for a break with my family, as well as doing more rehab with Rooster. We'd hired a couple of villas, and my phone was going all day. Selectors, friends, everyone with one burning question: 'Are you doing it?'

And I didn't know. I honestly didn't know if I wanted it. I kept thinking, 'I should, shouldn't I? It's the England captaincy.' I mean, it's the sort of job you say yes to because it feels like the right thing to do, even if it's not right for *you*. Even if I stuff it up, I have to be able to say I gave it a shot, don't I?

The team got announced at The Oval – sure enough, me as captain. I hadn't picked the side. Hadn't shaped the group. It didn't feel like *my* team. And I didn't have that relation-ship with the coach, Duncan Fletcher. Not a bad bloke, you understand, but not my bloke, if that makes sense. We were never properly aligned.

I even managed to mess up the announcement. I'd been growing my hair, but in trying to recapture something of the old me – the lad with the shaved head who played out of his skin in 2005 – I shaved it again. Only, I went too short, and I ended up looking like a Deptford bouncer. It didn't start well, and it didn't get better.

We barely had a build-up. Got hammered by the Prime Minister's XI in a warm-up game in Canberra. Marcus Trescothick flew home again. Harmy wasn't bowling well, but I still wanted him in. He's a confidence player, and when he's on, he's unplayable. But he wasn't on. And I knew it.

Then came the big moment. Press conference before the first Test, which would be at the Gabba. I get asked, 'Who's bowling the first ball?'

I say, 'Steve Harmison.'

Because that's what captains do, isn't it? You back your players. You trust them. And I trust Steve like no other. But as we walked out that first morning, I could see it – Harmy wasn't right, by which I mean, he was jittery and nervous. Not just butterflies, but full-on haunted.

Looking back, I know what I should have done. I should have taken the ball myself and said, 'Steve, I'll do this.' But hindsight's a wonderful thing and anyway, there's no way I could have brought myself to do that. Not because I didn't want to, but because I cared about him. Too much, probably. Besides which, a few nerves are nothing, especially not on a big occasion like that. He'd get over them, right?

Safe to say, he didn't.

He bowled. It sailed. It went so wide it didn't even land on the cut strip. And I was there in the slips, watching it like it's coming straight for me.

It wasn't just a shocking delivery – it was a sign.

We were off. Off the pace, off the boil, off the map. Right from minute one.

I tried to settle things. We actually got a wicket not long after, but it didn't matter. They tore us apart. I didn't bring myself on early enough with the ball. Tried to ease Jimmy and Hoggard in. Tried to protect Harmy. And I suppose I was trying to protect myself, too.

At the press conference after the Test, I was bluffing my way through it – saying we'd come back from one-nil down before. I knew I was talking rubbish.

After that implosion in Brisbane, we had to move on fast – next stop, Adelaide for the second Test. And for a brief, glorious moment, it looked like we'd got ourselves back into it.

We even set a trap for Ricky Ponting – a smart one, and credit to Matthew Hoggard for that. Hoggy bowled a slower ball into the pitch hoping Ponting would poke the ball upwards to the waiting Ashley Giles at deep square leg.

Sure enough, Ponting took the bait. Played the shot, just as we'd planned, straight to Giles. Except he ran in too far. Either way, it went down. Doesn't matter now. He didn't catch it. And we missed the opportunity.

From there, they rallied. We batted again, but the pitch slowed up and their bowlers – Lee, McGrath – just kept hitting the same spots. No easy runs, no rhythm. We lost wickets, couldn't push the score, and the whole thing ground to a halt. Then they chased down the target with time to spare, quick as you like.

We sat in the dressing room afterwards, stunned. My birthday, that was. Rachael had booked a table at one of the wineries, and I didn't get back to the room until two in the morning.

We drank, didn't say much. The mood was shot.

And then it was on to Perth.

CHAPTER 26

IT'S THE HOPE THAT KILLS YOU

Perth for the third Test. We'd already gone two-nil down and my body was starting to go with it. My knee was a mess – not screaming in pain exactly, but grinding away every time I bowled or batted, and I was having to bluff my way through. I couldn't show it. Couldn't say anything. Just had to get through.

We actually found ourselves in a half-decent spot at one point. I can't remember all the finer details – it's a bit of a blur now – but it wasn't too shabby, despite hundreds from Michael Hussey and Michael Clarke, until Adam Gilchrist came in to bat for the Aussies and blew it all up. He took Monty Panesar – our left-arm spinner – apart. It was sixes and fours all over the place, brutal stuff, one of the fastest Ashes hundreds ever, and it turned the whole game on its head.

After another hundred by Alastair Cook and a good

knock from Ian Bell, Kev got a few. I got a few. We were chasing in the second innings and there was just enough on the scoreboard to tease us. Not enough to think, *We've got this*, but enough to think, *Maybe, if something happens*.

And it's the hope that kills you.

By that point, I was all over the place. I nearly did something mad in that match – not in a dangerous way, just in a daft, defiant sort of way. I'd decided I was going to go out to bat in my cap, not a helmet, as some sort of statement. No idea what I thought I'd be saying, to be honest with you. I was sitting there in the dressing room, cap on, pads on, thinking, *Right, that's it. I'm doing this*. Wicket falls. I get up. About to go. Ready to make my statement.

And Duncan, the coach, just says, 'Where's your helmet?'

I say, 'I'm wearing my cap.'

He looks at me and says, 'Put your helmet on.'

So I did. Thank God. It was fast and bouncy and I'd have been flattened.

We ended up losing, of course. That meant we went three-nil down. And when the series is gone is when you start thinking, *Can we just go home now*? Because there's no way back from three-nil. There's no way you can save face.

But no. You've still got to do the full run. It's all part of the show. The series has been sold, the tickets bought, the schedule locked in. And so the next stop was Melbourne – the Boxing Day Test – and it was a circus. Ninety thousand people at the MCG, and I just wanted to curl up some-where and vanish.

Holed up in our apartments, Christmas was grim. My mum and dad had flown out to spend it with us, but I just broke; I remember sitting with my dad on Christmas Eve and bursting into tears – proper sobbing, and saying sorry. For what, I wasn't entirely sure, but it felt like I'd let everyone down – the team, the fans, my family, myself.

On Christmas Day, we had a training session in the morning – no escape from it. Then came the team Christmas dinner, sitting around a table with people I didn't really want to sit with, making strained small talk, passing the potatoes while everything felt like it was caving in.

Boxing Day rolled around. Fourth Test. The pitch was a mystery, and I didn't have a clue what to do if I won the toss – bat or bowl. I walked past Ian Botham and asked, 'Have you seen the pitch?'

'Yes,' he said.

'What would you do if you won the toss?'

He shrugged. 'I dunno.'

Brilliant. Thanks, Beefy.

I won the toss and chose to bat – shouldn't have. We were out there fielding soon enough and got battered for two and a half days. Matthew Hayden and Andrew Symonds both got big hundreds. All I remember was standing out there in the middle of it, surrounded by holidaymakers and England fans who'd flown halfway around the world for the big festive cricket tour – and there we were, getting taken apart. No hiding place. No off switch. Just relentless.

Sydney was the fifth and final Test, and by then it felt like a wake. Glenn McGrath was retiring. Justin Langer too. So it was all ceremonies and tributes – speeches, applause, end-of-an-era stuff. We had to give Langer a guard of honour, which I hated. He came out, soaking up the sentiment, and then Matthew Hayden tried to walk through it like he was part of the parade, too.

I looked at him and said, 'You're not fucking retiring.'

I just wanted the whole thing to be over.

We weren't good enough. The team lacked experience and belief, the dressing room didn't feel right, and I wasn't in a good place. I was drinking more, trying to escape, because there wasn't any help coming from anywhere else. Duncan Fletcher, the coach, was barely saying a word to me. No support, no encouragement – just silence. He kept his distance. Didn't want to know. A few of the lads had started disappearing into little groups, looking after themselves, and I was stuck in the middle of it all, just trying to hold it together. And of course the press were vicious – and I mean proper vicious.

The only one I really connected with out there was Steve Harmison. He was having his own battle, and I could see it, but he still stood up for me. Like, after the second Test, I didn't want to play. I felt done, but he stood up and said, 'He's playing the next one,' meaning that I wasn't quitting, I wasn't dropping out.

That meant a lot to me, that public backing from Harmy.

And of course the press were vicious – and I mean proper vicious. Not just the Aussie tabloids, though they were bad enough, with the headlines and the jibes, but the English press, too. It was like they enjoyed it. The old routine: build you up, knock you down.

All I knew was that 2006 in Australia had just about broken me.

CHAPTER 27

THE TOSS

More than most, I know how random life can be. How everything can change in a split second. I'm reminded every time I look in the mirror. Every time I look back on my career. How random and sometimes impulsive (and sometimes drunken – hello, Mr Pedalo!) choices go on to define your life from then on. Factors beyond your control. A toss of the coin.

So let's talk about that, shall we? Let's talk about the coin toss.

In cricket, you can prepare all you want, pore over data, analyse conditions, talk endlessly in team meetings, but there comes that moment before every match when it all boils down down to one thing: heads or tails.

The coin goes up, and for a brief second, it's out of everyone's hands. People make a lot of the coin toss, and rightly so. It can set the tone for the entire match.

Generally, I was always in favour of batting first. Most of us were. If you're offered first use of the pitch, you usually take it. The surface tends to be at its best early on. True, the first hour or two might offer a bit for the bowlers – bit of moisture, some seam movement – but once you get through that, the conditions settle. The sun gets on it, the wicket flattens out, and scoring becomes easier. But as the game wears on, the pitch deteriorates. Cracks open up, the bounce gets uneven, it starts turning more, and batting last becomes a nightmare. That's Test cricket: it evolves over five days, and you want to get in while it's good.

Of course, all this assumes that you're confident in your own batting line-up. And that, ultimately, is where so many coin toss decisions come from. Confidence – or lack of it.

When I captained, I usually had my mind made up before I even walked out there. You watch the pitch during the days leading up to the Test, you talk to your coaches and factor in the pitch conditions, the weather, everything. And nine times out of ten, the decision was clear in my head before the coin was even in the air.

But really, you still have to play well regardless. The toss doesn't win or lose you the game. It might give you an edge, but you've still got to get the runs, take the wickets.

Which brings me neatly to Brisbane, 2002. First Ashes Test. And one of the most infamous toss decisions in recent memory – Nasser Hussain at the Gabba.

At the time, I wasn't even playing. I was there, part of the squad, but physically nowhere near fit enough to join in. Earlier that year, I'd been diagnosed with double hernias by Dave Roberts, the Lancashire physio – we called him

Rooster. Top man. England wanted me to play the full summer schedule regardless. I soldiered through the series against India, playing while dosed up on painkillers and injections. By the final Test of that summer, I was in bits. I didn't even bother bringing my kit to the ground; I literally couldn't run. I sat on the grass during team selection, and when my name was called, I looked at the selector and said, 'Are you joking? I can't move.' But they wanted me to play. Another jab, another dose of painkillers, and off I went.

After that, I had surgery, but the damage was already done. My recovery was brutal. The hernias were fixed, but the knock-on effects lingered. I couldn't train properly. So, when the Ashes tour came around, I was taken along to continue my rehab, with a view to possibly being fit for the second or third Test. I still couldn't run when we landed in Australia.

The atmosphere on that tour was strange. Darren Gough was injured too, struggling with his knee. Michael Vaughan had knee trouble as well. We were this little injured contingent, working away on our own rehab programmes while the rest of the lads trained. One day, Duncan Fletcher, the coach – with whom I had a pretty fractious relationship at the best of times – came over to me during warm-ups. 'What are you doing?' he asked.

I said, 'I can't run.'

He looked at me confused. 'Yeah, but when you said you couldn't run, I didn't think you meant you actually couldn't run.'

I just stared at him. 'That's sort of what "can't run" means, Duncan.'

COMING HOME

By the time the first Test at Brisbane rolled around, it was obvious I wasn't going to play. But I was there, watching as Nasser walked out for the toss. Now, the Gabba is a belting pitch. Perfect for batting early on. In Australia, it's almost automatic: you win the toss, you bat first. Set the game up, post a big total, apply scoreboard pressure. That's how the Aussies do it, and they do it well.

But Nasser chose to bowl.

Now, people talk about that decision as if it was some spur-of-the-moment blunder. It wasn't. These things are debated, analysed. He'd have talked it over with Duncan Fletcher and the coaching staff in the days leading up to the match. The problem was confidence – or rather, the lack of it. Australia were so dominant back then, and I think the fear was: what if we bat first and collapse? What if we're all out before lunch? Better to bowl, stay in the game, ease into it. Try and contain rather than dictate.

But that's not how you beat Australia.

As it turned out, we got slaughtered. The Aussies batted, piled on the runs, and we were under the cosh from the off. I was sitting there, watching, frustrated and helpless. Simon Jones – a good mate of mine, quick bowler, great lad from Wales – was playing. I was pleased for him. Then disaster struck. Simon dived to stop a ball in the field, and his knee got stuck. Blew it out completely. It was horrific. A brutal injury.

We carried him off the field – me and a couple of the lads – and suddenly we were one man down. They needed a substitute fielder, so I got sent on. Fielding at slip at first, which was fine – you don't move much. But then they shifted me to deep square leg. The plan there is simple: if the bowler sends down a short one, the batter might hook it your way.

Well, that's exactly what happened. The ball went up, catchable, but I physically couldn't get to it. I hobbled after it, picked it up and threw it back. Nasser looked at me and shouted, 'What the fuck?' I shouted back, 'I can't run! I'm injured!' That was that. He sent me off. I was fine with it – didn't fancy fielding anyway.

That Brisbane Test summed up a lot of where England were at the time. On paper, we had good players – some very good players, in fact – but mentally we were miles behind. The environment wasn't right. We didn't believe in ourselves the way Australia did. They expected to dominate. We hoped to compete. And decisions like that toss reflected the mindset.

The Aussies would look at that flat Gabba pitch and see runs. They'd see the chance to set the game up, to crush the opposition with scoreboard pressure. We looked at it and saw jeopardy. The possibility of failure. It's a mindset thing. You can have all the talent in the world, but if you don't believe you're as good as your opponent, you're already behind.

I don't blame Nasser entirely. It's not easy standing out there with 50,000 people watching, cameras everywhere, knowing the pressure that comes with an Ashes series. He would have agonised over that call. And I've been in that position myself as captain: you win the toss, and everyone expects you to know exactly what to do. The truth is, sometimes you're not sure.

Later in my own career, I became more philosophical

about the toss. You can't control it. It's a 50–50. What you can control is how you play once the coin's landed. Win it or lose it, you've still got to perform.

But still – that Brisbane decision will always be one that gets talked about. Even now, people bring it up, and I get why. In a way, it was a snapshot of where English cricket was at the time. Fearful. Passive. Hoping not to lose rather than playing to win.

Since then, of course, English cricket has shifted. The mindset's different now. More aggressive. More confident. Look at the way we play today – there's no fear. We dictate terms, we take the game on. And funnily enough, once you approach things that way, the coin toss matters a little bit less. Because you're backing yourself either way.

That, ultimately, is the lesson I took from all those coin tosses, good and bad. Control what you can control. The rest – the random stuff – you just have to roll with. Like so much in life, really. One minute you're flipping a coin at the Gabba; the next you're being carried off with a bad knee; the next you're being sent off the field because you can't run. You can't script any of it. But you learn from all of it.

Heads or tails? You call it, you live with it, and you get on with the game.

CHAPTER 28

THE PEDALO INCIDENT

Stop me if you've heard this one before. I'm on the beach in St Lucia, pissed as a fart, trying to launch a pedalo into the Caribbean.

It's sometime after midnight – I think – and the sea is flat and black and still, apart from the gentle slap of water against the rocks. The air's thick, humid, that kind of tropical heat that clings to your skin and doesn't let go, and I'm barefoot, wearing a t-shirt and baggy jeans. I'm dragging a bright yellow pedalo backwards across the sand like it owes me money.

Behind, there's a row of bars with the music still going. Dancehall, I think. Or maybe reggae. Hard to tell with the way everything's spinning slightly. There are a few staff cleaning up, a couple of stragglers milling about, but otherwise it's just me and this stupid boat.

And the plan – if you can call it a plan (which you can't) –

is to paddle out into the harbour. I've spotted a yacht moored just off the marina, and in my rum-sodden brain, I'm convinced that Ian Botham's on it. I'm absolutely certain he is. And I'm thinking, wouldn't it be brilliant to turn up unannounced, give him a shock, have a bit of a laugh?

(Only, as it turns out, it's not Botham's boat. It's Tim Rice's. The lyricist. *Jesus Christ Superstar*. That Tim Rice. Which makes absolutely no sense and also makes perfect sense in the state I'm in.)

Either way, I try to push the pedalo into the shallows, but it's heavier than it looks. Every shove feels like I'm moving a fridge. I stop to catch my breath and sway a bit. I've got sand on my jeans and rum on my breath, and the boat still hasn't budged.

Then I hear someone calling my name. A voice from up the beach. Stern, sharp, cutting through the haze. I turn my head but everything's blurred. Can't make out the face.

Next thing I know, there's movement. People coming towards me. One of the security lads, maybe two. I honestly can't remember. Just shapes and noise and me, trying to pretend it's nothing, like I'm just having a stroll. Bit of late-night exercise.

I don't even remember being escorted back. Just fragments. A scuffed shin. A wet T-shirt in my hand. The faint smell of chlorine and smoke.

The rest of the night disappears.

* * *

It had started out innocently enough. We'd just lost our opening match of the 2007 World Cup to New Zealand.

I knew the boys were going out for a drink after the game, but for some reason, I decided I was going to stay in. We were right on the beach, my hotel room overlooking the sea; I'd just have a quiet night and enjoy the view.

I tried to stick to my plan, but by about 9.30pm the disappointment of losing – as well as getting a first-ball duck – was weighing heavy, so I headed out for a drink alone at a rum bar on the corner called Limeys.

One rum punch turned into two, three, four, five. I ended up in conversation with a couple of umpires. Around midnight, I knew the lads were in another bar, so I went to join them. About an hour after that, I realised I'd had far too much and just wanted to get back to the hotel. I staggered through reception towards my room, which meant walking past the beach.

And that's when I got the idea to go and visit Ian Botham.

I'd been doing a bit of swimming on the trip, but I wasn't confident in the water.

Boat, then. Right.

I saw a kayak at first but couldn't find any oars. The only mode of transport left was a pedalo. Bright yellow thing, bobbing about at the edge of the beach like it had come straight out of a kids' cartoon. I could use that to paddle out to Botham's boat and say hello.

Getting in was hard enough. Trying to get going was even harder. I floundered around for a few minutes, then gave it up as a bad job. As I stood in the water, the pedalo drifted out to sea, and before long a security guard was hauling me out of the water and back towards my room.

What followed was chaos. A beach attendant stopped me.

COMING HOME

I got hauled back again. No one got hurt. Nothing really happened. No yellow boats were harmed in the making of this anecdote. But someone made a phone call. From there, the whole thing took off, and by the morning, it was everywhere.

The headlines were savage. *Fred-alo* was the one that stuck. I'll admit now, it was funny – but back then, it felt like a punch to the gut. After all, I was vice-captain and supposed to be setting the tone. Sure enough, I got dropped for the next game, fined and marched out in front of the press to apologise like I'd tried to steal the Crown Jewels.

I remember sitting at that press conference, a bit hung-over and a lot ashamed, just trying to say the right things, trying to own it. But it was humiliating. I'd become a punchline. Again.

And it wasn't just the papers. The dressing room felt it too. Some of the lads backed me up but others didn't. Some looked at me like I was the problem – like I was dragging them down. And maybe, at that point, I was.

CHAPTER 29

ENOUGH

Drink. For better or worse, it figures large in my story, so let's give booze its own (but very short) chapter. First things first: I'll never say never, but as of now, I'm not drinking.

No dramatic moment. Not even the pedalo in 2007. No flashing lights or big rock bottom. Just a quiet reckoning. I looked in the mirror one morning – puffy face, sore head, that creeping sense of shame from not knowing exactly what had been said or done the night before – and thought, *I don't want this any more.*

Not 'I can't.' Just . . . 'I've had enough.'

Because I wasn't the guy with a bottle hidden in a drawer. I wasn't shaking in the morning or pouring vodka on my cereal. But I was the guy who couldn't stop once I'd started; the one who turned a couple of pints into ten, who took a good night and turned it into a bad morning. The one who drank to forget, not to enjoy.

COMING HOME

And for a long time, I told myself it was part of the job. Cricket? There was always a drink waiting – after the match, in the dressing room, on the bus, at the airport, in the bar. It was how you bonded, how you blew off steam. Then came telly, and it didn't slow down. If anything, it ramped up.

Filming *A League of Their Own* was like being strapped to a firework. It started with a glass of wine before the show, then wine during the show, then wine afterwards, and before you knew it, we had our own in-joke called Wine Club and none of us could remember who started it. There were nights with Whitehall and Corden and all the gang where we drank until dawn and laughed until it hurt – and yeah, some of those were magic.

But that kind of magic always comes with a hangover.

Not just the sore head, but the creeping self-doubt. That low hum of shame. The kind where you're replaying the night back in your head and wondering if you were just a bit too loud. A bit too much. A bit of a knob.

I started to notice I wasn't as sharp. Not as funny. Not as present. I didn't want to show up hung-over any more. Didn't want to keep apologising. And the truth is, I didn't like who I was on it. Not really. I thought I was being the life of the party. But more often than not, I was just a bit lost.

So I stopped.

Not right away. Took a few stuttering goes. A few 'I'll just have the one' nights that ended in doner kebabs and blurry cab rides. But eventually, I got there. I switched the wine for lime and soda. Started saying no. And surprisingly, I liked it. I liked waking up clear-headed. I liked being in control. I liked remembering.

The first dry shows on *A League of Their Own* were strange. You're used to that little warm-up buzz, the looseness that comes with drink. Without it, everything felt raw. Like trying to be funny with the volume turned down. I remember thinking, *This might not work*. But then it did. The laughs were still there. The joy was still there. I just didn't need a pint to find it.

There were still temptations, of course. Still are. The odd event, the odd afterparty, where the drinks are flowing and everyone's saying, 'Come on, just one.' And maybe I'm still the kind of lightweight drunk who might get caught up in the moment, who might be one sip away from back to square one. But I kept coming back to the same thought: I've had my fill. And if I never drank again, that'd be all right by me.

I missed some bits – the camaraderie, the ritual, the first cold sip after a long day. But I didn't miss the fallout. The fuzzy regrets. The ache in my bones the next morning. The uncertainty about who I'd been the night before.

These days, life is simpler. Fewer big nights, more early mornings. More time with the kids, more memories I actually remember. And for once, the story I am living feels like one I am writing myself – not just riding out.

So yeah. Drink. It figures in my story. It had its moments – some brilliant, some bleak. But it didn't define me then, despite appearances to the contrary. And it certainly doesn't define me now.

CHAPTER 30

A RESET

By the time that the 2007 World Cup had wrapped up – pedalo and all – I was on my knees. Physically, mentally, the lot. I wasn't just carrying an injury. I was carrying years of them. I'd been patched up, broken down and sent back out again so many times I'd stopped keeping count. The only real consistency in my life at that point was surgery.

The World Cup was supposed to be a reset. Instead, it ended with headlines, hangovers and the infamous pedalo.

The roots of it all lay back in 2005. Just before that incredible Ashes summer, I'd had an operation on my left ankle – a bone spur taken off the back, which had been causing me all sorts of problems. The procedure didn't go well. They left some fragments in there, and the worst part was that the bits they left in kept growing. Bone fragments – like weeds in concrete. Every time I ran in to bowl, they ground away inside the joint. And still, I got back in time for the Ashes. I was getting injected to get through it. Injections to numb the pain, not fix it.

After that, it was just one op after another. I reckon I had three on that ankle alone. One of the surgeons told me, 'It's all sorted.' But it wasn't. Another one gave it a go, then another. Eventually, I started to think they were just doing it for their CVs.

At some point, I was sent to a bloke in Northampton. The England physio lived nearby, so it made sense for him, I suppose. Didn't make much sense for me. I came out of that one worse than I went in.

Eventually, I gave up on all of them. I started working properly with the physio at Lancashire. You may remember him from a few chapters back – a fella called Dave Roberts, aka Rooster. He'd been England physio back in the days of Botham, and I'd known him since I was a lad. First crossed paths when I was 15, playing England age-group stuff. He was back around Lancs by then and basically never left my side. Bless him, he knew I needed sorting properly.

Rooster went above and beyond. He scoured the world for an ankle specialist who might actually fix the mess I was in. That's how we ended up flying out to Holland. The surgeon's name was Niek van Dijk – like Dick Van Dyke but not – very Dutch, and when we arrived, I knew we were in the right place. There was a Barcelona footballer sitting in the next room, waiting to be seen. Rooster clocked that they were trying to fob us off with Niek's number two.

He didn't have it.

'We've not come all this way to see a replacement,' he said, gruff as ever. 'I want to see Niek.'

They tried to explain how it worked, the process, the protocol, but Rooster wasn't listening.

'I want the surgeon,' he said.

Eventually, Niek came in, and Rooster laid it all out – the history, the failed surgeries, the fact that no one in England would touch it. The Dutchman listened, nodded once, and said, 'I'll lay him on his front, stick his ankle up, take the fragments out. You happy with that?'

I was. And he did. From that day on, the ankle didn't give me grief again.

Of course, then the right knee packed in.

That was the rhythm by then – fix one bit, another breaks. My body was just done. I reckon I had three dozen scans across my career, maybe more. Over a hundred cortisone jabs. Every joint, every limb, has its own saga.

I remember being back from the World Cup, needing more surgery, and then hearing that Duncan Fletcher had been sacked. Everyone gathered round when he told the team, last day of the World Cup in the Caribbean. For some of the lads, it was emotional. Vaughany was crying. Collingwood too – or trying to. Paul Nixon, who'd only been in the team for five minutes, was giving it a go as well.

Me? I was quietly delighted.

Not in a nasty way, not really. But I knew I wasn't going to get much more from Duncan. And I knew exactly what was coming next. He'd write a book, and I'd cop it in print. Funny thing is, he always used to bang on about how cowardly it was – criticising people in black and white when they weren't there to answer back. And then he went off and did exactly that.

I didn't read it. Didn't need to. I already knew what was in there.

I was injured, low and getting hammered in the press – especially after the pedalo thing. It became the short-hand for everything that had gone wrong. For my injuries. For missing games. For being drunk in charge of a pedalo. I started drinking more. I didn't want to be around cricket. I didn't know if I had it in me any more.

So I spoke to Rooster. I spoke to Rachael. And I said, 'Why don't we just go away for a bit?' The World Cup had finished, the headlines were out there, and I just needed out. We pitched it to the ECB. To my surprise, they bought in. I think they wanted me out of sight for a while too. So we packed our bags – Rooster, his missus, Rachael, the kids and me – off to Florida for rehab and sunshine and breathing space.

We rented a house on a golf course in Palm Beach. I didn't even play golf back then (that's changed), but it was perfect: gym on site, pool, big kitchen. And the weather was unreal. I was training every day with Rooster, sweating buckets. We'd have barbecues in the evening, Corona Light in hand, and I was getting stronger every day. Rehab was going great. There was a lad from South Africa who worked in the gym who knew who I was, and that was it – the only one. Americans didn't recognise me. No media. No fuss. Just peace.

And you know what? It was bliss. Proper bliss. Just me, Rachael, Holly, who would've been three, and Corey, 18 months. We were a family again. We even started looking at houses. The pound was two to one back then, and everything felt cheap, so I said to Rachael, 'Why don't we stay? Just buy a place, start again, open a café or something?'

She was up for it. Leave the madness behind. Why not? And for a moment, we meant it. We really did. But I was 28, and I still had something left. I wasn't finished yet.

So I came home.

By that point, Peter Moores had taken over as England coach. I already knew Mooresy from his time running the academy, and he was a good bloke – straightforward, decent, someone I got on with. So I went to see him at Loughborough. Funny thing is, I couldn't stand the place back then. Now? I live there. Spend half my time wandering around it these days.

Anyway, I sat down with Mooresy in his office for our first proper meeting, and I just laid it out. I said, 'Peter, I'm not sure I want to do this any more.'

'What? This meeting?'

'No. I mean this, as in cricket.'

He sighed. 'Why not?'

I told him everything. The injuries. The press. The booze. The misery. I told him how great it had been in Florida.

He smiled and said, 'I'll look after you.'

Just like that.

And I thought, *That's what I've needed. Someone to say that. Someone to mean it.*

I walked out of there thinking, *Right. I'm in.*

That was the start of something. I wasn't fully fit – was I ever? – but I was coming back. I played against South Africa that summer, and there was a spell at Edgbaston – bowling to Jacques Kallis, their great all-rounder – that I'll never forget. I gave him a proper working over. It wasn't express pace – 86–88mph – but it felt quick, and more than that, it felt good.

That was the best part. I was enjoying it again.

Didn't last, of course. Not for long. I got injured again not long after – now it's the knee. There was always something.

CHAPTER 31

THE BATTLEFIELD

It's Durban, September 2007. The first T20 World Cup. Yuvraj Singh, India's left-hander – all timing and fire – is facing Stuart Broad, England's tall, fresh-faced quick, still finding his feet. And Yuvraj just detonates. One, two, three . . . six sixes in a single over. Pure theatre. Brutal and beautiful. Stuart Broad never gets over it.

And what a lot of people don't realise is that it starts with me.

We're already out of the tournament, but still have games to play. My ankle's shot – properly gone – but I'm playing through it, barely able to bowl. Deep down, I think this might be it. The last game. And as a result, I'm in a dark headspace, full of pain and frustration and feeling sorry for myself. Yuvraj is batting. Strutting. Smirking. Playing well, as he often does. And something in me snaps.

We've got a bit of a running thing, me and Yuvraj. Banter,

mostly, though sometimes it veers into something more. Usually I get it right – walk the line without stepping over. But not this time. Today, I cross it. I can't even remember the exact words, but I know I threaten him. Not great, but I'm angry, bitter, wound up by the game, by my body, by everything, and I let it spill.

He doesn't take it lying down. He walks straight at me, bat in hand, eyes blazing, saying – apparently – 'You see this bat? You know where I'm going to hit you with it?'

The umpires step in before it kicks off properly, but it's close. Too close. And honestly, it's one of the few moments in my career I really regret. Because that? That's not cricket. That's not me either. But I can't pretend it doesn't happen.

Then comes Broad's over. Yuvraj on strike. First ball – six. Second ball – six. He's looking for me. I'm on the boundary, crowd behind me going mad – mostly Indian supporters in Durban. Third ball – six. By now, I know what's coming. The fourth disappears too. And here's the mad part: after that, I kind of want him to do it. Poor Broad. He's bearing the brunt of my idiocy – my moment of madness. Fifth ball – six. Sixth ball – six. History.

The ground erupts. Yuvraj gives it the big one, and rightly so. And me? I just stand there, unsure whether to clap, laugh, cry or walk off. It's a moment of cricketing genius, and I – muggins here – have helped spark it.

* * *

A few years later, we played each other again – a Test in India. Kevin was captain. I was bowling my 21st over and into another long spell. Yuvraj came out to bat and I ramped it up. Gave it everything. Touched 93, 94 miles an hour. He nicked one. Dropped at slip. We never said a word to each other the whole time, but when I finished my spell and dropped my head, he walked past, patted my back, and said, 'Fucking hell, it's tough.'

That's him. That's the measure of the man.

He was one of my great duels. Could destroy bowlers. Had that magical ability to hit balls no one else could even reach. I had success against him sometimes, got under his skin in a way that worked. Other times, he had me. That's what makes it a proper battle. He went through cancer and came out the other side. Fought. Survived. Came back. Played again. How can you not respect that?

India fans still give it the big one on social media – little digs here and there. But there's no hate. I look back and wish I'd handled Durban differently, but I also know that's sport, and life, too. You get things wrong. You lose your head. What matters is how you carry it after.

The truth about sledging is that it's not about being a hard man. It's about control. Knowing how far to go, and when to stop. There's no glory in tearing someone down just to win a game. But there is something glorious in the contest, the mental side, the chess of it all.

And when it's done right, it can elevate the sport.

While we're on the subject, I've always felt there should be rules to sledging. Not written ones, obviously. Just a kind of code, an understanding; like for example, you don't go after families. You don't bring up things that have nothing to do with the game. You don't try to destroy someone for sport. You keep it clever, if you can. Funny, ideally. And above all, you know when to stop.

That's the bit some people never got. They thought it was about being nasty. About winning the game in the corridor instead of on the pitch. But it wasn't. The best sledges weren't cruel. They were disruptive. Designed to knock you off rhythm. To make you question yourself. That was the point – not to break someone, but to unsettle them just enough that they forget who they are for a moment. And if you could do that, you were in.

But it has to be earned. There's no sense turning up on a field with your mouth moving faster than your feet. You have to back it up. That was something I learned quickly. You can't chirp and then disappear. If you're going to dish it out, you'd better be ready to cop it too.

That's why I always admired the Aussies. They gave it out but they stood by it. None of this 'white line fever' stuff – the idea that you can say what you like on the field and then shake hands after as if nothing happened. If it was personal on the pitch, it stayed personal. You didn't get to wipe the slate clean just because the game had ended. That's too easy. Too convenient. I wasn't about that.

There were times I got it wrong, when I said too much or took it too far – or both. But I always knew when I had. It sat with me. Still does. Durban, obviously, but others too – moments I won't repeat, not because I'm hiding them, but because I'm not proud. I've apologised when I've had to. And I've tried not to repeat the mistakes.

But when it worked? When it was just right? That was electric. There's a moment – a split second, really – when you know it's landed. You say something, the batter flinches or frowns or glances down, and you're in. You've got them thinking about something other than the ball. And in that moment, you've shifted the odds.

I'm older now, but when I think back on those battles – the words, the tension, the looks exchanged between overs – I don't think of them as dark moments. I think of them as part of the game. Cricket isn't just about stats, it's about will. And sometimes, that will is tested in words as much as in runs or wickets.

Sledging, done right, isn't the problem. It's part of the theatre. But it only works if you keep your humanity.

And maybe that's the bit I had to learn the hard way. The game can make you forget yourself sometimes. But it can also bring you back. If you're lucky, it hands you the moments that remind you who you are. Durban was one of those. And so was the pat on the back from Yuvraj, years later.

CHAPTER 32

A FIVE-FOR
AT LORD'S

I can't get my shoes on.

I wake up that morning in agony. Not just my knee but the rest of my body is hurting. I can hardly move or function until I've had my injection and painkillers. Rachael helps me out of bed, helps me get ready, gets me dressed and puts my shoes on. As I limp to the door to leave, she gives me a kiss on the cheek and tells me, gently, not to be a hero. But it's too late for that.

It's the final morning of the second Test of the 2009 Ashes at Lord's, and I'm sitting on the bench in the dressing room, grimacing as I try to work my foot into my boot.

Problem? My knee's locked up again, but it's worse than it was the day before. I've not had the meds yet – I don't want to numb it too early and have the pain return at an inopportune moment. But every movement sends a jolt through the joint, like metal scraping on bone. I glance up at the physio, shake my head. He just gives me that look – the one that says, You sure?

I'm sure.

This is Lord's. It's the Ashes. We've not beaten Australia here since 1934 – before the war – and I'm not sitting this one out. No way. Fuck that with a funny hat on.

By the time the painkillers do their painkilling thing, I'm a different man, and out on the field, something takes over. The pain fades, the crowd rises, and I'm in the zone.

First ball, I'm bang on the money – a fast, searing delivery, right on target. Then another. The rhythm kicks in, the adrenaline floods my system, and I feel like I've tapped into something deeper.

And I bowl. And the wickets start falling.

Wicket one: Simon Katich, who scoops it up and into the waiting hands of KP.

Wicket two: Phil Hughes, who gives it to Strauss for a catch.

Wicket three: Brad Haddin, caught by Collingwood at second slip.

Wicket four: Nathan Hauritz, bowled.

Wicket five: Peter Siddle. A beauty! Middle stump. I am mobbed.

And that was it. A five-for. A proper one.

And a five-for, for those who don't live and breathe the game, is five wickets in a single innings – a bowler's dream. Especially at Lord's. Especially in an Ashes Test.

And I'd never had one there before.

The thing about a five-for is it doesn't just change the

game – it defines it. Especially in a match like this, on that stage, against that team. You don't fluke a five-for. You earn it. Every ball, every bead of sweat, every aching sinew.

I'm bowling quicker than I have in years – 95, 96mph – and even Strauss comes over and asks if I need a break. I tell him no. Not today.

When I finally walk off, the crowd is on its feet and I can barely breathe. I don't care. We've won. Lord's has finally got its win.

*　*　*

It had started in Cardiff, and it hadn't started that well.

First Test of the series, and the whole thing felt off. The pitch was a road, flat as a pancake. It didn't feel like an Ashes venue – for me that's Old Trafford, the Oval, the traditional ones – but it was. And I'd worked like mad to get back for it. My knee was held together by tape and hope. I'd come through one last brutal block of training, got myself stronger than ever, and I was bowling like a man possessed. The batting had gone; I just couldn't move like I used to. But with the ball, I still had it.

I went hard at Phil Hughes and gave him a proper working over – short stuff, nasty angles, just relentless. I got him in the end, too, which was a message. We might've been underdogs, but we weren't rolling over.

And then came Monty Panesar and Jimmy Anderson and their famous last-wicket stand, where they batted out the final moments to secure a dramatic draw. That gritty partnership became iconic because everyone was tense, pacing, chewing nails. Jimmy was blocking like crazy, Monty was doing Monty things, and somehow – God knows how – they saw it through. It felt like a win, that. Not on paper, but just in the guts of it.

We had a few days off before the second Test, which was at Lord's. During the break I had a bit of a mad night out. How mad? Put it this way, it began by bumping into the lads from Kasabian (legendary party animals) and then continued when we were joined by the lads from Oasis, who, you may have read, are also partial to a drink or two.

Like they say of the 1960s: if you can remember it, you weren't there. And it was certainly true of that night for me.

Sure enough, I woke up the next morning stinking of booze and made a decision: this was going to be it – my final Ashes, my final Test summer. I told Strauss who wasn't keen on me going public, saying it would be a distraction. But I needed to be honest. I couldn't do another year of patching myself together.

And then Lord's happened.

Everything came good – that bowling spell on the final day, five wickets, the roar of the crowd, the feeling that maybe, just maybe, I'd timed it right. I could go out on top. I didn't say it out loud, but inside, I knew it.

After the match, Rachael and I went out with Piers Morgan and his wife. It was a good night. I sat there drinking bottles of red and pints of Guinness. Thinking, if that's the last big moment, I'll take it.

Ah, but next was Edgbaston. Third Test.

The story was the rain, mostly. My knee was hanging on, but only just, and I managed a few bursts, got through a few good spells. I tried to bat but couldn't plant my front foot, so everything was wrist and hope, and although I got a few runs, it really wasn't pretty. We battled hard and scraped a draw.

Scores on the doors: two draws and a win.

Headingley. The fourth Test. And I was desperate to play.

I told the coach I had one more in me, and I meant it. I nearly believed it. But Strauss and the backroom staff weren't so sure. They thought I was done. Too banged up and too far gone, so I got left out. I got the call: I was out. Not in the squad. Rested, they said.

I didn't kick off. Didn't argue. But I couldn't stay either. I packed my bag, gave a couple of quiet nods, and slipped out the back. Didn't hang around. Just drove. I don't even remember where to, not exactly. Just . . . *away*.

And then I watched from a distance as the whole thing unravelled. Bowling for the Aussies, Mitchell Johnson – who'd been all over the place earlier in the series – suddenly clicked. Found his rhythm. That slinging left-arm pace started swinging back in like a boomerang, and we had no answer. We made 102 in the first innings, which isn't even a decent Twenty20 score. They batted like gods. Marcus North made it look easy. Hussey found his hands again. We were battered. Inside three days, the Ashes were on the line all over again. It was slipping away.

There was only one left.

The Oval for the fifth. We went in level. Whoever won this Test won the Ashes.

CHAPTER 33

DIRECT HIT

I'm off like a shot.

I'm fielding at mid-on, not my customary slip because I can't bend down. And I'm moving before anybody else reacts. Ball hit square, just behind point, and I'm gone before anyone else has registered it. Doesn't matter that my right knee's shredded, doesn't matter that I've been hobbling between overs, teeth gritted and heart thumping – in this moment, I'm pure instinct. Hussey's nudged it toward me and called Ponting for what he thinks is an easy single, thinking I won't get there because I can't move. He's played it well – always did, especially when it mattered – just a push-and-run. But I'm already there, mid-on or thereabouts, breaking before most have even clocked the shot.

I scoop the ball on the run, turn, and let fly. The second it leaves my hand, I know.

Direct hit.

Off stump cartwheels and Ricky Ponting's diving, scrambling. But he knows. He's short. He's gone. And I've done him.

The Oval erupts. It's deafening – a wall of sound that hits you square in the chest. I stand there, both my arms in the air, and drink it all in.

Inside, though, I'm fizzing.

That was my last Test wicket. Or at least, the last act that mattered. No bowling involved – just a sprint and a throw, on one leg, in my final Ashes match.

Sweetest piece of fielding I ever managed.

And not a bad way to go out.

Good enough, I'd say, to bear repeating.

Not a bad way to go out.

* * *

Two weeks earlier, I'd been sitting on the sidelines at Headingley, sulking like a teenager.

I knew what was coming next. The Oval. Fifth Test, the decider, and just to add a bit of personal interest, my last Test match. I'd announced it before the series started, saying this would be the end of the road, and I meant it; I had nothing left to give. After all, I was already pushing beyond sensible.

But if you're going to stop, there are worse ways to do it than at a packed Oval, with the Ashes on the line.

I was patched up, of course. Injections, ice, stretches, strapping – the usual dance. Most importantly, mentally I was there. Focused. I didn't want to be a passenger. I wanted to contribute. To do something. I didn't have the gas to bowl long spells any more, and batting was more ceremonial than functional by then – one big swing and move on. But I still had moments in me. That was what I told myself.

And I got one. That run-out.

They were wobbling, and that run-out sent them over. Like the point that changes a Wimbledon final. It was a moment. You could feel the shift. The whole ground lifted. The lads came in from everywhere, as I stayed still and took it in.

It was Graeme Swann who spun us home. He was magnificent – flight, dip, turn, confidence. I just tried to keep the pressure on, plug an end, give him space to work. We hunted as a pack. You could feel it shifting back our way.

And then the moment – Ponting out, and not just out but done by something sharp and unexpected. That gave us the lift. The edge.

By the final day, the place was absolutely rocking. The Oval's my favourite ground, nowhere near as prim as Lord's and the noise there is like nowhere else when it's full. You feel it in your chest.

When the final wicket went, it was chaos. We'd won. We'd regained the Ashes. Two series wins in four years. We'd won with time to spare.

Michael Hussey was the last man standing – the one who'd made it look nervy, dragging the match deeper than we'd have liked. He was on 121, stubborn, calm, textbook. But then Swanny, who'd been twisting the screw all innings, found the edge. It wasn't a wild heave or a reckless swipe – just one that spat and caught the bat on the way through.

And Cook, close in at short leg, went low and sharp to take it.

That was it. Done.

The moment that ball nestled in Cookie's hands, The Oval blew up. Players in from all sides, sprinting, shouting, hugging. Staff on the balcony. Fans on their feet. It was one of those full-body-roar moments – no restraint, no planning, just unfiltered joy. The kind of moment you chase your whole career.

We'd bowled them out for 348, and won the match by 197 runs. But numbers barely mattered in that instant. What mattered was the feel of it – the way it landed. The way the last act came with drama and defiance. We weren't hanging on. We weren't crawling over the line. We were walking off as winners, chests out, series in hand.

The Ashes were ours. Again.

There was no giant celebration. Just that shared, silent look between lads who'd given everything. A few hugs, a few handshakes. I stayed out on the grass and took it all in. That was the end of my Test career. I wasn't sad, not really. I was spent.

People ask if I cried. I didn't. But I felt something deeper than that. Like closing a door you know you're never opening again.

I hung back for a minute. I stayed out on the field while the others started drifting off, just wanting to soak it in for a second. There was a big blue sky over The Oval, crowd still buzzing, that low hum of celebration in the air. I could see Rachael up in the stands, beaming, and the whole thing had a sort of golden glow to it. You know when a moment feels big, but warm, too? Like it knows it's going to stick with you. Bit like that.

And I didn't say anything. Didn't need to. No speeches. No waving bats or getting the lads in a circle. That run-out had said enough. That final walk off the pitch, under that sky, with the crowd rising – I let that be the full stop.

Later that night, the boys had a drink for me. As is customary, we had a get-together with the opposition and then, back at the hotel, we had the penthouse suite for the team, family and friends. Very different vibe to 2006. Rachael didn't leave my side. I had a knee operation planned for two days after the Test, but she brought it forward to the day after so I was nil by mouth by midnight – no repeat of last time. No drinking through the night, no bus parade, no pomp. Just the Lister Hospital the next morning to start the end of my career. They told me afterwards they'd found floating cartilage, bone fragments, all sorts. The surgeon said, 'How were you even walking?'

I just smiled.

I wasn't ready for the end – not completely. But if it had to be the end, at least it ended right.

CHAPTER 34

FREDDIE VS THE WORLD

Dennis Rodman, complete with trademark peroxide hair, multiple piercings and *multiple* tattoos, is lounging on a veranda in Laguna Beach, several sheets to the wind.

Oh, and he's setting $50 bills on fire – as you do.

Den's not smiling. It's a serious business this having-money-to-literally-burn lark. I've had a couple by this point – nothing mad, but enough to decide that asking him why he's burning money is a good idea. He looks up and drawls, 'It's only money,' and I – ever the diplomat – go, 'Yeah, but you asked for seventy grand to do the show and you've ended up having to take seven. Might want to hang on to that, Dennis.'

He's not laughing.

Dennis Rodman, by the way – just in case you don't know – is an American basketball player. Just not your average basketball player. Dennis Rodman didn't just rebound –

he transformed the game. He took the scrappiest, least glamorous job on a basketball court and turned it into theatre. He'd throw himself into bodies, chase lost causes like a man possessed, crash the boards with a kind of reckless devotion that made you stop and stare. There was an artistry to it, even though it looked like chaos. Rodman made rebounding feel like performance art.

And he did it all with a flair bordering on weirdness. After all, this is a bloke who once wore a wedding dress to promote his autobiography and claimed to be best mates with Kim Jong-un, all the time cultivating a look and persona that was totally out there.

So yeah, setting fire to his own cash isn't *totally* out of character. Still obscene, though. Offensive, even. I remember thinking, *Mate, if you don't want it, stick it in a charity box.* Not that they'd have one here. It's Laguna Beach, after all.

Meanwhile, our director is getting pinned to a wall by Rodman's security bloke, who looks like stone cold Steve Austin's older, angrier brother. Why? Search me. All I know is that the whole scene is unravelling. Rodman's roaring now, this bloke's breathing down my neck, and I'm trying to wedge myself between the two by the wall to stop it all going completely sideways.

And I'm wondering what possessed me to take up a career in telly.

The next morning we're meant to be filming. Ten o'clock call time. But 10am comes and goes and there's no sign of Rodman. Eleven. Still no appearance from the mercurial and flamboyant basketball ace.

So I'm about to go marching off to wake him up when

he eventually stumbles out looking like he's been dragged through a nightclub backwards. There's stuff everywhere – bottles, mainly, but God knows what else – and the place stinks, and I'm thinking, *We've got to fly planes today. Actual planes.* No word of a lie. We're supposed to be doing mock dogfights in the sky with a joystick and a bloke dressed like Tom Cruise telling us what buttons not to press.

So here we are, turning up for this flight experience, and the first thing we get is a briefing from the *Top Gun* bloke. Aviators, flight suit, silver hair, the whole bit. He's clearly seen things – you can tell just by the way he stands, that ex-military poise – and he starts laying out what we're in for, which involves handing us the controls (sort of) and going head-to-head in mock dogfights (again: sort of). The whole time, I'm barely holding it together, stomach already lurching. And then suddenly, Rodman, who's sitting there, wild-eyed and absolutely off his rocker, interrupts this hardened veteran with a loud, 'Shut up, you old fucker,' just to be a pain in the arse, as far as I can tell. Rodman is giggling, twitching, full of manic energy, totally on-brand. And I'm sitting there thinking, *We're actually going to put this bloke in a plane?*

Next thing you know, we're airborne, except that instead of enjoying the experience, I'm hunched over a sick bag, losing the contents of my stomach in slow motion while the pilots try to catch Dennis Rodman's plane, because he has – true to form – gone rogue, and if last night it felt like it could easily go completely sideways, well, today it has, it really has, and again I think, What possessed me to take up a career in telly?

And that was just one episode.

As I learned during the time I spent with him (mercifully brief), although Rodman could be brilliant, smart, funny and thoughtful, he also had a tendency to flip. One minute he was waxing lyrical about his mum, the next he was tearing into a stranger in the street. Madonna this, Carmen Electra that. It was like watching fame curdle in real time, and it was mesmerising, terrifying and even a little bit addictive. Must have been – I couldn't take my eyes off it.

That trip around America, which boiled down to six weeks of daft challenges, unpredictable chaos, me getting thrust into this bizarre travelling circus (oh, and doing a lot of drinking), was a proper TV baptism by fire. I had no script, no clue, no business being there really. But that was telly, apparently. Or at least, that was *Freddie vs The World*.

Like another time, we were in Mexico City, filming the first leg of the series. The plan was to start big – wrestling match, live crowd, full costume, the lot. I was in red Lycra and glitter, looking a bit too Freddie Mercury for my liking, and Goughy – Darren Gough, who'd also been roped in – was in tights too. It was meant to be scripted. Pre-planned. As in, 'a show'. But pretty much the second we stepped into the ring, it all unravelled.

The idea was that Goughy would get thrown around, I'd do a few moves, bit of crowd play, then we'd pull the plug. Except nobody told the other team. One of them started slapping Goughy open-handed across the face, again and again. Goughy was trying to laugh it off, and I was standing on the sidelines pissing myself until one of the wrestler's wives stormed over and started hurling abuse at us. In Spanish. Loud. I didn't know what she was saying, but I'd seen that face before – she was livid. So, still laughing, I lobbed something back. No idea what. Just sounds.

That's when her husband clocked me and gestured like he was about to shoot. Full-on finger gun, bang. We'd hired gangsters for security, the crowd was baying, and Goughy was still being chucked around the canvas like a sack of laundry, and at last I belatedly worked out that this wasn't theatre. Not any more. As another bloke gave me the gun finger, I decided that we had overstayed our welcome. It was time to go.

We legged it. Goughy grabbed the mic, gave it a bit of *Rocky*. 'Me and my friend here, it's been amazing, thank you, Mexico!' and we made like trees: straight into the dressing room, out the back, gone.

Next morning, we were cliff diving. Because of course we were.

The irony is, I'd only said yes to all this because I thought I'd be back playing cricket soon. At the time, 2009, I'd just stepped away from Test cricket, having made peace with that part of my career coming to a close. But the plan wasn't to walk away from the game completely. Not yet. I still had some gas left in the tank for what we call the white ball stuff – the shorter formats, One Dayers and T20s, where the ball's white, the pace is quicker, and the crowds come for the fireworks. There was talk of the IPL – the Indian Premier League – which had exploded onto the scene with its big-money contracts and carnival-like atmosphere. That, or maybe Queensland, over in Australia, who'd shown some interest. Both would've kept me in the mix, kept me competitive, but without the grind of the five-day format.

Around the same time, we – as in the Flintoff clan of me, Rachael, Holly, Corey and Rocky – made the call to base ourselves in Dubai.

On paper, it all stacked up. Tax-free earnings, a fresh start, the kids sorted for school – we'd even found them a place at one of those posh international jobs with a cricket pitch and compulsory sun cream. Everything looked lined up. Then bang – the knee went. Surgery the day after my last Test. Just like that, the cricket plan vanished.

We moved to Dubai anyway, but I hated it. I've said before that my criticism of Dubai probably says more about where I was mentally than anything else, but still – the sand, the skyline, the sense that everyone was trying to be someone they're not. It was like a witness protection scheme, except with room service. No one knew your backstory, so you could make one up. And most people did. I felt like I was walking around in someone else's shoes. The kids were at school, I couldn't drive post-op, so my days were a blur of physio, aimless conversations with virtual strangers, and long stretches of nothing. I felt properly adrift.

Even so, I still thought of myself as a cricketer.

I'd already done all sorts of TV work. *Cricket AM*, *Soccer AM*, daft sketches with Joey Barton or pretending to be a seal trainer, so I already had an insight. It was all nonsense, but it kind of stuck. People remembered the mucking about. It wasn't always the centuries or the catches – sometimes it was the pedalo incident that got me recognised. That still makes me laugh. Or wince. Bit of both.

Then came *Freddie vs The World*, with Rodman and all that madness. And through the chaos, I started to think, *Maybe there's something here.* Not coaching, not commentary (I'd tried commentary and hated it) but something that felt a bit more . . . me. Still competitive, still demanding, but not pretending to be something I wasn't. Not having to sound clever in a headset while secretly worrying I was just parroting clichés.

What I learned fast was this: telly, when it's good, has its own kind of rhythm. Not match rhythm, not dressing room rhythm, but something real, mad and a bit magic. And I thought, if I can survive Rodman setting fire to his own wages, maybe I can survive anything.

CHAPTER 35

A PROPER OFFER

So, back to Dubai, which was meant to be the launch pad. A way of buying time. The plan was that I'd step back from Tests, play some white ball cricket, earn a bit, and figure out what was next. That was the idea. Instead, it became a kind of limbo. The injury had taken the cricket away before I was ready, and Dubai – all glass and shine and reinvention – only magnified the sense that I didn't belong anywhere any more.

What hit hardest was the drift. Days without shape. The kids were at school, I couldn't drive, and I'd find myself pacing between the gym and the beach like a tourist lost in his own life. I missed weird stuff. I missed the rhythm of training, and the accountability. I even missed being tired, that kind of exhaustion that means you've earned your sleep. Now, I was just knackered from overthinking.

Then the telly stuff started trickling in, and I suppose, with hindsight, it was a kind of soft landing, a way of edging towards a new version of myself without admitting the old one was gone. As I say, I'd tried commentary too, and I gave it a proper go, doing bits in Australia, some work with Sky. I'd thought it would be a decent bridge – stay close to the game, talk about what I knew. But no. I hated it. Not just the job, but the version of me it brought out. The banter merchant. The court jester in a headset. I'd be sitting there, trying to be chirpy, while some former pro dissected a delivery like he'd invented reverse swing.

It's not that I didn't have thoughts. I did. (No laughing at the back.) But saying them out loud felt . . . false. Like I'd crossed over to the other side too quickly. I was barely out of the dressing room myself. Who was I to analyse lads still in the thick of it? I'd see someone edge one through the slips and think, *That used to be me* and then hear myself saying something empty like, 'He'll be disappointed with that,' and want to crawl under the desk.

There's a kind of distance you need to be a proper pundit. A coldness, maybe. I didn't have it. Still don't. And I didn't want to end up resenting the game because I was spending my time picking holes in people who were still living it.

The lowest point came during a commentary stint abroad. I won't say which game, but I remember sitting in the box, headphones on, and realising I wasn't listening to the match. I was listening to myself, trying to sound like I belonged, and trying to say something insightful while worrying I'd already become a parody. 'He'll be very disappointed with that,' I said, and as my co-commentator vigorously agreed, something inside me died.

So I started saying no. Not to everything, but to the

stuff that didn't feel right. I figured, if I was going to fail at something, it might as well be something I actually wanted to do.

That's when *A League of Their Own* came back around. I'd got the call about being a team captain a while back but said no at first. This time it was James Corden himself calling with what you might call a proper offer.

Even so, I still wasn't sure. Panel shows weren't exactly my world. I didn't know the rules. Didn't know if I'd be funny enough, sharp enough. But there was something about James – the way he framed it, the way he just seemed to *get* people – that made me think it might be worth a go.

So I'm like, *Okay, I'll give it a go.*

I didn't know it then, but saying yes would end up changing everything. Not just because of the success the show became, but because it gave me a bit of space to figure out who I was outside of cricket. Not all at once. Not cleanly. But enough to start again.

CHAPTER 36

WINGING IT

At first, I treated *A League of Their Own* like a bit of fun, just to see how it went. What I didn't expect was to find myself still there years later, gloves on, buzzer in hand, trying to guess the name of some Hungarian hammer thrower while Jamie Redknapp giggled like a kid.

Nobody knew what we were doing at the start. Not really. James had it in his head – the energy and the format, with its blend of sport and comedy – but the rest of us were learning on the job, aka making it up as we went along.

As a result, and to nobody's great surprise, least of all mine, the first series was chaos. You won't find it on catch-up anywhere, probably for good reason. The studio felt like a school play where half the cast had wandered in off the street. James was rock solid, of course. He was a massive star at that point, and the reason he'd risen so high so quickly was because he was an absolute natural in front of a camera.

COMING HOME

Me, not an absolute natural in front of a camera. Look up 'bloke winging it' and you'll see a picture of me on TV. I was floundering; Jamie too, in his own way. As a result, the show was a bit on the flat side. They used to ply the audience with drinks beforehand just to keep the atmosphere up and so the audience spent half the show getting up and down to go for a piss. If that was you – you didn't miss much.

Sometimes I just sat there thinking, *What the hell am I doing?* No dressing room banter to fall back on, no score to chase. Just lights, cameras and the sinking feeling that if I cocked it up, they'd all see through me.

Early days on the show, I kept pretty quiet. Didn't quite know where to pitch it. I'd say something that might've gone down a storm in a cricket dressing room, a bit of banter, a bit of cheek – and here it would be met with a stony silence. Different rules, I soon realised. Different crowd. So I held back, watched and listened. Spent that first series mostly feeling my way through.

Some of the comedians would come in fully loaded – gags prepped, punchlines polished. I tried that a bit, throwing out the odd line and hoping it would land, but it wasn't really me. What I came to realise was that the comedians *made* the show funny – that was their job – and sometimes your job was just to take the hit, be the punchline, roll with it. And that was fine. We'd all take turns being the butt of the joke. That's how it worked.

Funny thing, though – some comedians didn't love it when the tables turned. You'd give them a bit back, nothing nasty, just a nudge – and you'd see a flicker of something.

Bit fragile, some of them. Insecurity's not just for sports-people it turns out.

But over time I got more comfortable. I started doing things I never thought I would – singing, dancing, mucking about. The kind of stunts I'd normally run a mile from. But in that environment, surrounded by people up for a laugh, you get to a point where you just think, *Sod it*. We're all in the same boat. Might as well lean in and enjoy the ride.

There's a thing I've said before – that I'm not the loudest in the room by nature. I've always been a bit of an extroverted introvert, comfortable in the thick of it, but also happy with silence. What telly did, especially *League*, was give me a place to play both roles. One minute I'm in Lycra riding a tiny bike up a hill, the next I'm reflecting on why I packed in cricket earlier than planned. The switch became part of the rhythm. I also made some great, great mates in James, Jamie and Jack Whitehall.

But it didn't always feel natural. I'd come home after filming and feel flat. Properly flat. Like the adrenaline had worn off and I was left with the echo of who I'd just been on set. I wasn't pretending, not exactly – but there's a cost to being 'on' for hours. The laugh, the line, the big reaction – it takes something out of you. And when the cameras stop, you're still buzzing, but also empty.

There was a baby photo they found once – me, Butlin's, bonnie baby competition winner. James did a routine on it, and Jack nearly passed out laughing. It became a running gag. I had to start writing limits into the release forms. 'Two uses only,' I said, half-joking. It still turned up in the edit every other week.

COMING HOME

It didn't fix everything overnight. I still had days where I wondered if I'd become a novelty act. Still had moments where I missed the simplicity of cricket – ball, bat, scorecard. But gradually, a new rhythm took over. And it felt all right.

CHAPTER 37

IN THE RING

The lights are hot, brighter than I remember, and the crowd noise is a low, buzzing wall – not quite cheering, not quite booing, more like that thick hum before a Test match starts, when everyone's still finding their seats and working out who's opening. I can feel it in my stomach, the mix of nerves and adrenaline, as though I'm about to face my first ball of the summer.

Only this isn't Headingley or Lord's.

And I'm not holding a bat.

In fact, I'm walking through smoke, some daft music thumping behind me, gloves on, mouth guard in. Opposite me is a lad who's been shot four times, done time for GBH and works as a debt collector. I used to take a break for sandwiches halfway through the day. Now I'm about to get punched in the face in front of thousands of people while my mates laugh ringside. Welcome to boxing.

COMING HOME

* * *

Boxing wasn't even the plan. Not to begin with. It had started with wrestling, believe it or not. There I was, still technically living in Dubai, commuting to film *A League of Their Own*, flying business class on Emirates as part of a daft deal I had with some Sheikh – I wasn't earning much, so the tax thing didn't really matter, but I was drinking every day, not heavily, just enough to feel it, and I wasn't training, so I was getting soft, putting weight back on, you know the drill.

So, I thought, *Right, I need to get fit.* And I'd had just enough of a taste of telly by then to know how it worked. Once you're on screen, production companies will meet you – not because they've got a brilliant idea, but because they hope you might. So you sit in soulless offices with warm bottled water, and they smile and ask what you want to do next. Half of them have no idea who you are. The other half think they do and suggest things that have nothing to do with what you're about.

So I started coming up with my own ideas with my management team, Katie and Richard, thinking, why not? Someone'll bite. And I remembered how, as a kid, I'd been obsessed with WWF – what's WWE now. All the noise, the costumes, the chaos. So I came up with this idea: get fit and wrestle The Undertaker in Manchester.

The Undertaker hadn't been my favourite wrestler, but the one I really loved, The Ultimate Warrior, had passed away in 2014. The Undertaker, however, was still knocking about, still wrestling professionally, still a looming figure in the ring, and it felt like a storyline people could get behind. Big daft cricketer takes on wrestling legend. What's not to love?

So we wrote it up properly with Fulwell 73 – that's the production company James Corden was involved with – and I met the head honcho Gabe Turner, who's now knee-deep in everything from the Kardashians to whatever's trending on Netflix. We pitched it to Sky, and they liked it. WWE liked it too. So we were off. Dave Roberts, our old physio, hooked me up with a trainer and I got serious about it. Six weeks of hard graft in Dubai – back in the gym, lifting, sweating, feeling something like an athlete again.

Then came America. Two weeks at the WWE Performance Centre in Florida – that's the boot camp for every hopeful wrestler. This is where it gets serious.

With Mum and Dad looking after the kids, Rachael came too. They flew us over business class, met us with a flash car, took us to the hotel – all very la-di-da – until the next morning, I'm sitting in this limo thinking. *What the hell have I done?*

Yeah, I know. He does a lot of that, does Freddie Flintoff. And you're right. But I guess it's a function of stepping outside of your comfort zone. Having second thoughts is all part of the process.

We pull up outside the place – two huge units, all branded WWE – and as I'm sitting there in the car, the other wrestlers start turning up. And I'm not being funny, I wasn't even as big as some of the women. These people are *units*. Walking protein shakes. And I'm sitting there in my vest thinking, *Christ*.

You don't realise how small you are until you're in a room full of protein. The women looked like Olympians. The men looked like action figures. There were blokes doing lunges who had bigger thighs than my torso. I was there in my Matalan vest, thinking I might have brought a knife to a bazooka fight.

We walk in – me and Rachael – and every single head in the place turns to look. You've got to understand, this is where people go to *become* superstars. It's intense. Competitive. Everyone fighting for a slot on the main roster. And then there's me, some unknown English bloke waltzing in. I turned to Rachael and said, 'Go back to the hotel, love.' Not because I didn't want her there, but because I couldn't bear her seeing what might happen next.

So in I go. Guy meets me, all friendly. 'Hi, Fred. Great to have you; just get involved.' Which sounds fine until you realise it means: no instructions, no hand-holding – just get stuck in. I got changed, started doing the warm-up. There were two rings, people stretching and grunting and throwing themselves around, and I was just copying what the big Welsh lad next to me was doing, hoping for the best.

Then suddenly I was in the ring. I didn't know how it had happened, but I was in there for what felt like three days – probably an hour, maybe ninety minutes – and it was non-stop. You ran the ropes, someone ducked under you, you leapfrogged them, they leapfrogged you, again and again. I was dying. Then this lad tried to leap me and I was too knackered to lift my head, so I went face-first into the apron. Just bang – straight on the canvas. Welcome to wrestling, Fred.

And that was just the morning session.

In the afternoon, it was my turn to lift people – and here's where I messed up again. You didn't actually slam them. It was all choreographed: you bent, they pushed off your knee, and they fell in a way that looked good but didn't hurt. I didn't know this. So I was properly slamming lads into the mat, upsetting people left, right and centre. Unintentional, but still. The vibe was turning.

There was this one bloke, big lad, and he wouldn't leave me alone. Mugging me off the whole time – jumping in the ring, trying to pin me from behind, proper winding me up. I'd had enough. So I turned to him, loud enough for the whole room, and said, 'Mate, if you keep this up, you're going to have to put all your muscles on your chin, 'cause that's where I'm going to belt you.' And he stopped.

Because in that moment, I wasn't doing telly. I wasn't mucking about. I'd come to prove something, not get played for laughs. I might not have been a wrestler – not yet – but I wasn't going to be anyone's punchline either.

The mood in the gym shifted after that. I wasn't one of them, but I wasn't a joke any more either. I think they'd expected me to bottle it. Muck about, get the footage, disappear. But I didn't. I turned up, took my knocks, gave as good as I could. You don't win people over with banter in that place – you do it with bruises. And by then, I'd earned more than most.

And from that point, weirdly, I was all right.

CHAPTER 38

BEATEN UP

Next day, we're in a different part of the place – a 3,000-seater venue with a proper ring in the middle – and I'm paired up with this American lad, nice guy, who'd been out with an injury. We started doing technical drills. He was showing me the ropes, giving me an insight into how the whole thing worked. The moves, yeah, they were rehearsed, but it wasn't like every moment was scripted. There was a general idea, a kind of structure, but once you were in the ring, it was a dance. You talked to each other constantly – guided the rhythm, the timing, read each other's movements. It was physically brutal. Honestly, it was the hardest thing I'd ever done. I was absolutely done in.

By halfway through the day, my back was going. I'd taken my shirt off the night before back at the hotel, and Rachael had looked at me like I'd been dragged behind a bus. She didn't even say anything at first. Just gave me that look –

a bit of concern, a bit of *what are you doing, love?* Then she laughed. 'You look like beef carpaccio.' And she was right. I'd peeled the T-shirt off and it had stuck to my back like Velcro. You'd swear I'd been hit with cricket bats all day. And in a way, I had – the ropes, the landings, the canvas. Everything in that place wanted to flatten you. I was black and blue – just from running the ropes. You'd think it'd be padded, but it wasn't. It was like someone had been lashing you with planks.

I said, 'Let's go for some food, have a chat, try to decompress.' Had a couple of pints – not many, just something to take the edge off.

So I rolled in the next morning, back still howling, went straight to the main room and requested to see a physio.

I said, 'I think I'm having a back spasm.'

They all started laughing. 'Oh, the English boy's having a spasm.'

Like I was being soft. Great. But anyway, I got to see the physio and he got me lying on this table, face down, pressing around and I swear I could feel my ribs moving.

I said, 'Mate, I think I've broken my rib.'

He said, 'Nah, you'd be in agony if that were the case.'

I said, 'I *am* in agony. I want to cry. I just won't do it in front of that lot.'

They sent me off for an X-ray. I saw the specialist – full American cliché: huge desk, shelves lined with trophies and photos of wrestlers. He looked at the scan and said, 'You've broken two ribs.'

I said, 'Thought I had.'

He goes, 'So what do you do?'

I said, 'I'm a wrestler.'

He said, 'How long have you been wrestling?'

I said, 'A day and a half.'

And that was what did me in, really. Not the pain – I could live with that. It was the disbelief. The fact that I'd flown halfway round the world, dragged Rachael along for the ride, trained until my body gave up, and somehow still felt like a mascot in someone else's sport. I mean, these guys lived and breathed it. I was visiting. A tourist with busted ribs.

Back I went, X-rays under my arm, feeling vindicated.

'I've broken two ribs,' I told them.

They didn't know what to say. Weird sort of respect came from it – like, you stuck it out, you took your knocks, you kept going. And I had. Fair play to me. High-five myself. I'd acquitted myself well. I mean, I could barely move, but I turned up the next day anyway. Told myself I'd go in, see how it felt, then Rachael and I would head down to Miami for ten days and take a proper break.

That day was acting class. Every Wednesday, they got 50 or 60 of them into the big room with the ring in the centre and they all had to grab the mic and cut a promo – their little bit of theatre, their chance to show off their character. It was all improvised. No script. Just you and whatever you brought to the table. The idea was to stand out – didn't matter if people loved you or hated you, just don't be boring. That was death. Vanilla wouldn't get you on the roster.

I sat watching this mad procession of characters – all these big lads and women off in corners practising lines, hyping themselves up.

I was thinking, *This is properly weird* as one by one they got up and did their bit.

And then it came. 'Fred, you're up.'

'You what?'

No warning. I had a 20-yard walk to the ring to figure out what I was going to do.

So I grabbed the mic, and I launched into this ropey rap about being English, how I was here to sort everyone out. Not my finest hour. I got a couple of heckles – not friendly ones either.

I asked, 'Can I have another go?'

And this time, I dropped the act and started pointing people out in the crowd – just roasting them. Big heads, massive legs, weird arms – nothing nasty, just English humour. But they didn't get it. No laughs. Nothing. They just stared at me.

It was the opposite of a dressing room. In cricket, you landed a good line and someone threw it back twice as hard. There's like a snowball effect. In that room, every gag fell like a fridge into a pond. No ripples. Just silence. They weren't wired for laughs – they were wired for aggression, drama, characters with backstories. My backstory had bouncers and bingo nights. Didn't quite land.

I finished, sat down at the back, and I didn't even get the polite clap they gave everyone else.

Then at the end, this bloke comes over. 'What *was* that?' he says.

I shrugged. 'I don't know.'

He says, 'We really liked it. It was different. We liked what you did there.'

Then he asked what my plans were. I told him, 'Well, we've booked into the Delano in Miami and I've got broken ribs, so I think I'll sit by the pool with a bottle of rosé and some mussels.'

And that's exactly what we did. Ten days of sun, sea and agony. I couldn't move, but the rosé was cold and the food was good. Perfect.

Then WWE got in touch wanting to meet. They basically said, 'Look, we love what you did, but you can't release this documentary because it'll give away too much about how we work.'

Instead – and this bit floored me – they said, 'We want you to join us.' Full-time. Three-year deal. Access to the academy, fast-tracked to WrestleMania in 18 months. And the money . . . I won't name a figure (but it was huge).

And for a moment – just a moment – I thought, *What if?*

I had to really think about it. Eight million a year is hard to ignore, but so is the reality – if you sign with WWE, they basically own you. You're on the road 300 days a year. You don't get to pop back for the school run or nip to nets with your lads. It's a full-time lifestyle, and I'd started thinking seriously about moving back to England. The boys were showing an interest in cricket – you're not getting that in Florida – and I could see it for what it was. The injuries were horrendous, constant. I wasn't sure I fancied spending my late thirties running around in underpants, to be honest.

They told me 35 to 45 was the prime window for a wrestler, so I was right in the sweet spot. They laid it all out – massive market in America, decent one in the UK, big push into India – and said they could make their money back on me in no time. Get me in the big shows, use the cricket background, package me up. It was wild. They had a whole storyline ready. The English hero. Bit of posh, bit of grit. Red, white and blue trunks. Maybe a Union Jack cape if I really leaned in. Sir Fred, charging the ring with a cricket bat. I could see it – all the lights, the music, the pop from the crowd. And a small part of me – the bit that still liked making noise – was tempted. Properly tempted. But you can't do that life halfway. You're either in, or you're out. And deep down, I was already thinking about nets with the boys.

'I'll be Sir Fred,' I'd joked, 'and come in with a sword and a St George's Cross.'

Not sure if I meant it, but it sounded convincing at the time.

Then it shifted.

CHAPTER 39

ANOTHER ROUND

I was in London with my agent, Richard, who was working with Barry McGuigan at the time. You know Barry McGuigan: one of those fighters who felt bigger than the sport. A featherweight from Clones with dynamite in his gloves and a nation on his back, he won the WBA world title in 1985 at Loftus Road, beating Eusebio Pedroza in a sweltering, 15-round classic. At a time when Northern Ireland was tearing itself apart, he came out to '*Danny Boy*' and had fans on both sides of the divide cheering the same man. He didn't just win – he meant something. No doubt about it, I was a fan.

I didn't think I'd met him before – or maybe just briefly – but this time we were sitting round a table and Richard said, 'Say hello to Barry.'

So I did. I said, 'Hiya, Barry.'

He replied, 'All right, Fred. How are you?'

I started joking around, told him I was thinking of boxing.

He goes, 'Really? You want to box?'

I said, 'Yeah, I'd love to.'

And that was it.

Not long later I'd written up the idea that would go on to become *Flintoff: From Lord's to the Ring*. I pitched it. It was accepted. And two weeks after that, I was in a gym in Essex getting my head handed to me by a 20-stone Nigerian lad called Biggie, who was trying to turn pro. Five rounds of punishment. The cameras were rolling. My nose was bleeding. My head was thumping. I was sitting on the canvas at the end, thinking, *What the fuck have I done?*

(Of course I was.)

And Barry leaned in, cheerful as ever, and said, 'Good moves! You can take a punch.' Cheers, mate. Great news.

It was the start of a savage 12 weeks.

I'd convinced myself this was how I'd close the chapter. That if I could get through this fight, I'd finally earned the right to walk away from sport on my own terms. No selectors, no injuries, no headlines. Just me saying, 'That's it.'

But that's not how it works, is it? You don't get to write your own ending unless you're making a film. In real life, you keep turning the page hoping the next one makes more sense than the last. And boxing wasn't the ending. It was just another mad diversion on a map I was drawing in real time.

The training itself – yeah, it was hard. But it wasn't harder than cricket. I've been through hell on a cricket pitch – training, graft, the lot. What I'd never experienced, though, was fear. Not like boxing. That's different. I'd done pad work for fitness when I was playing, knew how to throw a punch, but I couldn't *box*. I had no grounding, no craft, no ring sense. Sparring was like turning up for a match without knowing the rules.

I'd go anywhere – East End, Aldershot, you name it – just to spar. Anyone who'd have me. At the Peacock Gym in London, I was just one of the bodies. Then I'd be off down to a military barracks, letting blokes in the Army punch seven shades out of me. I'd carry my own gloves everywhere, keep it controlled, keep it safe. Or so I thought.

I never got used to the conversations. Boxers only talk about boxing. It's all they want to speak about. Who they've sparred, who they've stopped, who ducked them, who they'd love to have a crack at. It's constant. At breakfast. In the car. Midway through a gym circuit. It did my head in.

I'd try to talk about the cricket, or ask how their kids were getting on, and they'd pull faces like I'd farted in the sauna. It wasn't personal – it's just how they're built. Boxing isn't a sport to them, it's a way of existing. They're still shadow boxing in their dreams.

Second sparring session, I'm in Aldershot again, facing a lad from Manchester who'd turned pro. We'd touched gloves before and I thought, fair enough, off we go. First punch – straight in my face.

It hurt.

I mean, it really hurt.

I could *feel* the knuckles.

After the round, back in the corner, I said to Shane, 'Mate, there's something up.'

He looks at me and goes, 'Yeah, he's stuffed you.'

Which in layman's terms meant either he'd taken padding out or he was using barely padded gloves.

I said, 'Can we go home then?'

Barry just grinned and shook his head: 'You've got four more rounds. Can't lose face.'

I said, 'I don't give a toss about face. I'm in a barracks, not Wembley.'

But I finished the rounds. And next day, I looked like I'd been run over. Nose gone, black eyes, headaches. Played in a charity match up in Sheffield with Vaughan, trying to act normal, but I looked like I'd done ten rounds with a truck. I turned up to a shoot looking like I'd lost a bet. One of the make-up girls took one look and said, 'Have you been run over?'

I said, 'No, sparring.'

She said, 'What's that?'

I said, 'Boxing, badly.'

At least with cricket, if you got hit, there's a story. Someone bowled a bouncer, you wore it, everyone nodded. Respect. But with boxing, you get filled in and nobody claps. They just stare. Wonder what's wrong with you. Why'd you do that?

God only knows the answer to that one.

The physical side was bad enough, but it was the mental side that broke me down. That's the thing about boxing. It hurts, yeah. But the pain's simple. You get hit, it stings. You breathe, you reset. Cricket pain is different – it builds in silence. Wears you down over months. Your form disappears and you've no idea why.

Boxing doesn't lie. You're either up or you're not.

And maybe that's why I stuck at it longer than I should have. It gave me something to grip on to when everything else felt slippery.

Every day I'd drive from Cobham into East London, knowing I was about to get filled in. One lad was six foot nine, Ukrainian, hit like a horse. Another day, my usual partner didn't show, so I sparred with this beast – 120 kilos, pure muscle, known for knocking lads clean out in sparring, which you're *not* supposed to do. He got me on a bad day – I was already struggling mentally – and he just unloaded. He hit me clean, I flew across the ring. And he just kept coming. I thought, 'You can't hurt me more than I'm already hurting.' But he did his best. I took it all. I just kept getting up.

I dropped nearly 20 kilos. I looked ripped in the pictures – all lean muscle, no fat – but the truth is, I was as weak as piss. My body was there, but my soul was running on fumes. I looked in the mirror and saw abs. Proper abs. The sort I'd never had even when I was playing. I should've felt proud. I didn't. I felt hollow. Like the training had peeled off all the fat and muscle and left just the shell. The outside looked bulletproof. The inside was shattered.

I'd spent weeks getting filled in by lads I wouldn't have dared speak to in a pub, dragging myself out of bed with migraines, ribs on fire, no appetite, and no idea why I was doing it any more. But I still turned up. Still kept training. Because I thought, *If I can just finish this, maybe I'll feel right again. Like the old me.* The real me. Who was that, though? I wasn't sure I knew.

CHAPTER 40

THE FINAL FIGHT

The fight itself? That was something else. I ended up in the ring with a lad who weighed 18 and a half stone when he was 15. Proper lump. It was at the Manchester Arena, sold out crowd, lights, ring walk, cameras – the full works. Backstage, I wondered how it was going to sound when muggins here appeared.

And I soon got my answer. The noise when I walked out was unreal. A proper wall of sound. People were on their feet, lights flashing, music thumping. It felt like a home Test, but on acid. The announcer was shouting my name like I was a gladiator. And I was there thinking: I used to check the wind direction before bowling my first over. Now I was touching gloves with a bloke who'd been shot and didn't blink.

And I was bricking it. Not just nerves – actual, genuine *What the fuck have I done?* I was pacing the dressing room like a caged dog. I tried to look calm, nodded at the camera crew, giving it the thumbs-up like I was about to run a fun run. Inside, I was shaking. My hands wouldn't stop twitching. Every time I sat down, I stood up again. I kept checking my gloves like something might have changed. I knew I was fit. I knew I'd trained. But I also knew I was one punch away from blackout. And I didn't want to go out cold in front of 10,000 people and everyone watching at home. That sort of thing stuck with you. It goes on YouTube.

I wanted to bottle it, honestly. I kept thinking, *How do I get out of this without looking like a right twat?*

But there came a point where I'd committed – and something just flipped in my head, and adrenaline took over.

After that, I don't remember much of the fight, just flashes – being knocked down, seeing my mates round the ring pissing themselves laughing, hearing Barry yelling instructions at me. I'd fought the week before in a gym in Ireland, when I went up against a Marine and boxed really well and felt sharp. But come the big stage, I just got carried away. I should have knocked this lad out, had him wobbling, but the occasion swallowed me, and my technique went out of the window, heart took over, and I started windmilling a bit. It got messy.

There's a famous Mike Tyson quote: 'Everybody has a plan until they get punched in the face.'

I now know *exactly* what that means.

He caught me behind the ear – just a glancing one – but that's enough. All your equilibrium goes. I ended up on my arse, blinking, trying to work out how I'd got there. It didn't even hurt. Instead of pain there was just confusion.

That's the weirdest thing about being knocked down. You'd think it'd be pain or panic. But it's not. It's like being unplugged for a second.

I was blinking, trying to find the floor. My legs didn't feel like they were mine. It's like your brain takes a second to reload. I could hear Barry shouting, the crowd roaring, someone banging on the canvas. And still, I was floating. Then bang – it clicks. You're back. You stand up. You lie to the ref. 'I'm good.' You're not. Looking round at all these faces gurning. 'Get up,' someone shouted. So I did, and I won the fight on points in the end. Got dropped in one round, won the others.

Afterwards, I sat on a plastic chair in the back corridor of the arena, wrapped in a towel, soaked in sweat, and shaking like I'd just come off a roller coaster. I wasn't buzzing. I wasn't celebrating. I was empty. Like the fight had pulled something out of me I didn't know was still there. Barry came in all smiles, slapped me on the back. I could barely lift my head. Just nodded and stared at the floor.

I'd done it. I'd gone the rounds, although it felt more like survival than victory.

And it was strange, the whole thing. The press conference the day before was surreal – me in a hotel, sitting at the top table with all the promoters and journos, opposite this fella they'd found for me to fight. He was a wrong 'un, the lad they found for me. Proper bit of work. Debt collector, four bullets in his back, done time for GBH. And there I was in my whites a few years earlier, sipping tea on the pavilion steps. Felt like two different planets. He had a glint in his eye like he still had one more fight outside the ring, and I had no idea what I was doing there, smiling for the cameras like it was a charity bake-off.

Then they do the face-off, all testosterone and posing, and Barry's whispering, 'Don't turn away first. Hold the stare.' I'm just standing there thinking, *Please turn away. Please turn away.* And he did. Small wins.

All told, I liked the training, I liked the discipline, but not the chat. Not the culture. Even sparring – I'd be in Battersea going up against rugby lads on their lunch break. One of them, I caught clean on the chin, legs started going, and Barry shouts, 'Finish him!' But I couldn't. Just put my arms around him. It felt wrong. The bloke had just nipped out from work for a bit of fitness. Didn't seem right to try and knock him into next week. I didn't have that killer instinct.

But no, I wasn't launching a boxing career. One fight was enough. Besides which, I had torn my shoulder in the second. I could barely pick my right arm up and had to put my hand in my pocket before I had surgery two days later (which then revealed a whole world of mess in my shoulder). Maybe part of me fancied another go, just to do it better, more controlled. But it's a different world, and not one I really belonged in. I'd done it. I'd got in the ring, got up off the canvas, won the fight, and shown myself what I could take. I'd proved the point – just not sure who to.

Maybe that was it. Maybe I was still trying to answer questions nobody had asked. Trying to prove I was still tough, still capable, still worth something without a bat in my hand. The fight wasn't about him. It wasn't even about boxing. It was about control. About facing something brutal and not backing down. And when it was done, and I'd walked away with my face intact and my name on the card, I finally let out a breath I hadn't realised I'd been holding for years.

CHAPTER 41

HONESTY

The Hidden Side of Sport was a documentary that started, like most things around then, with me pitching an idea. What it was, I'd started thinking seriously about mental health – not just mine, but what I'd seen in other blokes, teammates and mates in sport.

Nowadays, mental health is, I'm happy to say, very much on the agenda, but back then it wasn't something people talked about much. It wasn't on panels or in headlines, not like now. You had Ricky Hatton talking a bit, and a few others, but it was still mostly in whispers.

I didn't set out to make it about me. I wanted to talk to other people, hear their stories. I wrestled with whether to include my own stuff. Part of me thought, *Just shut up and ask the questions. Stay behind the camera.* But it started feeling dishonest, like I was hiding again – and that was the whole problem, wasn't it? We all keep hiding.

But the more I spoke to people, the more I realised I'd

been through a lot of the same stuff – I just hadn't had the language for it. I'd had periods where I wasn't right, felt low, angry, anxious, all of it, but I'd thought it was just me being crap. When I started doing this thing, it brought a lot to the surface.

One of the weirdest things was hearing other people say stuff I thought only I'd felt. Not just the sadness or the stress – but the shame, the pretending, the weird fog that descends when you're meant to be on top of the world.

Some stuff I hadn't even thought about for years started cropping up. Old feelings I'd boxed away. Days I'd written off as 'just a bad mood' suddenly looked different. I wasn't going into this thing expecting therapy, but I ended up talking about things I'd never said out loud. Not even to myself, really.

I'd sit there nodding, thinking, *Bloody hell. That's me.* And that's when it clicked – maybe I wasn't crap. Maybe I was just human.

The show wasn't slick, either. We didn't have a massive crew or a big glossy budget. A lot of it was mates, favours, borrowed time. People showed up because they cared. We were filming in scrounged rooms, editing on fumes, and still somehow managing to land proper names. It felt more like a mission than a programme.

One of the first people I interviewed for the documentary was Ricky Hatton. I've always liked Ricky. Our careers ran alongside each other. We're both from the North West, both came up at the same time, had a few nights out together over the years. He's this proper fighter, all heart and guts, but also really funny, warm, vulnerable.

So when he talked about his struggles, it floored me. Made me like him even more. And it didn't feel like an interview. It felt like two lads in a pub, quietly admitting we'd both had a wobble. He opened up, and without meaning to, so did I. I think that was the moment I realised I wasn't just presenting this thing – I was in it.

Then there was Vinnie Jones. That came about in a weird way. I was in LA, filming, and I popped in to see Piers Morgan – I know, I know – because I wanted a media perspective. How the press writes about mental health, that sort of thing. While I was there, he says, 'Have you spoken to Vinnie?' I hadn't. So he gives me his number. I ring him up and he says, 'Yeah, come round – but we've got to be done by 7.30, it's poker night.'

So I drive up to this house – middle of nowhere, proper LA hills – and it's like this mad scene from a film. Vinnie's in the kitchen telling me his story, which is powerful and raw and everything you wouldn't expect from Vinnie if all you know is the hard man image. But then the poker crowd start turning up – a weird mix of actors, dodgy 1980s football managers, the bloke who played Pepe in *EastEnders*. Just chaos. We wrap the interview, and somehow I end up staying for poker.

And it's around that time that my mate Gabe – who worked with James Corden and knew David Beckham through him – gets a call. David rings him and says, 'What are you up to?' Gabe says, 'I'm round at Vinnie's but it's poker night.' David goes, 'Great stuff, come round mine when you're done.'

So off we go. Next thing I know, we're pulling up outside this enormous house in Malibu. David and Victoria are renting Steven Spielberg's place. Actual Spielberg. We walk in and there's Victoria, holding Harper, just being . . . normal. Lovely, actually.

She says, 'You hungry?'

I go, 'Yeah.'

She says, 'I'm making David a pizza. I'm having fish. What do you want?'

Like it's a Tuesday in Bolton.

We have a bit of food, a few laughs, then go and watch football in Spielberg's cinema room. Big projector, reels with the titles of all his films – *Jaws*, *E.T.*, *Indiana Jones* – just stacked in the back like it was Blockbuster. I didn't even know what game we were watching, I was just sitting there thinking, *What is my life?* Sharing a beer with Beckham in Spielberg's house, the night before I'm due to fly back and finish editing a depression doc.

It stuck with me, the whole evening. That contrast between what people show and what's really going on. The gloss and the graft. That's what the doc was about, really. Pulling back the curtain. Letting people say, 'Yeah, me too.'

And then it was back to grey rooms and hard drives. The editing was its own slog – long days, tiny tweaks, trying to balance clarity with care. I didn't want anyone coming off badly. That was the rule: if someone trusted us with their story, we looked after it.

After the edit, I had a few days where I felt like I'd been hit by something heavy. Not regret – more like an emotional hangover. When you say all that stuff out loud, it doesn't just disappear. It lingers. But so did the relief. I wasn't carrying it on my own any more.

By the time the doc came out, I think I'd been diagnosed with depression – or maybe just after. Either way, it was a relief. Suddenly it wasn't just moods or weakness, it was something with a name. You could do something about it. Understand it. I didn't want sympathy – never have – and I didn't want to make it about being brave, either. It wasn't about big speeches. If anything, filming taught me how to talk smaller. Less dramatic, more honest. Just saying, 'Yeah, I've had bad days,' or 'Sometimes I don't know what I'm doing,' felt like a bigger deal than any confessional monologue. That's what landed. The small stuff. People say, 'Oh, you're brave doing that.' I wasn't. I just didn't want to pretend any more.

But I was nervous. I worried how people would take it. You've spent your whole life being one version of yourself – tough, driven, in control – and now you're on telly talking about how you weren't always okay. I thought maybe it'd shift how people saw me.

But you know what? If anything, people were kinder. Not only that but they wanted to share. So many people said to me, 'I've felt like that too.' Blokes I'd never have expected. Ex-players, cab drivers, teachers, dads on the school run. They weren't all deep chats, just little nods. As if me saying it out loud had given them permission to feel it too.

If I could go back and talk to the bloke I was at the start of that doc – still second-guessing it, still worried people would laugh or turn away – I'd just say, 'Say it anyway.' Because what came back wasn't judgement. It was recognition. Quiet nods. People saying, 'Me too.' That's all I needed, really. I didn't fix anything. But I felt a bit less alone. And judging by the reaction, I wasn't the only one.

CHAPTER 42

GOING WILD

We're floating down the Amazon on a houseboat with hammocks slung across the top deck and a crate of Bushmills rattling in the corner. It's late, the sky's dropped down like a lid, and I'm sitting up there with the environmentalist Rob Penn, cameraman Mungo, the director and the soundman, passing the bottle around and watching the river move. You can't see where it ends, or where it started, just endless water and green and heat. It feels still, but underneath it all is this hum of frogs and birds and something bigger, probably watching us.

It's quiet, not because there's nothing going on, but because we're too knackered to speak. That's what it's like out here – full on, full-time. And we've got 1,000 miles to cycle.

* * *

COMING HOME

That trip to the Amazon was part of a two-parter we did for Sky, looking at the damage being done to the rainforest and why some people were trying to fix it by planting trees, while others were cutting them down to survive.

I knew nothing going in. No angle, no expertise, just curiosity. And that's been the best bit about telly, really. The chance to see the world, to ask questions, to end up in places you didn't even know existed. I'd have happily done it without the cameras, to be honest. Just to be out there, properly out there.

Rob and I cycled the last 1,600 miles of the Trans-Amazonian Highway – which is 5,000 miles long – and we finished where the road just sort of gives up and dumped our bikes at the river where they never quite got round to building the bridge to Peru.

Along the way, we met everyone: loggers, ranchers, miners. In other words, the kind of people you might expect to be the villains in all this, but they were anything but. They were warm, welcoming and desperate to tell their side. And once you listened, it made sense – not in a 'yeah, go ahead, tear it all down' way, but in a 'we're just trying to survive' way. It wasn't evil, it was economics.

The trickiest bit was with one of the Amazonian tribes. We'd been told there was a barrier on the road and we'd need to negotiate to get through. Fair enough. We were there to hear their story. But when we sat down with the elders – language barrier, everyone whispering, very formal – they said they wanted 100 grand. For what, we weren't quite sure. Just to talk? To camp? We spent five hours trying to work it out. Felt a bit like Dennis Rodman all over again. We were there to help, not exploit. But sometimes, those lines get blurred. Everyone's trying to protect something.

Still, I loved it. Proper adventure. Me and Rob got on like a house on fire. And the show went down well. So we did more – *Lord of the Fries*, which was my idea: me and Rob driving a chip van around the UK, then later a barbecue truck through Australia. We did beauty spots in Wales, Scotland, England and then drove from Melbourne to Darwin, flipping burgers and handing out chips. Sounds daft, but it's one of my favourite things I've ever done. Just us, good food, cracking views and a bit of proper graft.

I did another one too – *Alone in the Wild* for Discovery. They were on the lookout for someone to drop into the middle of nowhere and see what happened, and I'm not sure I was the answer, but I gave it a go.

I ended up in the Okavango Delta in Botswana, just me, a camera and a week of surviving on my own. The area I was in wasn't open to the public. You needed a special permit to even camp there. No footpaths, no signs, just bush and predators and silence. I kept thinking, this isn't a TV shoot – this is trespassing with permission.

I had two days of survival training, then they dropped me in this incredible patch of land where only wild animals went. Special permit job. I filmed it all myself. I drank straight from the river – couldn't be arsed boiling it (but don't try this at home, folks). For food, I had a bag of rice and not much else. I didn't even bother cooking most of the time. I'd nibble a few dry grains and call it dinner. I wasn't starving, but I wasn't far off it either.

It was mad. There were hyenas getting closer each night,

giraffes wandering past the tent, lions underneath me, elephants charging – all of it real – no crew, no lifeline.

I camped by a watering hole and watched a giraffe come down to drink every evening like clockwork. At night, I climbed a tree and slept there to keep away from the predators. Terrifying. But also . . . something else. Freeing, I suppose. That's the bit I didn't see coming. In between the panic and the weird hunger and the elephant dung, there were moments of complete calm. I'd be crouched by the river, washing a tin, and suddenly everything would go still – no pressure, no noise in my head.

It didn't last long, but when it came, it was clean. I hadn't felt that for years.

Off the back of that came *Freddie Flintoff Goes Wild*, my own series. The pitch was simple: take me somewhere remote, stick me with a local guide, and let me learn how they live. Bit of survival, bit of travel, some hard questions. The idea was to mix adventure with insight. In reality, it often turned into me sweating in the wrong shoes and trying not to fall off things. I walked through Tanzania with a Masai guide, wandered the wilds of Canada and Australia, and hacked through the jungle in Borneo. (That was the toughest one. Proper humidity, constant bugs, soaked to the skin within minutes. At one point I stepped in something and my leg disappeared up to the thigh. Took two of them to pull me out. I asked what it was, and they said, 'We don't go that way.' Cheers, lads, thanks for the heads-up.) Incredible experiences.

But honestly? Terrible telly. It didn't cut well. Too slow, too quiet, not enough jeopardy for a trailer. I wasn't dramatic enough. There were no arguments, no tears, no crocodile bites. Just me, a bloke with a backpack, learning how to light fires or track something I'd never heard of. But that was the point, I think – it wasn't about spectacle. It was about showing up.

So no, not a great TV event. But for me? Brilliant. My guide was awesome. Barefoot half the time, moving through the bush like it was his back garden. I turned up with kit and bottles and gadgets, and within an hour I was following him, empty-handed, trying to keep up. He barely spoke, just pointed or grunted. But every so often he'd say something that stuck – usually about animals, sometimes about people. Okay, tell the truth, I can't remember anything now, but at the time it felt very profound.

That's the best thing about the TV stuff. Not the lights or the studios or the recognition – but the chance to see and do things, that no one tells you is even possible when you're growing up in Preston. I wasn't home as much as I should've been during those years. It started to feel like the old days – always packing, always chasing the next thing. One shoot would finish and I'd barely unpack before flying off again. Different reasons now, but same rhythm. That creeping guilt when you hear your kid say, 'Are you going away again?' and you don't have a good answer. Always away, like when we were playing – three months here, another trip there.

The difference this time was that I wasn't chasing applause. I wasn't even sure what I was chasing. But I knew I didn't want to perform any more – not the way I used to. I just wanted to be where I was, not faking anything, not fronting. That took longer to learn than it should have. But now, finally, I'm finding myself more at home. And I like it. I really do.

What those years gave me, more than any headline or shot of the jungle, was space to reset. A bit of perspective, chipped out one trip at a time. And the realisation that being lost isn't always a crisis. Sometimes it's just a signal. Sometimes you need to drift a bit before you can come home properly.

CHAPTER 43

THE FIRST RETURN

I don't really count it, to be honest. The return to cricket. Not properly. But it happened. And it came from a few different places at once – the itch, the unfinished business, the fact that I'd got ridiculously fit training for the boxing (even if I was light and not exactly strong).

I think the seed had been planted before the fight, that quiet thought: could I actually play again? It circled me silently. I remember walking with the kids – same path as always, the girls pedalling ahead, me dragging my feet behind.

I was muttering to myself, low enough so they wouldn't hear. 'Sometimes you can't have it all your own way.'

I was trying to let it go, to file Lord's under 'done and dusted'. But I couldn't. It still gnawed at me – the sense of being cut out, of unfinished business that wouldn't leave me alone.

My knee was still wrecked, of course. I'd had this mad operation called an osteotomy – they break your leg, straighten it out, take a chunk from your hip and jam it into the knee, then clamp the whole lot together with bolts running down your shin. The surgeon told me I'd never run again. No skiing, no nothing. But when I asked him straight – could I try cricket? – he just said, 'You won't do it any more harm. If you can stand the pain, go ahead.' Which is as green a light as I've ever needed.

The shoulder was another matter. I'd detached it in the second round of the boxing match. I couldn't even lift my arm afterwards. I walked around all night with my hand stuffed in my pocket like it was nothing. I had surgery the next morning – they patched it back together and did a microfracture op to try and rebuild what was left, but found so much damage from my cricket days that there wasn't much to work with. I ended up in a sling, again.

So it wasn't like I jumped straight back in. It took a couple of years, and even then it started as a whisper. I was coaching my kids – well, watching them get coached – and feeling that tug. I'd always offered to help at Lancashire. Always wanted to stay involved. My kids had come through the club and I'd watched every training session, every drill, and every time I'd say, 'If you want a hand . . .' But it never really led anywhere. Felt like I was invisible sometimes.

So one day, I just turned up to a net session, spoke to Glen Chapple who was coaching, and said I'd bowl a few if they fancied it. Nothing serious. Just larking about. The ball came out all right. Not like the old days, but decent.

Then I picked up a bat and had a knock on the machine –

one of those bowling machines that fires balls at you in the nets, quick as you like, same spot every time. No need for a bowler, just you and the rhythm of the thing. It's how you find out if the hands still work, if the feet still move, if the eyes still pick it up early enough. And I felt something. Not fireworks, but a flicker.

Then came a couple of Wednesday night games for a local side. No connection to the place, really – just a chance to see if the fire was still there.

First game, I wore my England helmet – the one I trusted – and made 20-odd. I bowled a bit and thought it went okay.

The keeper started giving me grief about the helmet. I said, 'Mate, I've been sledged by the best in the world. I'm not taking it from you. And if you're going to do it, don't ask for a selfie after.'

I didn't need that. I wasn't there for the circus.

Then came the MCC thing – that Rest of the World match. Sachin Tendulkar was involved, and I thought, if I don't try to get in, I'll regret it, so I phoned John Stephenson and said I wanted to play.

He seemed keen – until he said Mike Gatting was picking the team. Me and Gatt had history. I'd sledged him as a teenager, and he'd got his revenge on an Under-19s tour by running me into the ground.

Sure enough, the call came while I was driving with the boys in the back. 'It's down to Gatt,' John said. 'You're not in.'

Gut punch. The look on the lads' faces killed me. I'd built it up – Lord's, dressing rooms, legacy – and just like that, it was off. So I pivoted. If the MCC didn't want me, maybe Lancashire would.

Sure enough, I played a couple of seconds games and sneaked into the first team. The first of those was at St Anne's – Saturday afternoon cricket, second XI stuff. My bowling was decent enough to take three wickets, but the best bit was my grandad being there. First time he'd watched me in years. I'd been away so long, and there he was, back on the boundary, watching me send them down. That meant more than anything. I wasn't trying to be flashy – just hit a length, kept it straight. And for a moment, it felt like the old days.

Finals Day came around. It nearly didn't. Just before I was due to return for the firsts, I went over on my ankle during a fitness test. Sprained it badly. Sitting there afterwards, ankle strapped, wondering if I'd made a mistake. Maybe this whole comeback idea really was daft.

But I'd come too far to back out now. I figured if I was going to fail, I'd rather do it on the pitch than be sitting at home second-guessing. I wasn't in the semi-final squad, just there as part of the group. Then someone pulled up injured, and I got the nod. No kit. Borrowed boots from Tom Smith, grabbed a bat, ran around like a fan who'd won a contest.

I was half-dressed, sprinting round the outfield to get changed, laughing at the absurdity. Twenty minutes to the final, no time to think, no time to stew. It was chaos – the sort that suited me, weirdly. I think if I'd had hours to prepare, I'd have overthought the lot.

I'd had just one net session before that day – literally one. But something happened. The ball came out quick. Faster than I expected. High 80s. I could see the lads watching – not just looking, but really watching. I caught a few nods, some raised eyebrows. It wasn't much, but it was enough. I hadn't felt that ripple of belief in a long time. Made me feel like a player again.

First ball – Ian Bell. Drives it straight up in the air. I suspect he thought it would be faster. Dreamland. Then came a beamer – waist high, smacked for six. Next ball: free hit, six again. My tidy spell turned to mush. Didn't bowl again.

Batting at eight, came in far too late. I said to Jordan Clark, 'I'll knock one, you go big.'

He looked at me and said, 'You're Freddie fucking Flintoff. *You* go big.'

So I did. I hit a few sixes, brought us back. We needed 14 off the last over, and I still play that over in my head, every ball. I made some poor calls, couldn't get back for a second run when I needed to, and the game slipped.

Still stings. Even when things seemed to go okay, the mental side hit harder than I expected. There were moments in the dressing room – laughing with the lads, talking rubbish, feeling part of it again – and then I'd be sitting there afterwards, boots off, lights dimmed, just staring. Wondering if I still belonged there. Wondering if that version of me – the one who thrived under pressure – was long gone.

But that match lit something. It gave me a bit of myself back. Not everything – but enough.

Enough that when Brisbane Heat rang, I said yes.

CHAPTER 44

BACK DOWN UNDER

Yes to what?

Yes to flying out to Australia. Yes to playing in the Big Bash. Yes to late nights and quick turnarounds and the kind of cricket that doesn't give you time to overthink. They wanted me as an overseas pro – come out, slot in, bring a bit of experience, a bit of firepower. Live in Brisbane for a few months, train hard, play harder. It was short-form cricket, high tempo, a different rhythm to the long-form grind I'd grown up with – but the basics were still the same: watch the ball, back yourself, commit.

And maybe, underneath all that, I was saying yes to something else too. A chance to see if I still had it. Not just the game – but the hunger.

It was autumn 2014, so, at the same time, I was filming *Lord of the Fries* for Sky, driving a chip van round the North. One minute I was dishing out battered sausage to pensioners in Scarborough, the next I was bowling in front of 20,000. It was surreal, like living two parallel lives, neither of which made much sense on their own, but together somehow added up to something.

I was only supposed to play three or four games in the Big Bash, or the BBL, in Australia. Stuart Law – who I knew from Lancashire – was coaching. He's a great player and a great bloke, so I wanted to do right by him.

But it wasn't easy. The cricket side of it, anyway. I'd gone over thinking I'd play three, maybe four games, ease in, get my bearings. But no – as soon as I got off the plane, it was, 'You're starting.' The other overseas player, I think it was Sammy Badree, had done himself in. So I was in from game one.

Batting, I could get by. Not brilliant, but I had shots, had timing, still had a bit of presence at the crease. Bowling, though – that was hard. My pace had gone. No denying it. I'd always been a bowler who relied on speed, and now that edge wasn't there. I could feel it, and worse, others could too. It's not that I wasn't trying – I was. I was grafting. But you can't graft your way back to 90mph. It either comes out or it doesn't. And for me, it didn't.

It stung especially because Stuart was the coach. He was the one who got me out there, and I felt like I owed him. Still do. And I think – I know – I let him down a bit. Not because I wasn't up for it, but because my body couldn't do what my head still thought it could. That's a lonely place to be. You're standing out there, trying to hide that you're a few clicks short, hoping the next ball doesn't expose you. Horrible.

The dressing room wasn't helping. There were a few lads – younger ones – quietly turning on the coach. Whispering, undermining. And that shocked me, genuinely. That's what I'd expect in county cricket at its worst, not in Australia. You always think of Aussie teams as tough, honest, upfront. No bitching, no side. But this wasn't that. It was messy. I saw Stuart trying to hold it together and I felt for him.

Still, there were bright spots. We lived in sun-scorched Surfers Paradise, right on Queensland's Gold Coast, for six weeks. Unreal. Can't knock that. And I got mic'd up during games – part of the deal was doing commentary as I played. I wasn't sure at first. Felt like a gimmick. But actually, it helped. I'd be talking as I faced up, or between deliveries, just nattering – and I realised it made me play better. It took the edge off the nerves. Distracted me in a good way. Reminded me of when I was at my best, singing at the crease, staying loose.

There's one game where I'm fielding and I'm singing 'In the Ghetto' by Elvis, which was probably my biggest contribution to the Big Bash. On air. Live. I commentated when I batted, describing the field change, what shots I'm looking to play, then taking guard again. Bonkers, but fun. I didn't realise how much I missed that feeling – being in the moment, properly in it. Not analysing, not commenting from the outside, but *doing it*, however scrappy it was.

The Aussies seemed to take to it. I struck up a nice thing with Mark Waugh in the box – him deadpan and straight, me jabbering away. Mark Waugh – the laconic, no-nonsense former Test opener; straight-talking, grumpy Mark – but it worked. We bounced off each other. He was one of my heroes growing up, and now we were on the same broadcast, which meant a lot.

Australia's always been complicated for me: 2005 – that series made me; 2007 – the worst tour of my life; 2009 – a high again, bowing out on my own terms. And through all of it, the Aussie crowd was what it was – loud, brutal, partisan . . . but fair. If you fronted up, they respected you. If you gave it everything, they saw it. And they have a weird soft spot for flawed people. People who fall over, then get up again. Warne, Symonds, blokes like that. They're drawn to the mess and the glory. Put it this way, they loved the Fredalo story Down Under.

That trip, even though the cricket was patchy, I felt like I'd earned a bit of that back. They saw me for what I was – a bloke having a go, not pretending, not hiding. I wasn't the player I used to be, but I was still trying. Still in the arena. And that counted for something.

I wasn't chasing the old days any more. I wasn't trying to be the bloke with the armband, taking the final over, arms raised. I just wanted to be in the moment. To give it a go. And I did. That, more than the wickets or the runs or the noise, was the win.

I came home feeling grateful. Not for the stats – they were forgettable – but for the chance. For the people. For another swing. I don't like missing out on things. I can handle failure. But not trying? That's what does my head in. So I went. I played. I gave it a go.

And if that was the last proper game, I'm okay with that.

CHAPTER 45

KING OF THE JUNGLE (PART ONE)

They sit me down in this big wooden chair like I've just won *Gladiators*, stick a daft crown on my head and hand me a trophy that looks like a prop from a hen do. There's jungle confetti – which is basically dry leaves – falling from somewhere, and I'm trying to work out how the hell I've ended up here. Everyone's clapping, someone's crying, and I'm sitting there thinking, *I've just spent six weeks being bitten by midges and pretending I'm afraid of frogs, and now I'm King of the Jungle.*

Right.

* * *

When I got back from the Big Bash, I thought I was done with mad ideas for a bit. I'd just spent six weeks in Australia trying to resurrect my bowling, walking around Surfers

Paradise like a bloke in someone else's career, and now I was back in the UK, thinking maybe things might calm down. But that didn't last long.

It started with a whisper – the Aussie version of *I'm a Celebrity . . . Get Me Out of Here!* was starting its first ever series. They'd been teasing it during the cricket coverage, just little hints – a cricketer's going in, mystery contestant, all that. Everyone assumed it was me. It wasn't. It was Merv Hughes. But the more I denied it, the more it looked like it *was* me. Like that Shakespeare line: 'The lady doth protest too much.' It felt a bit like that.

Anyway, that first series came and went, but I was back home, doing bits and pieces. I think I was promoting the chip van show – or maybe something else, I honestly can't remember – and I was lined up to go on *The Jonathan Ross Show*. Just another day.

I did the taping, it went all right, and then afterwards I walked into the green room and Katie, from my management team, was sitting there with Rachael. I clocked them chatting, laughing like they'd been up to something. Katie looked up and said, 'You're going to LA for two days.' I went, 'Am I?' She said, 'Yeah, you're interviewing Will Smith.' Brilliant. 'And after that, you're going in the jungle.'

What?

I said, 'No, come on. That's not me, I'm not doing the jungle.'

I'd been asked before to do the UK one but I'd always said no. Not because of the show itself – I can handle being uncomfortable, eating bugs, all that – it's the attention. The circus around it: the front pages, the opinion pieces, the press camped outside your house. I didn't want any of that. Believe it or not – and I have to keep telling people this, else they won't believe it – I don't actually like being the centre of attention, far from it.

They were keen, though, and Katie said, 'If it goes well, it might open doors. If it doesn't, it's in Australia – no one over here's watching.'

Fair point.

So I said, 'Go on then.'

Off I went, and the next thing you know I was sitting in the back of a car on the way to camp, thinking, *What the hell am I doing?* when it suddenly hit me: *I'm going on a reality show, in a jungle, wearing red trousers.*

They took me to this house on the edge of the Kruger Park – a beautiful spot, the kind of place where people usually go to shoot game, not film telly. And everyone was dead nice. Proper welcoming. I started thinking, *You know what, this might actually be all right.*

Then they handed me my kit for the press shots – the red combat trousers, the vest, the silly hat, the backpack – and just like that, everything changed.

As soon as that outfit went on, you stopped being a person. Honestly. I wasn't Fred any more, and I certainly wasn't Andrew. I was a contestant, a gimmick, something for the telly to chuck into the jungle and laugh at. It was like someone flicked a switch. One minute I was chatting to producers, thinking *This'll be a laugh*, the next I had 'Vote Fred' slapped across my chest and people were looking at me like I was a full-time idiot.

And this was *before* I even got to camp.

Because – of course – there was a challenge first. They don't just drop you in. They've got to build it up, make a meal of it. I got paired with this woman called Julie Goodwin – lovely woman. I didn't know who she was at first, but it turned out she was a *MasterChef* winner, a big name in Australia and proper famous. She was older than me – funny, warm and dead sweet, a bit of a mum figure – and we got on straight away.

The challenge? Sit in a pitch-black cave for 12 hours. No lights. No clocks. Just darkness. We were allowed out four times for five-minute toilet breaks – that was it. I remember thinking, *Right, here we go. This is the real jungle now.*

I kept waiting for them to start dropping spiders or snakes on us – something nasty. Julie didn't seem fazed. She just sat there like, 'Isn't this lovely?' And I'm beside her sweating, picturing a tarantula crawling down my spine.

Before you go in, they give you a form to fill out – list your phobias, things you can't stand. I wasn't stupid. I didn't put down 'dark' even though I'm not keen, because I knew they'd jump on that. So I lied. Wrote 'frogs'.

The joke was on them though. I don't mind frogs. Later on, they chucked a load of them on me and I had to pretend to be horrified. *'Oh no, not frogs.'* Ridiculous.

But that cave . . . it really got to me. Not because of what *did* happen, but because of what I thought *might* happen. That's how they get you. The waiting. The second-guessing. You spend 12 hours flinching at shadows and imagining centipedes in your socks. That messes with your head.

COMING HOME

I thought the worst was over once we left the cave – the spiders, snakes, whatever else they had lined up – but no, the real weirdness started when we walked into camp.

No one knew we were coming. Me and Julie – we were the drop-ins, the late arrivals. And walking into that clearing . . . it was surreal. You'd seen it on telly a hundred times, that familiar jungle set-up – and now suddenly, *you're in it*. Part of the furniture. There was the fire pit, the sleeping mats, and the rest of the cast – half of whom I'd never even heard of.

The first face I recognised was Merv Hughes. Big moustache, bigger presence. He was a former Aussie fast bowler – fierce on the field, funny off it – and I'd loved him as a cricketer, all fire and flair. We hit it off straight away. Ended up sitting together most of the time, just laughing, really.

The rest of them? All lovely, I'm sure. But it wasn't my world. A couple of presenters, someone from *The Brady Bunch*, a few Aussie TV types. I was polite, friendly and did my bit, but I wasn't there to get stuck into camp gossip. I didn't want to be that bloke constantly talking just to get airtime. If I had something to say, I said it. If I didn't, I kept quiet.

And I was very aware that every word out of my mouth was being recorded. Always on, always watched. It does something to you, that. Makes you think before you speak. Not in a fake way – I wasn't trying to play a part – but just in a *don't be a prat* kind of way.

The first two weeks were all on a set fee – decent money. After that, it switched to a daily rate based on whether you survived the vote. So I thought, *All right, I'll bed in, do the time*, and then give it a proper crack.

And you know what? It was a bit of a breeze. People were already tired and hungry when we arrived. Me and Julie, we'd been fed before we got there. Speaking for myself, I had a bit of energy and the clarity to match. Everyone else was two weeks into deprivation, and it showed.

The thing that struck me was how people tried to present themselves. You could see it – everyone had this version of themselves they wanted to be seen as. Well, that might have been the plan when they first went in? But after six weeks in a camp? That mask slips. You go back to who you really are. I watched that process happen to the other contestants.

Merv, though. I could've sat with him all day. He was exactly what you'd want – funny, loud, blunt, but with a real warmth underneath. He told a story about Chopper Read – the Aussie criminal who cut his own ears off – and did an impression that apparently didn't go down well in the edit. It looked like he was being aggressive, which he wasn't. That's the gamble with reality TV – they cut the way they want, whatever fits their – wait for it – 'narrative'.

Merv got voted out eventually, but not before he'd put in a good shift. Legend.

While others were losing their minds over food, I just saw it as an opportunity. A bit of a detox. A break. How often do you get to stop completely? No phone, no emails, no schedules. I thought, *Brilliant – I'll catch up on sleep, drop a bit of weight, earn a bit of cash. What's not to like?*

Nearly got myself kicked out, mind. I smuggled in a stash of sleeping pills. Hid them round the rim of my hat. I'm not proud of it, but I needed something to help me get off to sleep that first week. I also had my phone in my pocket when I arrived. I kept hold of it for a bit and then handed it in. Probably for the best.

There was one moment – they were all moaning about food, again – and one of the TV presenters started talking about staging a strike. Get the press involved, make a statement, that kind of thing.

I just looked at them and said, 'Right, let's go. Let's do it now.'

They all went quiet.

'Come on,' I said, 'this'll play great. Loads of starving people around the world, and here's a bunch of over-paid celebrities in the jungle refusing to eat their rice. Cracking look.' Which had the desired effect. It was never mentioned again.

I was cheeky in other ways too. I figured out the smoking thing quickly – they allowed it, but you had to go outside the gate. So I had my routine: every day I'd wander out, light one up. One after breakfast, one after lunch, one before bed. Became a rhythm.

But the best bit was the water.

See, everyone else was boiling water every day, trying to stay hydrated, but I clocked that the medical hut was only 200 yards away from where I stood smoking. I noticed that it wasn't an especially secure medical hut.

What's a bloke to do?

Sure enough I popped the window, climbed through, filled my bottle from the cooler. Cold water. There was fruit too – bananas mostly – and I nicked a few of those. Bliss.

Twice a day I did that, for a while. And no one knew. Not at first.

Eventually I told Julie. She was struggling with the heat, the dehydration. So I said, 'Give us your bottle,' and came back with it filled, fresh and cold.

'Where did you get that?' she said.

I just winked. 'Don't you worry about that. Twice a day, kid.'

I even got friendly with the runner – a young South African lad – who'd sit and chat with me outside the gate. Lovely bloke. He started bringing me little extras.

And the anti-poaching lads too – the ones with rifles, keeping us safe from lions and whatever else. I'd go sit with them for a bit, chat, have a laugh. I liked that. Felt normal.

Chris Brown – the Bondi Vet – was the host. Lovely fella. Smooth, charming, had the whole country swooning. I never saw much of him, obviously, but when I did, he was good as gold.

Especially when I worked out how to *really* game the system.

CHAPTER 46

KING OF THE JUNGLE (PART TWO)

It took me a couple of weeks to figure out how it worked – I mean, what you could actually *do* to make it yours. Because most of the time, it's a bit out of your hands. They cut it, shape it, reframe everything in the edit.

But there's one bit they can't fiddle with – the live stuff. That's yours. That's where I realised I could have a bit of fun.

It started with Chris Brown, the Bondi Vet – model, actor, looked like he'd been carved from mahogany. I mean, just absurdly good-looking. And, as it turned out, a really nice bloke. So I started leaning into it – complimenting him, saying he'd clearly been grown in a lab, asking if he had a button that made his eyes sparkle. All a bit tongue-in-cheek, but he didn't know how to deal with it. No comebacks, no banter. Just sort of sitting there blinking.

And I thought, *This is my in.*

So every morning, when the cameras went live, I'd give him a bit more. Break the show down while it was happening, mess with the format, chip away at the edges. And it worked. It was daft, yeah, but it gave me a bit of control. Everyone else was waiting around to be picked for challenges, but I was treating it like a late-night radio show. Just having a laugh.

The challenges themselves – you *wanted* to get picked. Not because they were fun – they weren't – but because it meant a day out. You got to leave camp, see new faces, stretch your legs. Bit of excitement. I did a few – one hanging under a helicopter, trying to grab stars, then dropping into a lake. Apparently it had crocodiles in it. No one mentioned that beforehand.

And yeah, I'd hoped I might get to meet a lion cub. Some of the others did. They got these little safari-style challenges – cuddle a baby cheetah, feed a giraffe. Me? I got the jungle spa.

It started with – wait for it – frogs. Loads of them. I had to lie back in a sink while they poured frogs on my face and I tried to fish out stars with my hands. Then came the insect helmet – big astronaut-style thing, thousands of bugs poured in, and I had to find the star with my *mouth*. I don't even like insects, but when there's a camera three inches from your nose, you just get on with it.

Next was a box full of what they said were rats. But let's be honest, they were telly rats. Cleanest, fluffiest rats you've ever seen. Like they'd just come off a Disney set. Then came the tubs. Fish guts, animal offcuts, some kind of jelly made from horror. I had to dunk my head in and fish the stars out with my teeth. Then a shower – not with water, no – a shower of what I can only describe as liquid bin juice. All over me.

And the host, Chris Brown, just stood there smiling, wide open. So I grabbed him and smeared it all over him. Just slathered it on. He had no chance.

Then came the eating trial. I don't mind that stuff as much. Had to eat a giant slug, a cockroach. You do it quick, try not to think, and hope it doesn't fight back. But the worst was the drink. Looked like a smoothie. Pint glass. Had to down it in a minute. Sounded doable . . . until I realised what was in it.

Fish guts. Cow intestine. Cockroaches. Maggots. Bits of a dung beetle – pre-beetle, just dung. They blended the lot and handed it over like a protein shake. I got three-quarters of the way through before the gags started. Couldn't finish it. Felt rough.

So I turned to Chris and said, 'Go on then, you try.'

And to be fair to him, he did. He picked it up, had a sniff and nearly vomited on the spot. Fair play, he even tried to sip it – until he gagged and had to bolt behind a tree. Full meltdown.

While he was retching behind the bushes, I walked over to Julia – one of the co-hosts – and just carried on presenting. Did his link for him while he was being sick. Felt like a solid day's work.

But it wasn't all a laugh. There was one moment, a bit of proper needle with the contestant Barry Hall, an Aussie Rules bloke. Big lad – six foot five, bald, even his muscles had muscles.

I knew nothing about Barry but thought he was a mate because he seemed to get on well with me and Merv. And turns out he'd come in on edge. His wife had just left him, apparently, and he was stewing. Turns out he'd boxed.

I used to sit on his bed sometimes to chat with Merv. Didn't think anything of it. One day he snaps – tells me to get off his bed. I think he's joking, so I laugh it off. He says it again, serious this time. Third time, he properly squares up. I get off. He's pulled aside by production, warned about his behaviour.

Later that day, I went back and sat on the bed again – just to chat with Merv.

Barry came over and said, 'I've asked you politely. If I tell you again, I'll ask the ladies to leave and I'll kill you.'

Right there. To my face. On telly.

I looked at him and thought, this is real. If he comes at me, I'm going to have to defend myself. And it'll be on *live television*. Great.

He didn't, in the end. But it hung in the air. Never really settled after that. Mad.

I knew I wasn't right after the Barry thing. I got off the bed and just sat on my own for a bit, not sulking, not being dramatic, just thinking, *I don't want to be here*. That shook me up, and it stayed with me. The day carried on, the show carried on, but for me, it had dipped. I wasn't enjoying it any more. The charm had worn off, and I kept thinking, *This is going to end badly. Unless I land the luckiest punch in history, I'm getting filled in.* I didn't want that.

But weirdly, that threat – that moment – had gone massive outside. It turned out that back in Australia, Barry's threat to kill me was front-page news. I didn't even know. I was just cracking on in camp, then a week later I'm chatting to one of the quiz show hosts they brought in for one of the daft games, and he says, 'Mate, that was everywhere.' I was like, *Oh, great*. But it fizzled out again. These things do.

And then – somehow – I ended up winning it. Not quite sure how. I never felt like I was playing the game; never tried to charm anyone. I just did the time. Didn't complain, didn't fake it. They sent me off to the waterfall two nights before the final – bit of a jungle tradition, quiet moment to reflect, bit of peace. But I knew something was up.

As I was walking there, I thought, 'Rachael's going to be here, isn't she?'

Sure enough, there she was, sitting on a rock, looking as unsure about it as I felt. So although what they wanted was the big emotional reunion, slow music, maybe a few tears, what they got was me going, 'You all right?'

And her going, 'Yeah, are you?'

Then she said, 'Come on, give us a hug.'

And that was that. No drama. Just us. I think they were hoping for a bit more telly.

They also made us do a roast. You draw a name out of a hat and have to do a celebrity roast for them – like the Comedy Central ones, but in the jungle. I got Chrissie Swan – didn't know much about her. Came second in *Big Brother*, apparently. Nice enough, but didn't do much around camp. So I wrote this daft thing, completely made up, imagining what the actual winner of *Big Brother* must be doing now. Something about a caravan, loads of dogs barking, a chip shop that went bust. Just rambling.

Everyone laughed.

Then one of the contestants turns to me and says, 'How did you know all that?'

I said, 'Know what?'

She goes, 'The woman who won it – that *is* what happened. She lives in a caravan, had a chip shop, struggled.'

I couldn't believe it. Pure fluke. Landed on the truth by accident. Felt awful. But what can you do?

So yeah, I won. They sat me in the big chair, plonked a ridiculous thing on my head, handed me a trophy that looked like a giant vibrator, and said congratulations. I just sat there, not knowing what to do. Didn't feel like a win, didn't feel like anything really. Bit daft. But it led to something.

Off the back of it, I started working more in Australia. I presented an entertainment show called *The Project* for 12 weeks – Tuesday and Thursday nights. Then came *Ninja Warrior*. I'd pop back and forth, take my mate Paddy with me, and the family would come out for six or eight weeks. I was never away too long. And it worked, actually. Felt like a detachment from everything else. A proper sideline.

That's the thing I liked – I was earning over there, living over here. They might show *Ninja Warrior* on ITV at 8am on a Sunday, but no one really watched it. Not properly. Which suited me just fine. I wasn't getting recognised on the school run. I could do the work, bank the money and keep things quiet. That's the balance I liked.

I nearly did the UK jungle one year. Came close. But I didn't in the end. Just didn't fancy the circus. Over there, it felt more contained. Less hysteria.

Strictly? They used to ask all the time. Threw money at

it, tried everything. I said no. Not because I hate dancing – well, I *do* hate dancing – but because I don't want to learn routines, I don't want to do those cringey bits to camera, and I definitely don't want to become part of that machine. I just don't care about it. And they don't get that. They keep asking. My agents Richard and Katie don't even bother setting up the meetings any more. They know.

That's the thing – I'm not desperate to be on telly. I'm not chasing it. Katie laughs about it. She says, 'You turn down everything and they still keep asking.'

But I'm just being honest. I don't want to be that bloke who says yes to everything. I've got a complicated relationship with the whole thing.

If it ends, it ends. I'll be all right. I was a half-decent cricketer once. I'm happy with that.

CHAPTER 47

A NEW KIND OF TOUR

The lights are down. There's a photo behind me – big, soft-focus, supposed to be my fiancée. Music swells, a sort of soft rock power ballad, the kind of thing you'd expect to hear in a karaoke bar at half-eleven on a Friday. I'm standing centre stage, back to the crowd, trying not to sweat through my jacket.

I know what's coming. I've known all day. Course I do, I've performed this song maybe 50 times by now – matinees, evenings, Tuesdays in wherever, Saturdays in somewhere else – but it never gets easier. It's *my* song. The one where the spotlight comes down and I've got to carry it. No Jodie Prenger to save me. No duets. Just me and this bloody key change.

The cue hits. I turn slowly. Face the crowd. There's a woman in the front row already laughing. I haven't opened my mouth yet. I spot someone holding up a programme and pointing at my face like they still can't believe it.

'That's him,' you can almost hear them whisper. 'That's the cricketer. What's *he* doing here?'

And I open my mouth.

The first note's always the hardest. If I catch it, I'm away. If I don't . . . well, then I've got three and a half minutes of floundering.

And you know what? There's no backing out. No drinks break. No umpire to save me. Just a thousand people staring, and a song I wish was in a slightly lower key.

But here's the thing – I hit it. Not clean, not beautiful, but solid. I'm on my way. I can feel it. I start moving, hand gestures I've half-learned, mimicking what the pros do. The crowd's with me, kind of. They're not here for *Les Mis*. They're here for a laugh, maybe a bit of warmth. And maybe, just maybe, I'm giving them that.

When it finishes, I hold the last note like I've seen on telly, then drop my arms and nod like I meant to do all of that. Lights fade. Applause, thankfully. I walk off, sweating, knackered, slightly elated. Not because I nailed it, but because I got through it.

This wasn't the plan. Not even close. But somehow, I'm in *Fat Friends: The Musical*, touring the UK, doing two shows a day and living on hotel chicken. And if you're wondering how the hell that happened – so am I.

* * *

It started with a meeting I didn't really understand. I was in Australia at the time, filming *The Project*, in and out of the country, and Katie rings to say, 'When you're back, Lynda La Plante wants to meet you.'

I knew who she was – the *Prime Suspect* writer – but I didn't know what it was about. Still, I said, 'Yeah. Go on then.'

She lived up to her billing.

Put simply, Lynda La Plante is a force of nature. She's got this booming voice, like someone who's been holding court for decades, and a look that says she's already decided whether you're worth her time. And if she *has* decided you are, then God help anyone who gets in her way.

She wrote *Prime Suspect*, of course – that gritty, game-changing cop show in the 1990s. Helen Mirren as DCI Jane Tennison, glass of Scotch in one hand, bag of chips in the other, trying to do her job while every bloke in CID tried to make her life hell. Proper drama. Not flash, not sentimental. Just hard-nosed stories, brilliantly told. And it changed things – not just in telly, but in how women in the force were seen. La Plante wasn't just a writer – she was a statement.

So I showed up to see her and a casting director and three hours later I was still there watching as she did impressions of me from *A League of Their Own*, her arms flailing, mimicking my Lancashire accent, taking the piss, basically.

Now Lynda, in line with her being an insanely talented crime writer, is as sharp as anything, completely bonkers in the best way, and at some point in the middle of all this chaos she said, 'You should act.' And not in a jokey way. She was serious. Not only that, but she wanted me in a lead role.

Which was like, *Woah*, because when Katie had said, 'You've got a meeting with Lynda La Plante,' of course I'd thought it'd be about a part, but something small, a copper in the background maybe. I didn't think I'd be considered for a lead role.

Lynda tells me she's written the prequel to *Prime Suspect*. It's called *Tennison*. ITV are backing it, going to film soon. I go, 'All right, brilliant.'

And she says, 'I want you to play a guy who's six foot four, ginger, drinks too much, smokes like a chimney, screws up relationships, screws up everything really. Depressive. Violent when it suits. But good instincts.'

And I'm thinking, *Right. That sounds . . . familiar.*

She says, 'I want *you* to audition for it.'

I told her I was off to Australia in a few days.

'Do it from there,' she said, like it was nothing. I said, 'Yeah, all right then. Why not.'

A few days after I got to Melbourne, the script arrived – two scenes, no context. I had no idea what I was auditioning for; no clue what the set-up was. But I learned them anyway. Then I was told I had to fly to Sydney for the audition.

The casting agency was one of the big ones – the kind of place that represented Thor. Not the character, the bloke. Hemsworth. One of them, maybe all three. Either way, it was a proper operation.

When I arrived, they sent me round the back where an acting coach was waiting. He seemed friendly enough. I sat down and said, 'Look, I've got the script, but I've no idea what I'm doing here. Never done a casting in my life. Is it on Zoom? Is it filmed? What's the process?'

He told me we'd run it through. I asked if he'd do it once first so I could see how it was supposed to go. He gave me a

look and said, 'That's not how we do it in the acting world.'
Fair enough. Lesson learned.

We started running lines. He nodded and said, 'Not bad.
Just relax a bit,' and then told me to do ten press-ups.

I asked why.

'To get the energy up,' he said.

I told him energy wasn't the issue, but I went along with
it anyway. Did the press-ups. Then we got going properly.

There was a reader on the other end, maybe meant to
be Jane Tennison, though I still wasn't entirely sure. We
had two scenes. One was in a car, talking through a case.
The other was a drunk scene, which I leaned into. Bit of
method acting. I had plenty of reference points. It actually
went okay. The coach said, 'That was good. I think you
might get this.'

I went away feeling – not confident, exactly – but not
terrible either.

A few days later, I got a call back. Two more scenes. This
time, I decided to lean into the role a bit more. I picked up a
cheap shirt and tie and a ropey old jacket – proper detective
gear. Bit of a look. Weirdly, it helped.

Same set-up as before – session with the coach, another
run with the reader over Zoom. I did all right again. Then
one of the agents from the same firm that handled the
Hemsworths came in and started asking whether I had any
representation. I thought, 'Here we go.' It felt like something might actually be happening.

And then – silence.

I went home, and after a while, I heard that Lynda
had gone into bat for me. ITV had said no – said I was

too much of a risk. I was told that things got fairly fiery between them.

And that was it. The part went to someone else. *Tennison* got made without me.

But for a minute, it had felt real. Like the door was open and I'd just stepped through it – only for it to quietly shut again before I could take the next step.

CHAPTER 48

PLAYING THE PART

How did all this lead to me singing in front of an audience? We're getting there. Still on the run-up.

So with Lynda's words of encouragement ringing in my ears, I found myself an acting coach in Manchester – proper no-nonsense bloke, not one for rolling around on the floor pretending to be a tree, and we started off by working through scenes. Stuff from *Happy Valley*, gritty telly. Nothing flashy. Just learning.

I liked it. He brought a mate in one day – a casting director – and after watching me do a bit, the casting director said, 'You want to try for something?'

Why not?

He rang Kay Mellor. I got a script. Next thing you know, I'm in a strange little room full of people at computers, with a camera in my face, reading for the part of a registrar in *Love, Lies and Records*. I didn't know what I was doing, not really, but I gave it a go. Read the lines. Tried not to look terrified. Kay was warm. At the end she says, 'Have you ever thought about doing musical theatre?'

I said, 'Yeah.' Which wasn't true. It had never crossed my mind. I mean, why would it? But when someone's asking and Nick Lloyd Webber's in the next room, you don't say no.

So I walk through, and there's Nick – Andrew's lad – sitting at a piano, and I'm suddenly in a new audition, reading songs from *Fat Friends: The Musical*.

There was one called 'The Only Fool Is Me', and another, which was a duet with a vicar. She asked, 'Which part do you want?'

'Kevin?' I said, and I have no idea where that came from. She nodded. Like, leave it with me.

Sure enough, I got both jobs. A small part in a romcom series *Love, Lies and Records*, and the lead in *Fat Friends*.

The TV bit in *Love, Lies and Records* had changed – at first it was supposed to be opposite Anna Friel, but she pulled out and they recast and they ended up with Ashley Jensen, who was great, but not right for my love interest, hence me getting shunted off to play a footballer getting married. The whole experience was as flat as my performance. I didn't love it.

The musical of *Fat Friends*, however? Different story. I'd said yes to a month residency in Leeds, but then Kay talked me into a six-week tour – proper theatres, mostly northern venues.

It was only when the script arrived that I started to panic. I'd never done theatre. I didn't know the rules. So I fell back on what I knew – I learned it. Every word. Every scene.

Turned up to rehearsals thinking I'd nailed it. But everyone else was still on the page. They looked at me like I was trying to upstage them. I wasn't. I was just trying to survive.

Then came the singing. I had three songs – two duets and a solo. The duets I could just about blag. Jodie Prenger – absolute force of nature – carried me. Sam Bailey too. Incredible voice. Even Curly Watts could hold a note. Then there was me. First time I sang in front of the cast, I was shaking. Tried to do this half-speak, half-sing thing. The musical director said, 'You're singing this. Hit the notes.' So I gave it a go.

The solo – 'The Only Fool Is Me' – was the real test. Like I say, it was lights down, spotlight on, big photo of my onstage fiancée flashing up behind me. I'd stand with my back to the crowd, then turn as the music started. Just me, on a stage, trying not to crack. Some nights I got through it. Others, my voice went, or I forgot the words, or missed the cue. I'd make it up. Ad-lib. The crowd laughed. They were forgiving. Theatre crowd, but more *League* than *Les Mis*. But backstage, I felt it. They were watching. Not always with kindness.

There was this moment after lunch one day – I walked into the green room and the place just went silent. One of the girls said, 'We were talking about stunt casting.'

I said, 'Let me guess – me?'

No one said anything. I thought to myself, 'You lot crack on with your little musical in front of no one. I'll go home.'

Only been doing it two minutes and already a diva.

After that, it eased. They saw I knew exactly what I was. I wasn't pretending.

Eight shows a week. Double up Thursdays and Saturdays. Sunday off. I was on £1,500 a week – which sounds all right – but I was spending more than that on hotels. No chance I was staying in digs. But some of the cast – they were on £200 a week, maybe £400 if they were lucky. Travelling, sorting food, doing the graft. It didn't sit right. The producer was pulling in cash. The kids onstage were scraping by. The system was broken.

They had Equity meetings. I wasn't invited. I didn't have a card and didn't want one either. I wasn't in the club, and I didn't need to be.

I didn't fall in love with theatre, nor did I miss it when it was over. But it did something. It changed how I felt about nerves.

And people say, 'You've played in Ashes Tests – how can you be nervous doing this?'

But it's different. In a Test, you've trained. You've got a bat, a helmet and a team behind you. Onstage, it's just you, a mic and a soft rock ballad you feel like you've only half-rehearsed. And if you mess up, there's nowhere to hide. Especially when your mates are in the crowd. They tell you the truth.

The one thing I *did* like – acting. That bit got to me. Not the musical stuff, but the idea of playing someone else, drawing on your own bits. Because it's all just versions of yourself, really. That's what I've learned – acting, telly, sport – it's all just using who you are, tweaking it slightly, putting it in a different context. The nerves, the pride, the trying to stay calm when you're not.

I did one more thing – a short for Sky called *Burt & Me*,

which was just me and a dog on a beach. No big moment, no punchlines. Just sitting there, watching the tide. I liked it. Played it straight. Nobody saw it, mind you, but that's not the point. I did it. And I still think about doing more. I've half-written some bits – sitcom ideas, dramas. If I did it again, I'd want to go heavy. Something serious. Something real.

But I'm 48. I've got a wife, kids and responsibilities. I'm not going to drama school. If I was 28, maybe. Maybe I'd have had a proper go. But I've done more than I ever thought I would. From *A League of Their Own* to singing onstage, to quietly talking to a dog on a beach. It's been weird, but it's been something.

And I can still hum the tune from *Fat Friends*.

CHAPTER 49

TOP GEAR

I'm standing in a field near Leicester, trying not to fall over the words in a script or the bonnet of a Dacia Duster. It's a screen test for *Top Gear*. They've handed me a sheet with all the car's selling points and asked me to drive around and talk. I'm not entirely sure where I'm meant to be looking.

Chris Harris is already there. I'd seen enough of his stuff to know he was the real deal – proper motoring journalist, knew what he was talking about. We did a short piece together – bit of a fun thing, nothing too staged – and I liked him straight away. He was sharp, dry, a cricket fan too, which helped. We had a laugh. No performance, no pretending. It felt easy.

Then they peeled us off to film some links. I was given a script and had a look through it – read all the info about the Duster, what it could and couldn't do. It was all there, but it wasn't me. So I said to the producers, 'I've been reading your script, but I'm not going to use it.'

They looked at me.

'What?'

'I've got the points, I know what I want to say. I'm going to freewheel it.'

Because here's the thing: if I got the job, I wanted it being myself. And if I didn't get it, fair enough – but at least I'd have done it my way.

What they don't know – and what I probably shouldn't admit – is that I'd already spent a fortune trying to land this job. When the application came round, there was a section asking what kind of cars you had. Now, I had a couple. Nothing flash. But I thought, *They're not going to give it to someone with a Kia and a family saloon.* I already had a family 4x4, and I'd picked up a four-seater Ferrari. Might've had a Lamborghini at one point, though I barely drove it. Got carried away. But it looked good on the form.

It seemed to go well. I got on with Chris, liked the crew, and when I left, I had that little flutter of hope in my chest. The way they were talking, I thought, *I might have this.*

Then . . . silence. Two weeks passed. Then four. Then six. I figured it was gone. I'd chased it hard – more than I'd chased anything in telly before – and nothing had come back.

Then one day we're in the car, driving through Altrincham. Rachael's at the wheel, one of the kids is in the front, and I'm in the back seat. The phone rings. It's Richard, my agent.

'Can you speak on your own?' he asks.

'No, I'm in the car.'

So I ask Rachael to pull over. I get out and walk to the pavement, phone to my ear.

'I've got news for you,' Richard says. 'Great news. You've got the *Top Gear* job.'

* * *

Here's the thing – I'd wanted this one. Most telly jobs, I'd kind of fallen into. Someone calls, asks if I fancy it, and I go, yeah, why not? But *Top Gear* – I chased that. Bought the cars. Took the screen test. Said yes with my chest. And when it came through, I was made up.

It felt like a proper job. Full on. Rehearsals, schedules, long days on set. I got to drive some brilliant cars, travel a bit and have a laugh with Chris and Paddy. I liked them both – Chris especially, sharp and straight, no messing. But telly's not sport. In sport, it's on you. You shape it. You know where you stand. With telly, it's different. You say a line, forget it, say it again. Someone says it's brilliant – even when it's not.

I remember early on – might've been *League* – I sat through a whole shoot and barely said a word. Felt like a spare part. End of the day, someone comes over and says, 'That was fantastic.' I thought – are you winding me up?

Telly's edited. It's subjective. They can cut you to look funny or flat, clever or clueless, and you've no say in the outcome. You're just one piece in the machine. You get recognised more for a Morrisons Christmas ad than for the Ashes. People still come up and say, 'Loved you in that one with the turkeys!' Cheers. I also took five wickets at Lord's.

And my mum – bless her – she still asks, 'Have they not

asked you to go on *Strictly*?' Or 'What about *The Wheel*?' I've been asked. Loads of times. And I always say no. Not because I think I'm above it. I just don't want to. Doesn't feel like me.

My dad never said much. Didn't judge. Didn't praise either. When *Top Gear* came through – nothing. When it ended – still nothing. But now I'm back coaching a bit, just quietly, he seems happier. Not in a big way. Just a look. A sort of settledness. And I get that. Because cricket – for all the stress and the sting – it was real. Telly never felt the same. It always felt . . . disposable. And I don't say that bitterly. Just honestly.

I've had good moments on screen, and worked with some great people. But after the crash things slowed. I had to stop. Reassess. You can't barrel on like nothing's changed after something like that. It forces you to ask questions. What am I doing with my time? What am I chasing?

And maybe that's the truth of it. You keep saying yes – not for money, not for the profile – but because you think the next thing might be it. The one that fits. But half the time, you don't even know what you're chasing. Only that it's not this.

I loved parts of *Top Gear*. The freedom. The noise. The daftness. The moments where it felt like it really was just mates mucking about in fast cars. But I also knew, deep down, that I wasn't that guy. Not full-time. Not forever. Although I suppose you could say that fate stepped in where that was concerned.

CHAPTER 50

FIELD OF DREAMS

I didn't really know what I was starting, if I'm honest. *Field of Dreams* began as a loose idea – a notion, more than anything – and like a lot of things I've ended up doing on telly, it wasn't something handed to me. I tend to come up with the concepts myself, the ones that aren't formatted already. Stuff like the bulimia film, the depression documentary, the fish and chip van one, the boxing – they were mine. *Field of Dreams* too. Not in a grand ownership way, just . . . this was something I felt. Something I wanted to explore. It started with cricket, but it didn't stay there.

The idea at the beginning was pretty straightforward – there are kids out there who don't get a shot at cricket, not because they don't love it or have potential, but because the game just never reaches them.

I thought: *What if there's a lad in Preston, proper talent, who's never had a chance to play? Never picked up a bat.*

That was the original spark. Go and find them; see what's there.

But then we started. We kicked off by meeting the kids, talking to people, and it shifted – like it always does when you get close to the ground level. The real story wasn't about unearthing the next professional. It wasn't about talent at all, really. It was about access. Belonging. About giving something back to the game that gave me so much, in a way that made sense in the present.

When you grow up in cricket, there's more to it than runs and wickets. You get a sense of place. You get mates, a structure and people looking out for you. That dressing room feel – it stays with you. And I could see straight away that what these kids needed, more than anything, was a place like that. Somewhere to show up and be part of something. Somewhere to matter.

We didn't do an open call and hope for the best. It wasn't just posters and turn up if you fancy. We reached out. We asked schools, youth clubs, community workers: who would benefit from this the most? Who's drifting? Who's not getting the chances? And they came – some invited, some just turned up – but each one brought a story with them. They'd all been written off in some way. Labelled troublemakers. Difficult. ADHD, autism, behavioural stuff. The kind of kids who'd heard 'no' more than any child should.

The first open day was at Preston Cricket Club. Some of the kids couldn't play for toffee – I mean, no technique, no experience – but that wasn't the point. You could feel it, straight away. There was something there. They were sharp, curious, they had something about them. Disillusioned, maybe. Detached. But not beyond reach. Just . . . untapped.

One lad stuck in my mind – Ethan. First session, he turned up in a puffer jacket, ear pods in, beanie pulled low. Everything about him was saying 'don't engage'. And my instinct, if I'm honest, was to go over and say, 'Take your jacket off, lose the headphones, hat off, come on.' But something stopped me, because I realised – that's not misbehaviour, that's his armour. He's nervous, he doesn't know anyone, doesn't know what this is. He's clinging to what makes him feel safe.

So instead, I just asked him – what are you listening to? It was 2Pac or something, not really my thing, but we had a chat, just small talk. And that was the crack in the door. He kept his music on for the session. No problem. Next time, he came back – no headphones. Session after that – no jacket. And you see it, gradually, like a flower turning to the light. He's in. He's part of it.

That was the lesson, really. You've got to meet people where they are. You can't help someone if you don't know them. And it's the same with coaching – you learn quickly that shouting instructions doesn't work if the person in front of you doesn't trust you. You've got to earn it.

There were days I'd get in the car afterwards and just think – what am I doing? Tear my hair out. Not because of the kids, but the scale of it. The responsibility. But bit by bit, you see it working. You see them showing up again and again. You see them laughing, mucking in, learning. And yeah, playing some cricket too. Not brilliantly, not always, but with heart. With hunger. And that's worth something.

By the end of the first series, I wanted to take them away. To India. That was the plan. A proper trip, something bigger than just nets and games in Preston. Show them the world a bit. And we'd told them – this is happening.

But life had other plans.

CHAPTER 51

KEYSEY

Before we go on, a quick word on Rob Key, who although he hasn't had a proper mention yet, has always been a part of this story.

Keysey came into my life properly in around 1997 when we were both in the Under-19s, and from day one he had this ability to make me feel like things were going to be all right, even when they obviously weren't.

At the time, I was still finding my feet – young, homesick, not quite ready for the idea of touring life – and if I'm honest, I wasn't sleeping well. The hotels were strange, the walls were thin, and I'd lie there staring at the ceiling, convinced something bad was going to happen. It sounds daft now, but I was genuinely scared of the dark.

What made it worse was that this wasn't a new thing for me – I'd had trouble sleeping since I was a kid. I used to sleepwalk and get panicky at night, and even now I might struggle when I'm indoors and the lights go out. It started after I watched *The Exorcist* far too young – messed me up a bit, that film. My mum used to lie next to me until I drifted off, just to settle me.

When he heard that, Rob mocked me ruthlessly. And then said, 'Well, you can kip in here if you want,' and shifted over in his bed to make space. As you can imagine, he still mocks me about this, and rightly so. I've told this story on Jonathan Ross when I was on with Kevin Hart who found it very funny indeed, and it seems the more I tell it, the more tax I put on it.

Joking aside, that's what mates are – someone you can turn to. And that's Rob all over. He's been that steady presence for as long as I can remember – funny, dry, always ready with a one-liner but also the kind of mate who turns up, listens, and holds his nerve when everything else is going sideways. We were thick as thieves, me and him and Harmy, and we probably did ourselves no favours career-wise, always joking, always up for a laugh. Looking back, I know we probably wound a few people up. But I wouldn't trade it. Mates over politics, every time.

Keysey could play, too. Seriously play. He got 200 against the Windies once, and a 90 not out that should've kept him in the side. But he had a couple of off games after that and Duncan Fletcher didn't need much excuse to move him on. It still stings a bit, how that went down – I always felt like my friendship with Rob probably counted against him. But he never held it against me. That's just not who he is.

And years later, when I was out of the game and unsure if I'd ever come back, it was Rob who reached out. Rob who opened the door. Rob who said, 'Come on, let's get you back in cricket.' Which, when you think about it, isn't all that different from what he did all those years ago in that Under-19s hotel room. Just a quiet gesture that said: you don't have to go through this on your own.

These days, we spend more time together than ever – working, talking, finding new ways to take the mick – and if you stick with this book long enough, you'll see how that relationship circles back again. Not everyone sticks around. He has.

And he was there, when this happened . . .

CHAPTER 52

AFTERWARDS

Covid's over, you numpty.

It starts with a voice in the crowd.

'It's finished, you prick. The fucking pandemic is over.'

We're leaving Headingley – me, Keysey and the kids – threading our way through the usual end-of-play throng towards our van.

I've got my snood pulled up, glasses on, bucket hat pulled low. It's not exactly subtle, I know, but it's not for show. It's my armour. Just survival.

It's the only way I can leave the house.

The comment lands like a jab. I stop. I turn. There's a group of lads behind us – early twenties, maybe – swaggering like they've had a few. One of them's smirking. He's the one who thinks that I'm still scared of Covid. And I'm just standing there, rooted to the spot, my daughter at my side, and my brain stuck somewhere between fight and freeze.

I don't go straight at the guy. But I don't walk away either. I just stare. There's something fizzing inside me, something I've been bottling for months. All that effort to stay calm, stay quiet, stay hidden – and now this. I edge closer. I hear Keysey behind me, saying something – calm words, fatherly ones – but I'm not really hearing them.

For a minute, maybe more, I stand there with my face covered, adrenaline thumping, thinking stupid things. Should I pull the scarf down? Make a scene? Show him who I am, whatever that means.

One of them gives me a shove. It's not violent – not really – just a nudge.

'Kids, get in the van,' I say, still not looking away. I keep staring. And that's when it hits me – I'm not angry at them. Not really. I'm angry that they caught me off guard. Angry that I still care. Angry that it still hurts.

We walk away.

Back in the van, there's silence. I'm sweating. My daughter Holly says something about the bloke being a knob, and I smile.

'Shouldn't have stopped,' I say.

But underneath that, there's something else. Something I hadn't felt in a while.

I was still in there.

*　*　*

After the crash, I disappeared.

Not in a dramatic way. I just sort of . . . vanished. From view. From life. I didn't leave the house except for medical appointments. I didn't go out. I didn't socialise. Rachael was holding everything together, and I was stuck in this tiny orbit of bedrooms and the downstairs sofa. My whole world had shrunk to two rooms and a hundred thoughts I didn't want.

It wasn't fear, exactly. It felt more like erosion. My confidence was gone. My curiosity was gone. I'd wake up eventually, around half ten or eleven, and even though I didn't want to get out of bed, I would. I had to. I didn't want the kids to see me like that. Then I'd go downstairs and plant myself on the sofa, and that's where I'd stay – sometimes till midnight. No plans. No goals. Just getting through.

Some days, I didn't even know what I was watching. The screen would be on but my mind wasn't really there. I'd cry at the strangest things. A story about a kid with a cleft lip. An appeal for a donkey sanctuary. The tears would come from nowhere. I wasn't sad about the ad. I was just cracked open, emotions leaking out from somewhere I couldn't quite name. I'd cry without knowing why. That became the rhythm: numbness, then flood.

There were days I'd drift off in front of the telly. Others, I'd just sit there slack-jawed, not really watching anything. The silence in the house was deafening. The hours slipped past without shape. Outside, the world carried on. Inside, I was paused.

I watched everything. Every box set. Every streaming service. *Cobra Kai*. All of it. Stuff I'd never normally bother with. I couldn't handle anything violent. Couldn't manage car crashes or chase scenes. Some adverts were too much – especially the charity ones with kids or animals. I'd have to turn them off.

The meds didn't help. I was on strong painkillers and Diazepam. At first, they took the edge off. But then they took everything. I became a zombie – just staring at the telly, flicking between screens, waiting for the day to end.

And all the while, I felt invisible. Not just hidden – but erased. That's honestly how it felt. People wanted a photo. A glimpse. I just wanted to disappear.

Months later, I had to go down to London for a medical appointment. Rachael sorted it all out. We went full stealth mode – blacked-out van, back door entry, the lot. Paparazzi had been hanging around the village, following us in cars. That bit really got to me. Not just for my sake – but for hers, for the kids'.

They were circling like carrion. I could spot the same cars idling at the end of the road. Same tinted windows. Same engines running. I hated what it meant. That my pain, my healing, had become someone else's spectacle. Not a person trying to recover. Just a scoop. Just a shot.

After the appointment, I popped into the agency office. They'd made a bit of a thing of it – nobody else in, nice food laid out. Just something different. I remember walking in, face mostly covered – snood up, glasses on, bucket hat pulled low. Richard Thompson was there. He told me that my old mate Rob Key, now the managing director of English cricket – like I didn't know – was in the building.

'Wanna say hello?'

Keysey. Of course I did.

I walked into the room. Everyone went quiet. It was awkward for a second. Then Keysey grinned.

'Bloody hell,' he said. 'It's the Invisible Man.'

And just like that, for the first time in months, I laughed. Properly laughed. Not a half-smile. A big, full laugh. I couldn't stop. Under the scarf, I was giggling like a kid.

That moment saved me, in a small but important way. Because it was normal. Stupid. Funny. Human. And it came from someone who knows me better than most. We played together, lived in each other's pockets for years. If he could laugh, maybe I could too.

We ended up chatting for ages. Just the two of us, talking cricket, talking nonsense. He said he was going to be watching the next Test from the Lord's offices.

'Why don't you come and watch with me?' he said. 'No one'll bother you.'

So I did.

I sneaked in round the back, slipped into the office and sat with him all day watching the cricket. My lads were out in the stands, coming back and forth, grabbing food, giving me updates. At first, it felt weird. But then it felt okay. And eventually, it even felt . . . nice.

There's something about the rhythm of Test cricket. Long days. Slow moments. Spells where nothing happens, and then out of nowhere – magic. It matched how I was feeling: mostly still, sometimes sad, occasionally lit up by something unexpected. I had forgotten how calming that could be.

Sitting there with Keysey, half-watching, half-talking, I felt more like myself than I had in a long time. Not fully back. Not fully me. But close enough to notice. Close enough to think, maybe, there's a way forward – even if it's not the way back.

That was the start. And not even that ugly incident at

COMING HOME

Headingley set me back. Bloody hell, it was like me and cricket had been messaging each other on Facebook and then taken the plunge and met.

CHAPTER 53

INDIA

Circling back to *Field of Dreams*, I had been due to take the lads to India in March 2023, the crash having happened in December of the previous year.

And I'll be honest, in hospital I was still telling myself I'd make it. Set myself this impossible goal – get fit, get ready, still go.

But that was the drugs talking, I think. That foggy, post-op optimism. As they wore off and reality crept in, I started to feel it. Not just the pain, but the guilt. The weight of having told these lads we were going.

And then not knowing if I could follow through.

I was desperate to go. Truly. But I didn't know if I had it in me. And what made it worse was the thought that these lads – they'd already had people give up on them. I couldn't be another one. I didn't want to be the bloke who stood in front of them and made promises and then didn't turn up.

COMING HOME

That haunted me more than the accident in some ways.

It's always been like that for me. Cricket, telly, whatever – I end up in these situations where, just before the thing happens, I have this moment. I don't want to do it. Like, I really don't. Could be a stunt on *Top Gear*, a race on *A League of Their Own*, standing onstage at the Palladium – I have this feeling: *Get me out of here.* And then, at some point, something kicks in. That bit of me that says, you're here now, you've made your choice, get on with it.

With India, that switch took longer. Too long. And that bothered me. Because I was waiting for it to arrive – that flicker of self-belief, the instinct to crack on – and it wasn't coming. That scared me more than I expected.

I've never really seen myself as a presenter. Still don't, to be honest. Every time I'm handed an autocue I think, *What am I doing here?* I fluff my lines more often than not, especially now with the eyesight – still seeing double half the time. I'll be standing there, reading about someone from *Love Island* and just thinking, *What the fuck?*

And I know that sounds like I'm fishing for compliments, but I swear I'm not. I've said no to so many things thinking that'd be the end of it, and yet they keep asking. It's baffling.

So with *Field of Dreams*, it couldn't feel like presenting. If it started feeling like a TV show, I wasn't interested. The idea from the beginning was: let the kids do the doing. Stick a camera on them, see what happens. That's it.

* * *

My first time back on camera after the accident was a year afterwards – January 2024 – in Preston. Me telling the lads we were going to India again. I didn't think they'd expect me to turn up – part of me didn't expect it either – but I did. And the reaction . . . well, they were just lads, weren't they? Brilliant in their own way. Some were clearly relieved I'd made it. Others didn't quite know what to say. But there was a warmth there, that unspoken thing you get when people have been through something together.

But then we got to India and that first morning, I was supposed to film something on my own. Just a bit in a park, me setting up some cricket, nothing major. Only I couldn't do it. I was walking round, completely unsure of myself. Anxious. Didn't know what I was supposed to say, didn't know if I wanted to be seen. I was terrible. That bit never made it into the final cut. Didn't need to.

That's been the thing all along with *Field of Dreams* – it's not about me. From the first series, I was asking the editors: take me out of that bit, cut that down, let the boys speak. My job was never to be the centre of this. It was to help them find their voice. To give them space and comfort to be themselves, to bring the best out of them. Anything else – my bits to camera, the reflective stuff – that could come later. Or not at all.

There was a director who came on board for India, and he was meant to be directing me, but I only let him do that for a day. After that, I stuck him on the kids. Not because he wasn't good, but because I don't want that kind of directing. I'm not there to be moulded or polished or made into something I'm not.

There was this one bit – we were filming street cricket in India – and the lads were having a proper game, natural, energetic, and the director tried to jump in wanting another take, or to stage it differently, and I just said, 'No. Mate, get out of the shot. These kids are playing. This isn't TOWIE. We're not faking moments for the camera. This is what matters – this is real. You don't mess with that.'

That was the battle sometimes – me and the production company pulling in different directions. They wanted telly. I wanted truth. For me, those lads had to feel safe. Comfortable. If they said something or opened up and later felt they didn't want it out there, that was fine. I wasn't chasing tears. Not like some of the stuff I've seen on other shows, where someone gets emotional and the producer's rubbing their hands, thinking they've struck gold. Nah. These were real lives. I didn't want gold, I wanted honesty.

And the thing is – these kids were brilliant. Genuinely funny. Genuinely bright. They weren't hard to film, they weren't characters you needed to enhance or manipulate. You just needed to give them space. Let them be themselves. And when we got to India, it became something else altogether. Like *Field of Dreams* crossed with the *Marigold Hotel*, but seen through the eyes of teenagers. A travelogue, but sideways. We weren't sightseeing. We were living it. I spent two and a half weeks with them, eating every meal together, staying in the same place, breathing the same air – and I loved it.

And yeah, it was therapeutic. Not in a big dramatic way, just . . . gentle. Grounding. Because India was different for me this time. As a player, I'd barely seen it. You'd be locked away in hotels, security everywhere, fans outside the windows. Thousands of them. You open the curtains – there they are. You try and go for a walk, you've got a mob behind you. It wasn't bad, just intense. I never really got to wander. Never got to just . . . be.

This time, I did. The cricket generation's moved on – these kids now, they don't know me like the old ones did. I've changed. My face, my body – everything's different. And that gave me something I didn't expect: freedom. I could go out shopping, take a stroll, soak it in. The production company probably weren't thrilled – I think they were hoping for a bit of fanfare, a bit of recognition – but I was fine with none of that. I didn't want to be the centre of attention.

More than that, I felt part of a team again. And that's what I miss. Doesn't matter what the setting is – cricket, telly, whatever – I'm always looking for that team feeling. Even in filming, I gravitate towards the camera guys, the sound techs, the runners. I want everyone to feel like they're involved. Don't care if you're the director or the kid holding the boom – if you've got something to say, say it. Some of the best ideas come from places you least expect.

We had that in India. The whole crew got on with the lads, properly. No egos. No one above anyone else. It was a little travelling unit, messy and brilliant, and I found a lot of comfort in that. It gave me something to hold on to at a time when I wasn't sure what I had left.

There was one day in particular – we visited this orphanage. Kids from the slums, some born on the street, no parents, just survival from day one. They'd been given a chance – a proper education, a safe place – and you could see it in their eyes, the way they held themselves. They knew what it meant. They weren't wasting a second. That hit me hard. Hit all of us, really.

Because the lads I brought out – they'd had their struggles, yeah. But they'd also had chances. People who cared. Systems, however flawed. Seeing those kids in the orphanage, it was like a jolt. A reminder. If you get an opportunity, grab it with both hands. And the lads took that on. You could see it shift something in them.

And for me? It was the same. I'd been through something, no doubt. Half a face is different now. But I'm not dead. I'm still here. Still standing. And I've got this – this thing I can do now. It's not cricket. It's not presenting, really. But it's something. And I owe it to myself, and to them, to see where it goes.

India gave me that. The trip gave me a mirror, a pause, a moment to say – right, what next? And for once, I didn't feel like I needed to run from the answer.

CHAPTER 54

WHAT'S NEXT?

There were moments, especially with the new director, where *Field of Dreams On Tour* started to veer too close to that classic telly template – bit of a walk and talk, like *Escape to the Country* but with cricket pads – and I hated it. I told them straight: this is not for me. That stuff's not who I am and it's not what the show's about. So instead I just stuck close to the boys. And once that settled in, the whole trip opened up. They grew in confidence, and I grew with them.

Watching it back – which I don't usually do – was strange. I've never liked seeing myself on screen. Like, even in the cricket days, I didn't watch my own innings. Never watched the TV stuff much either. But this one felt different. I had a few reasons. I wanted to check we'd done right by the lads. That nothing had crept in that might embarrass or expose them. And, if I'm honest, I wanted to see myself. See what I looked like.

Because there's what you think you look like, and there's

what the camera shows. And post-accident, that difference can be stark. You get used to the angles at home – you know where to stand, how to glance. But in a new mirror, or on a screen, it can hit you all over again. I remember getting my hair cut and catching myself from a new angle. Didn't like what I saw. So watching *Field of Dreams* was part of coming to terms with that too.

And here's the thing – I quite enjoyed it. Not my bits so much, but theirs. There were 12 of them, going off in little groups, doing things I hadn't seen – shopping trips, adventures, moments I only heard about afterwards. Watching it back gave me a chance to see what I'd missed. To see them shine. And that felt good.

We're on to series three now – not broadcast yet, but nearly there. This time we've got three teams: one from Manchester, mainly Newton Heath lads who've moved to Blackley Cricket Club, one in Bootle and Liverpool, and a girls' team from Blackpool. It's grown, quietly. Organically. And we were meant to finish last year, but it's not that sort of project. It finishes when it finishes.

That's one of the hard things about it – defining the end point. With shows like this, you've got to be careful. You can't just swoop in, give them a glimpse of another life – cameras, travel, attention – and then vanish. That's what I worry about. You can't pack up and disappear. You've got to think about what happens next.

Because now the kids are asking, 'What's next? Where are you taking us? And the truth is, I don't know. The India trip was unique – magical, even – but we're not doing that every year. So where does it go from here?

It's captured a bit of imagination. The prime minister, Rishi Sunak, mentioned it in Parliament.

It's a crossroads, really. You could take this and build something big – an organisation, a programme, a proper movement. But then you need funding. You need partners. And as soon as you bring all that in, it changes. Not always for the worse, but definitely changes.

It's a labour of love, and it's growing, but I've also got a life outside of this. So you start asking yourself the big questions – do we bring in the ECB? Do we form a partnership? Do we turn it into something formal? And I don't know. I genuinely don't.

What I do know is that it's evolved. It's grown in a way that's been really special. But we've hit that moment now – the moment where it either becomes something structured and lasting, or it stays as this passionate, messy, brilliant thing. Either way, it needs a plan. Needs clarity. Because I can't do it all on my own. And if we go again, we need help. Professional help. Structure. A team behind the team.

And maybe, in some strange way, that's the full circle. From one cricket club in Preston, to India, to Number 10 – all off the back of an idea that started with nothing more than a sense that kids deserved a shot. Deserved to belong. And maybe that's the bit I hang on to, whatever happens next.

CHAPTER 55

BACK ON THE PITCH

It wasn't really a job offer. Not officially. It was more like a nudge. A gentle hand on the back from someone who knew the landscape and knew me better than most.

Rob Key said, 'Why don't you do a bit with the Under-19s?'

We'd been sitting together at Lord's, just watching the cricket. I was mostly quiet. He was half-working, half-watching. We let the rhythm of the day and the game carry the conversation. He didn't push. He just floated the idea. Like you might suggest going out for a walk. And at first, I didn't say yes. Didn't say no either. I just sat with it, let it hang in the air.

The idea of coaching had been there for a while, tucked away somewhere in the back of my head. I'd done a bit before – a short stint with the Lions in Abu Dhabi. But this felt different. This was post-crash. Post-hiding. This was now. And that made it harder. I wasn't just rusty. I was uncertain about everything.

But okay. I'll give it a go. Do one match.

In the hotel before the game – Beckenham, it was – I couldn't settle. I was restless, pacing the room, trying to talk myself into calm. But it wasn't cricket that was making me sweat – it was the thought of walking downstairs the next morning. Into that breakfast room. Into the eyes of people who hadn't seen me since.

What do I wear on my face? Do I go masked up? Should I wear the glasses too? Will they be wondering? Staring? Whispering? The questions kept circling. Over and over.

In the morning, I must have tried to leave the room ten times. Each time I reached for the handle, something in me locked up. Like a hand braced against the door. Not yet. Not ready.

So I'd turn. Sit. Stand. Walk a few steps. Tell myself I was being ridiculous. Try again. It wasn't panic in the traditional sense – not a full-body jolt or meltdown. More like a fog. Thick. Quiet. Suffocating. I wasn't afraid of being judged. I was afraid of being seen.

I knew that downstairs there was a room full of people – players, coaches, staff. I couldn't bear the idea of being looked at. Not even in a bad way. Just looked at.

In the end, I took a breath. Pulled the snood up. Adjusted the glasses. Opened the door. And went.

Nobody batted an eye.

Not one. A few nods. A couple of quiet hellos. But mostly, the lads just carried on eating their breakfast. And honestly, that was perfect. I didn't want a fuss. I didn't want sympathy. I just wanted to be there.

The rest of that day was a bit of a blur. Not dramatic. Just busy. A little foggy. I was quiet. Probably a bit stand-offish. I was still nervy, messing with the scarf, pulling it up and down depending on who I was near. But I was there. Around cricket again. In the dressing rooms. On the edge of the nets. Watching. Listening. Trying to find my feet.

And here's the thing – none of the lads cared what I looked like. They weren't clocking the scarf or the glasses. They weren't whispering. They weren't staring. They were just getting on with it. Talking about their cover drives. Grumbling about the spinner who'd had them in knots. Asking if I'd seen their last innings. Should I be playing that one on the front foot? Or the back?

They weren't waiting for some old version of me to walk through the door. They just wanted a coach. A bit of guidance. Someone to stand next to the net, nod when they got it right, pull a face when they didn't. That was it.

And once I realised that, something in me softened. Just a little.

I started to breathe a bit easier. Not all the way. But enough to let the snood slip now and again. Enough to let the glasses slide down.

There's a photo from that trip I saw recently. Me and a young lad who'd asked for a picture. In the photo, I've still got the snood up and the glasses on. But you can just about tell it's me. I remember thinking at the time, he probably doesn't know who he's standing next to. And that was all right. I didn't need to be recognised. I just needed to be there.

After that, I started doing a bit more. I went down to Brighton with them and did a few more sessions. Found a bit of a rhythm. And little by little, something inside started rebuilding. Not the old me. Not the pre-crash me, or the version people saw on the telly, but something steady. Something real.

In the background, the noise hadn't stopped. Paparazzi were still hanging around the village. Cars idling outside the house. Some of them even followed Rachael. One time, we had to go to a medical appointment in London and ended up doing a full cloak-and-dagger job – back of a van, trying to lose the tail. They followed us for miles before giving up somewhere outside Stoke. It was relentless. That kind of attention, when all you want is peace, it starts to feel personal.

Even at matches, I found myself scanning the crowd. Not the players but the crowd. Always wondering – does someone have a phone out? Are they pointing it at me? What angle would they get? It doesn't take much to knock you off balance. That kind of tension – it sticks.

But the more time I spent with the lads, the more I forgot about all of that. Not always. But sometimes. Moments would sneak up on me. I'd be sitting on the balcony with them, half-watching a session, and suddenly I'd realise I hadn't thought about my face, or the cameras, or the accident in over an hour. It was just cricket. Just the day in front of me.

There was something in that. In letting the game take over. In being asked about footwork instead of flashbacks. It didn't make the trauma disappear. But it quieted it. And maybe that was enough. I didn't need to be fixed. I just needed not to be drowning.

I started going to more matches. Watched most of the Ashes that summer. Started at Lord's. Then Birmingham. Then wherever I could. Still hiding away in the boxes, but I was there. Among cricket people. Among people who knew me from before, who didn't make it a thing.

And that's what got me, in the end. The people. Coaches. Players. Old teammates. They made space. Let me sit in silence if that's what I needed. Let me talk when I wanted to. No questions. No drama.

And the dressing room – God, I'd missed that. There's nowhere like it. People say that all the time, but it's true. It's not just a room. It's a world. A kind of sanctuary. Once you're inside, you're one of the group. There's safety in that.

The dressing room isn't just a space. It's a line in the sand. When I was playing, I hated anyone crossing it. Sponsors. Cameras. Even family sometimes. Unless you were part of the group, you didn't come in. It was sacred. Still is.

That's what saved me, I think. That there was still a door I could walk through and be met with nods instead of questions. Didn't matter what was happening outside. On the pitch. In the papers. In my own head. Inside that room, you had each other. And that meant more to me than I can properly explain.

I'm not saying everything was fixed. I was still skittish. Still anxious. I still had days when the idea of walking into a breakfast room made me feel sick. Still couldn't handle certain scenes on telly. Still wary of the mirror.

But there were signs. Little flickers. Moments of life.

Hints of something returning. Of me coming back, or at least finding some version of me who could get up, face the day, and give it a proper look in the eye.

Then the England set-up rang. Asked if I'd come in to help out.

And this time, I didn't flinch.

CHAPTER 56

LETTING GO

I walk into the cricket ground and there it is again – the glance, the softening of eyes, the hand on the arm. Someone, usually well-meaning, says, 'Are you all right?' and I nod, of course I nod, because what else am I going to do? But inside there's this flicker – not quite annoyance, not quite gratitude – just something that wears at me.

Like I've become the crash.

Not Fred. Not the lad from Preston.

Not the cricketer or the dad or the bloke who's spent years trying to get things right. Just the accident. Just the bloke who nearly died. And didn't.

I know people mean well. I get that. But it's hard when every room you walk into tilts a bit, just because of what's happened to your face, or what they've read or what they *think* they know.

Most days I don't feel broken. Not even close. But the

world keeps handing me the mirror, showing me this version of myself I'm supposed to be living inside – fragile, grateful, surviving. I'm not hiding. I'm out in the world, doing the work, getting on with it. But every so often, something comes back – a dream, a memory, something from underneath – and there I am again, in it. Not for long. Just long enough. And then I shake it off, breathe it out and carry on. Because that's what I do now. I carry on.

There was a stretch just after it happened when I was full of anger. I didn't show it much, but it was there. Not just at what happened – though yeah, that too – but at the way it played out afterwards. The silence. The speculation. And when I agreed to do the documentary for Disney, I told myself it was a chance to speak about it on my terms. Get it said, then move on. I didn't want it to be *about* the accident. I didn't want long, drawn-out shots of me wandering around the house or stroking a dog like I was in a trailer for a sad film. I wanted it referenced. Not romanticised.

I'll be honest, what I hadn't really planned for was how much of the show would end up focused on the crash. I thought there'd be space for other things – for the cricket, for talking about people I've played with or looked up to, maybe even a few of the good stories. I wanted it to be a celebration, not of me, but of the sport, the life I've had in it and the figures I've encountered (how this book has turned out, I hope); instead, it became something else. It became a story about trauma.

And now, even months later, I walk into places and I can feel that's what people are seeing first – the bloke who had the crash. Not the rest of it.

It was the same when I did the depression documentary, *The Hidden Side of Sport*. I remember that shift. The way people spoke to me afterwards. A bit slower, a bit softer, like I might break if they used the wrong words.

I appreciate the care, I do. But it's hard work. I've got mates, people who know how to take the piss and keep me grounded. That helps. But outside that circle, I sometimes feel like I've been nudged into a role I didn't ask for. Like I've become this symbol of something, when really, I'm just trying to work it all out like anyone else.

Lately, people ask if it helped – talking about it, going on Jonathan Ross, doing the Disney documentary. I suppose, in parts, maybe it did. But I don't think of it like that. There's no clear line, no moment where I think, 'Right, that's sorted now.'

Recovery's not like that. I don't even know what recovery is supposed to mean. I'm not stuck at home with the curtains drawn, but I'm not floating around in a haze of positivity either. I have nightmares. I get flashbacks. Then I crack on. That's the rhythm now. No big breakthrough. Just doing the next thing, and the thing after that.

And the weirdest bit is, sometimes I don't even feel like it's mine to explain any more. Like the story belongs to other people now – the viewers, the papers, whoever wants to write their version. And me, I'm just in it, trying not to let it define everything.

And even when I was doing press – going out and talking about it, putting the story out there – there was a bit of me that felt strange about the whole thing. Embarrassed, even. Because I'd had this crash, yeah, but then I'm the one getting a documentary out of it, being talked about, paid for it, while the people who actually *did* something – the nurses, the surgeon, the ones who looked after me every hour of the day – they go home and do it all again the next shift. One of the nurses sat with me through the night, kept me company, calmed me down when I was climbing the walls. That's her job. That's her life. And I've no idea what she's going home to, what she's dealing with. It makes you think – not in a throwaway 'Oh, life's short' kind of way, but properly. You start seeing things differently. Or maybe just more clearly.

Has it changed me? Yeah. I think so. It'd be hard to go through something like that and not come out the other side with something shifted. I don't work as much now, and I work at things I want to do. I've got more time with the kids, with Rachael, with my mates. More time to just sit with people, rather than constantly running off to the next thing. And I'm more grateful for that now. Not in a big, spiritual way. Just quietly. I notice it.

I think I'm a bit more mellow now, though I still have my moments. I've always had that edge – that bit of fire – but it's not running the show any more. If you'd met me before all this, I don't think you'd have found me full of myself or belligerent, not all the time anyway, but maybe a bit more driven in a way that wasn't always helpful. I'd come home and just collapse into a chair, drained. Like I'd switched off a version of me that existed for everyone else.

TV's a weird one. I used to feel like I had to keep saying yes to things – keep it going, keep the momentum. *Top Gear*, game shows, whatever came next. It was like this unspoken pressure to keep proving something. And now, I don't feel that. I'm not chasing any more. I'm not sitting around waiting for the phone to ring. If something comes along and it feels right, great. If not, I'm all right. That's a big change.

It's even changed how I think about coaching. I reckon if I'd been coaching ten years ago, or maybe even just before the accident, I'd have been a very different kind of coach. Sharper. Harder. Probably a bit too intense. I'd have pushed players like I pushed myself – all effort, all in, no room for slack. But now I see it differently. Part of that's just getting older. And part of it's the people I'm working with now – Rob Key, Baz McCullum – the way they talk about the game, the environment they create. It's not about softening standards or lowering the bar. It's about understanding where pressure really comes from. It's about recognising that some players don't fail because they don't care – it's the opposite. They care so much they get in their own way.

And that's what I try to remember now. That letting go a bit – not of the ambition or the drive, but of the fear – can actually help people play better. Not because they're not trying, but because they're finally free to try properly. That's what I've learned, I think. That and the importance of time. Giving it. Taking it. Knowing that some things don't need fixing, they just need space.

So, yeah, I'm not the same as I was. Still me, still stubborn, still daft at times. But quieter inside. Slower, in a good way. I look at life a bit differently now – not like I've had an epiphany or found all the answers. I haven't. But I've stopped chasing. That's enough for now.

CHAPTER 57

PASSING IT ON

By the time we did the first series of *Field of Dreams* – in other words, *before* the accident – I'd already been edging back towards cricket. Not playing, obviously, but being around it again. Thinking about it. Feeling it stir. I'd stepped away from the game for a long time. Not out of bitterness, not really, just other things taking over – telly, family, noise – but the cricket was still in me. Always was. And that project, those kids, they pulled it back out.

It feels strange now, looking back. Strange how it all lined up – how I was just starting to reconnect with the sport when the accident came in and smashed everything up. And yet somehow, that didn't stop the thing. If anything, it deepened it. Sharpened the reason I was doing it.

Working with those lads – and some of them had incredibly complex needs, whether it was autism, ADHD, broken home lives – it changed something in me. Or maybe it just revealed something. I didn't want to be another adult who gave up on them. Another voice telling them off or writing them off or bollocking them for something they couldn't control. I started realising how easy it is to go after the behaviour, but not the cause. These aren't bad kids. They're kids. They're hurt. Or misunderstood. Or just left behind.

And what I learned – and it's something I've carried straight into coaching – is that if you don't really know them, then you can't help them. You can't just lob instructions at someone and expect change. You've got to listen. You've got to care. That's what mattered to me when I was young – when someone genuinely gave a toss – and it's the same for these lads. Show them you're in, and they come with you.

I reckon the accident fast-tracked a bit of that. Or maybe it just stripped things back. It took away the distractions and gave me a lot of time to think and to go over who I was, how I'd done things and what actually mattered. And the stuff I used to obsess over – the winning, the proving people wrong – it doesn't drive me any more. Or if it does, it's a quieter hum.

What I'm doing now, it gives me a purpose. It's not about me. Not really. And I like that. Whether it's working with kids on *Field of Dreams* or coaching The Lions, I get something from helping other people find their thing. Seeing them grow. Seeing them enjoy something that gave me so much, in a way that feels like it matters now. I'm not chasing England jobs or dreaming about press conferences. I've done that bit. These days, I'm just enjoying it. Keeping my head down. Getting on with it.

There's something nice about not being the main event

any more. Not needing to be. That was the thing with *Field of Dreams* from the start – I didn't want it to be my show. I didn't want long shots of me walking into the sunset or making big speeches. I just wanted to be there, helping them speak, helping them find something. And now, with the coaching, it's the same. I get to work without the cameras in my face, without the media circus. I'm not doing interviews. I'm not playing the role. I'm just doing the work. And I like that.

I'm coaching now in a way I never imagined I would. More patience. More empathy. More awareness that what's going on in someone's head will always matter more than how they hold a bat. And that came from the kids. That came from *Field of Dreams*. They opened that door again. They showed me what cricket can still give.

And maybe that's the biggest thing – it gave me something back. After everything. After the silence, the recovery, the not knowing what came next. Cricket found its way back to me. And now I get to pass it on. In whatever way I can.

CHAPTER 58

COMING HOME

What's next? Well, at the time of writing, I'm looking forward to the Lions' trip to Australia. It's proper cricket, and I'm proud of what we're building there. I'm not employed in the old-fashioned sense – more like I'm committed. They give you a minimum days thing; I end up doing double, some paid, some not. Doesn't matter. I care about the team. I care about England cricket.

That's the difference now – I'm not chasing anything. Not trying to land a big franchise job in some faraway league. Not looking for the next headline. What I want is for these lads to come through, not just to play for England but to be ready. Embedded in the right culture. Able to walk into that dressing room and not flinch.

I'm also working on something with the surgeon who fixed my face – Mr Jahrad Haq. Might be a project around helping kids globally, showing the work these surgeons do. I was lucky after my crash. I had access to the best people. Not everyone gets that. If there's a way to shine a light on it, to use what profile I've got for that, then that's what I'll do.

And yes, that means revisiting the accident. But I do that anyway. It's always there, in some form. But you meet people who've had it worse. And you realise – whatever you've been through, someone else is carrying something, too. Might not look the same, but it weighs just as heavy.

That's what struck me filming *Field of Dreams* again. One of the kids lost it one day – real anger, and I got it. I've felt that. And maybe I couldn't fix it, but I could say, I know. I've been where you are. That counts for something.

It also made me think about what I'd have done if it hadn't been cricket. What then?

Truth is, I don't know. I mean, I had mates who worked proper jobs – steady, grounded stuff. Builders, factory lads, shop workers. I always sort of envied that. They'd do their shifts, then head to the social club at the weekend, have a few pints, watch the footy, have a laugh. There's something to that. Something simple and honest. No chasing. No headlines.

I think I'd have been all right. I was happy working at Woolworths. Get on my bike in the morning, do the shift, head home. I liked it. There's a rhythm to it. And in some ways, I think I'm still chasing that kind of simplicity now. Even with things like *Field of Dreams* – it's never been about me. It's about the kids. The worst bit's having to film it. But without the filming, it doesn't exist. So you do it. But the bit I like is the people, the process. The feeling of doing something that matters.

COMING HOME

When I started out in cricket, it was all about winning. That's all I wanted. Lancashire and England – they were my two teams. That feeling of belonging, of being part of something. That's what I craved. I didn't care about the rest. I just wanted to prove myself. Sometimes I wonder if I even liked having something to push back against – a coach, a critic, someone I could stick two fingers up to and say: I'll show you. Probably did. Stubbornness has always been part of the deal.

But I'm different now. Coaching's changed me too. It's not about winning any more – not in the same way. It's about creating space. Letting players breathe. Helping them enjoy it, because I've learned that's when people are at their best – not when they're grinding themselves into the ground trying to win, but when they're lost in it. Present. Smiling. That's when it happens.

The thing is, when you've had all the noise – the telly, the headlines, the crash – you start to see through it. You watch a chat show now and think, *What are we all doing?* Just talking for the sake of it. Making stuff up. Trying to be entertaining. I used to feel like I had to be that. Now, I just say what I say. If that's enough, great. If not, I'll get off. I've learned that a bit late, maybe. When you're younger, you chase everything. Money, status, the next big thing. I did that. Got a bit of money early on, didn't handle it well. House, cars, all on tick. And the cricket suffered. Someone told me, sort your game out and the rest will follow, and they were right. Now I tell the young lads the same thing.

Be happy. Be decent. Work hard. Let the rest come.

That's where I am now. Back in cricket, back where I

belong. Not for the headlines or the nostalgia. Just because it feels right. It's like coming home.

And sometimes, I think of that little lad in the tracksuit – the one at Harris Park in Fulwood, standing on the boundary, heart thudding, not knowing where to stand. First time out, pads too big, heavy bat, out first ball. One and done. But he was there. He turned up. And he thought, *Next time*.

This is the next time.

It's not about chasing dreams any more. It's about living them, quietly, and helping others do the same. That's enough. That's more than enough.

Coming home. Yes, that's exactly what it is. That's exactly how it feels as I put the kit on piece by piece. Socks first, rolled tight. Then the bottoms – still a bit damp from yesterday – and the old tracksuit top with the stretched cuffs. Clipboard under one arm, cap in the other. There's no music right now – sorry, Johnny Cash – just the quiet rhythm of it. A kind of ritual. The same every morning, give or take. And I like it that way.

The building hums behind me as I make my way down the corridor – the low clatter of cups, a radio crackling in the physio's room, the muffled thump of someone knocking catches in the indoor nets. I push through the doors and step out into morning.

The pitch opens up in front of me – wide, green, cut sharp – and for a second, I just stop. That smell of cut grass hits me, thick and sweet, and I swear it takes me back in a heartbeat. Back to Harris Park, me in my Man U top, first game ever. Some mornings feel like that. Like time folding in on itself.

The light's coming in low behind the sight screens – soft

and white, like it's leaking through the canvas. There's a mist hanging just above the square, not quite lifted yet, and the dew's still on the rope. I see shapes moving – a batter stretching, a couple of bowlers lobbing balls to each other, a keeper crouched down in quiet conversation. There's laughter already – proper belly stuff – and the occasional sharp sound of bat on ball. Someone's shouting for a catch. Someone else is telling them they're dreaming.

I walk across slowly, boots crunching on the gravel, clipboard swinging at my side. No rush. It's early yet. But there's a feeling in the air – possibility, maybe. The good kind of tension. The sense that something's about to begin.

This is the part I love now. Not the matches or the crowds or the cameras. Just this. The morning. The work. The chance to make something happen. Not for me any more, but for them. I get to help. I get to shape. I get to give a bit of what I've had.

And as the sun starts to lift behind the pavilion, catching on the edge of the covers and throwing long shadows across the grass, I take a breath and head out into the light.

ACKNOWLEDGEMENTS

I'd like to thank Rachael, my family, friends, coaches, teammates, and the opposition: without them there would be no story to tell.

Special thanks also to Andrew Holmes, the team at Bonnier, and Madison, Katie and Richard at M&C Saatchi Talent.